Tales
from the
Expat
Harem

Tales from the Expat Harem

Foreign Women in Modern Turkey

ANASTASIA M. ASHMAN

JENNIFER EATON GÖKMEN

SEAL PRESS

Tales from the Expat Harem
Foreign Women in Modern Turkey

Copyright © 2006 by Anastasia M. Ashman and Jennifer Eaton Gökmen
Turkey map © 2006 Avalon Travel

Some photos and illustrations are used by permission and are the property of the origi-nal copyright owners.

Published by
Seal Press
A member of the Perseus Books Group
1700 Fourth Street
Berkeley, CA 94710

ISBN-10 1-58005-155-3
ISBN-13 978-1-58005-155-2

9 8 7

Library of Congress Cataloging-in-Publication Data

Tales from the expat harem : foreign women in modern Turkey / edited by Anastasia M. Ashman and Jennifer Eaton Gökmen.
p. cm.
ISBN-13: 978-1-58005-155-2 (pbk.)
ISBN-10: 1-58005-155-3 (pbk.)
1. Turkey—Social life and customs—20th century. 2. Turkey—Social conditions—20th century. I. Ashman, Anastasia M. II. Gökmen, Jennifer Eaton

DR432.T29 2006
956.104'086'91—dc22
2005023859

Cover design by Suzanne Albertson
Interior design by Margaret Copeland/Terragrafix, Berkeley, CA
Cartographer: Kat Smith

Printed in the United States of America by Worzalla

To our Turkish husbands, families, friends, and neighbors
—with love and appreciation.

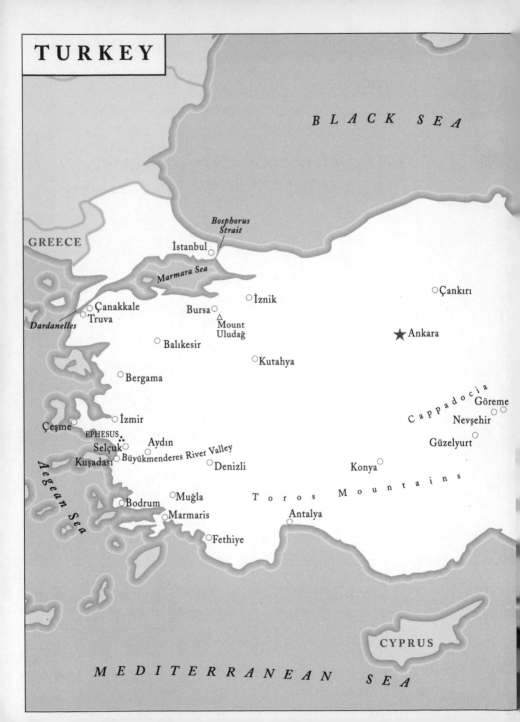

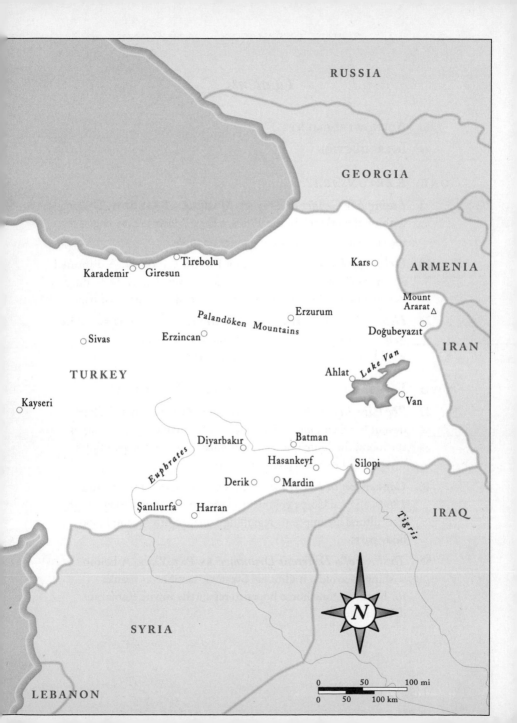

Contents

Acknowledgments

$\mathcal{E}$xperiencing the land of Turkey, its culture and people, has been an extraordinary gift. May this anthology be our grateful reciprocation. We feel blessed that people from all quarters—scholars and artists, writing and expatriate groups, foreign service professionals, the news media, the contributors themselves—grasped the innate value of this project and helped us bring it to life by selflessly donating their time, effort, and resources.

We would like to thank our tireless agent, Jonathan Lyons at Curtis Brown and McIntosh & Otis, for guiding the project as it grew.

We are indebted to families and friends for their inspiration and support, especially Monika Ashman and Ingrid Kai Liiv, who supported from afar; Joan and Dennis Eaton, Yüksel and Dr. Sami Gökmen, Elif Shafak, Mine Toker, Arzuhan Yalçındağ, and Celyn Alpauti for direction and encouragement; Mukkades Akça of Mozaik for pro bono public relations; Leslie Dann and Guido Cruz for design work; Andréa Bucci for an inspirational photo of İstanbul; Jennifer Lawler for her steady industry advice; Gökalp Bayramlı, Dr. John Israel, and Banu Tesal for translations; and Ebru Keni, Banu Önür, Dilek Bıçakçı, and Seda Domaniç for generous professional mentoring.

For publicizing the project, much credit goes to the expatriate community in İstanbul and throughout Turkey; multicultural Turkish organizations like the Turkish-American University Association and numerous Turkish-American social groups; publications for the foreign community in Turkey, like *Time Out İstanbul* and *The Guide;* and other community groups, like the alumnae of Bryn Mawr College. Thanks to Lisa Öz for her support; to John Scott, editor of *Cornucopia* magazine, for spreading word to connoisseurs of Turkish culture worldwide; and to news, politics, and entertainment journalists who covered the creation of the book—Nicolas Cheviron, Gülızar Baki, Nazire Kalkan, Didem Ünsal, and Eylem Bilgiç.

We are gratified by the support of experts in Turkish politics, society, and culture; women's studies; and expatriatism; who graciously read early versions of the collection and offered promotional reviews. Thanks to Karen-Claire Voss for inspiring our mention of the liminality of Turkey.

Thanks are also due to those who inspired our love of words and convinced us of their power, like Western Michigan University English Literature Professor Mike Jayne, whose tuition fostered Jennifer's dedication to the study of literature and writing; and General Wesley Clark, the former NATO Supreme Commander, whose campaign for the American presidency fired Anastasia's hopes for a more diplomatic world.

To Brooke Warner and Marisa Solís and all the people at Seal Press, our thanks for believing in the book.

Introduction

If there were ever a place tailor-made to play host to wanderers, travelers, and those pursuing lives outside their original territory, surely Turkey is that place.

The perpetual evolution that travel and cultural assimilation visits upon the foreign-born women in this collection echoes the continuous transformation that envelops the entire country. As a threshold to worlds East or West, depending on which way one faces, Turkey is itself a unique metaphor for transition. Forming a geographic bridge between the continents of Europe and Asia, as well as a philosophical link between the spheres of Occident and Orient, Turkey is neither one of the places it connects. Similarly, foreign women on Turkish soil are neither what nor who they used to be, yet they are not fully transformed by their brush with Turkey. Our Expat *Harem* women are on the brink of reclassifying themselves—challenged to redefine their lives, to rethink their definitions of spirituality, femininity, sensuality, and self. Aligned in their ever-shifting contexts, both Turkey and the expatriate share a bond of constant metamorphosis.

Delirious with influenza, a friendless Australian realizes the value of *misafir perverlik* (traditional Turkish hospitality) when she's rescued from her freezing rental by unknown Anatolian neighbors bearing food and medicinal tea; a pregnant and introverted Irishwoman faces the challenge of finding her place in a large Black Sea family; a Peace Corps volunteer in remote Eastern Turkey realizes how the taboos of her own culture color her perceptions; and a liberated New York single questions the gallant rules of engagement on the İstanbul dating scene, wondering whether allowing herself to be treated like a lady makes her less of a feminist.

These are among the tales from the Expat *Harem*. The titillating, anachronistic title acknowledges erroneous yet prevalent Western stereotypes about Asia Minor and the entire Muslim world, while also declaring that our storytellers share a common bond with the denizens of a traditional Turkish *harem*.

Much like the imported brides of the Seraglio, İstanbul's 15th-century palatial seat of the Ottoman sultanate, our writers are inextricably wedded to Turkish culture—embedded in it even—yet forever alien.

If a *harem* in the time of the sultans was once a confined community of women, a setting steeped in the feminine culture of its era, then today's Expat *Harem* surely follows in its tradition. Virtual and mainly of mindset, this newly coined community of expatriate women in modern Turkey is conjured by the shared circumstance of being foreign-born and female in a land laced with the history of the *harem*. Like the insular life in the Seraglio of the past, foreign women in today's Turkey can often be a self-restricting and isolated coterie, as newcomers are initially limited in independence and social interaction due to language barriers, cultural naiveté, and a resilient ethnocentricity. *Tales from the Expat Harem* reveals both the personal cultural prison of the initiate and the peer-filled refuge of those assimilated. Our *harem* is a source of foreign female wisdom—a metaphoric primer for novices and a refresher for old hands.

Our Scheherazades, our modern-day counterparts of that historic *Arabian Nights harem* storyteller, are drawn from a worldwide diaspora of women whose lives have been touched by Turkey. When our call for stories reached them, through networks of people and computers, we heard from a multitude of expatriates—women in West Africa, in Southeast Asia, in America's Pacific Northwest—all desiring to be counted and to recount their sagas. By telephone from her home in California, an artist who studied illuminated manuscripts at Topkapı Palace was the first to admit the precious affliction she shares with many of her *harem* sisters: "Turkey gets into your blood. I'm an addict now."

As editors we faced the delicate task of administrating the Expat *Harem*'s stories, preparing womanly wisdom for safekeeping. Managing the epic enterprise, with its ticklish spectrum of cultural appreciation and feminine self-portraiture, our nights were nearly as sleepless as Scheherazade's. For months we coaxed diplomats, nurses, chefs, and others to explore and express their truths about Turkey in a culturally balanced tone. Some were not professional writers, and some were unable to commit their tale to paper. Of those who did, only a fraction survived the editing process. But affinities emerged as each woman divulged her internal journey and lasting emotional connection to the place and its people. Systems engineers and hoteliers, missionaries and clothing designers, artists, journalists, and others—all share a fierce affection for Turkey. Revealing what Turkish culture has yielded in their lives, they unspool humorous and poignant adventures at weddings and workplaces, in cobbled Byzantine streets, in Ottoman bathhouses, and at boisterous bazaars along the Silk Road. In an atmospheric travelogue through a countryside still echoing the old ways, through Giresun and Göreme, they transport us on emotional journeys of assimilation into friendship, neighborhood, wifehood, and motherhood. As modern women in the real world, they take us along on their quests for national identity, business ownership, and property possession.

What follows is a literary version of the virtual, modern *harem*'s never-ending gathering of women—day melts into night and relaxed feasts spur spirited conversation, with diverse company reenacting scenes of cultural contrast and discovery. Turkey is a veiled place that insists on being uncovered; the country rewards seekers. And in the process of discovering Turkey, the contemporary women of the Expat *Harem* unmask themselves as well.

In narratives illuminating imperfect human nature and the fullest possible cultural embrace, our Scheherazades wrestle urges to overly exoticize the unfamiliar and strive to balance self-preservation with the fresh expectations placed on them by Turkish culture. Some delve deep into interiors of country and psyche, like the shy teacher transformed by the full-frontal impact of a 13th-century central Anatolian *hamam*. Others teeter on the comic edge of a cultural divide, like the archaeologist who sparks hilarity in the trenches at Troy when vaudevillian pantomime has to suffice until her language skills improve. In attempting to reconcile countless episodes of unconditional native generosity, the women of the Expat Harem learn to accept a new emotional calculus. A midlife dancer mincing her way through the alleys of İstanbul's bohemian Beyoğlu district to the beat of a *darbuka* drum invokes Mary Oliver's poetic revelation, one that echoes in every tale from the Expat *Harem*: "I was a bride married to amazement."

ONE

Kervansaray

Traveling across the country, one witnesses places that still echo a way of life centuries old. Steeped in history, the Turkish landscape offers the curious explorer adventure on Anatolian homesteads, intrigue amid the country's natural spectacles, and exposure to some of the great wonders of the world.

Losing My Gender at Troy

BY MAUREEN BASEDOW

*M*any people tell me they wish they were archaeologists like me. They imagine a life spent delving into the mysteries of the past with the high style of Indiana Jones. I am the last person to disabuse them of their fantasies. In fact, after twenty years of digging mostly in Turkey, I am happy to confirm that archaeology is indeed a life of challenge and adventure.

But I don't always explain that by "challenge" I mean enduring a fourteen-hour bus ride with a nasty case of food poisoning, or staving off delirium while standing eight hours a day in the blazing sun, or rinsing in a trickle of reeking green water every evening. When recalling my most amazing finds to the lay-person, I rarely include the unhappily unearthed poisonous snakes, centipedes, spiders, and scorpions. Daily life experiences like these do not fit the image of the profession held by outsiders.

When I talk to Americans and Europeans about my experiences with the traditional village men who worked closely with me at Troy, my stories do not match their expectations. Even my Turkish friends are surprised by my tales, for my relationship with these rural workmen was antithetical to the accumulated wisdom of the ages, the opposite of what a young Western woman in similar circumstances should expect.

I had been warned about Turkish village peculiarities. In advance of my first season at the site outside modern-day Truva, urban Turkish friends said I would need eyes in the back of my head in the villages, explaining that the smallest incorrect gesture could offend—or even worse, indicate my immediate sexual availability. Never sit down, I was told, in a posture that suggested I was relaxed and "ready for it." Don't even lean against a tree. Never, ever bend over—which, short of the ground rising up to meet me, would seem to preclude me from doing any actual archaeological work.

In an interesting convergence, the Americans and the more religious among my Turkish acquaintances thought it very unlikely that a group of Muslim men, however *Atatürkçü* (committed to the modernizing ideals of the republic's founding father, Atatürk) they might be on the surface, would accept supervision by an unmarried Western woman. After I got married, the site director notified me the village men would not continue to work with me unless my husband was present. When I became one of the few members of the excavation to move from the archaeologists' camp into a nearby village, I was informed that my workmen's wives would disapprove and no one would want to dig with me. All of these warnings may have been based in rural cultural realities, but for me, none came to pass.

Shackled by preconceptions from sources I was inclined to believe, I walked out to my first trench assignment at Troy with a stiff stride—and a lowered gaze, since I had been warned that to look someone in the eye was a sexual invitation. Frankly, I was terrified. It did not help that my assigned trench was out of sight, more than a hundred meters from any of the other trenches, in the middle of a shoulder-high wheat field. No tourists would walk by during the entire season. The site director would seldom visit, since there was no road to the area and he wasn't expecting very much from my trench. I also knew next to no Turkish, outside of greetings and the numbers *bir* through *dokuz* (one through nine). On that first morning I had to ask one of the Turkish trench supervisors the words for "trowel" and "dig." He responded that the only words I needed to know were *daha çabuk* (faster), *gidiyoruz* (we're going), *iş başı* (start working), and *paydos* (stop work). Apparently this vocabulary summed up the relationship between the majority of supervisors and the village workmen.

That first day, I picked up my six workmen outside the equipment room. They had been pulled from the general ranks that trooped up the road to Troy at 5:30 AM. A Turkish supervisor gruffly pointed to me and then to the equipment I'd assembled: two rusted wheelbarrows and the absolute worst of the dig equipment piled in a spiky heap. They began to load the equipment into the barrows. I was already sweating. Sometimes it was cool in the mornings at Troy, but not this first summer, which was one of the hottest on record. Dressed in long baggy pants and a white long-sleeved men's shirt bought at the bazaar in Çanakkale, I wore rubber-tire sandals—another local purchase—and a long scarf tied more like a messy headband than a proper head scarf. My workmen wore old suit jackets and pants with shirts like mine underneath. Two of the older ones wore tight-fitting wool caps that they never took off, even on the hottest days. All were physically small—and at five feet, seven inches, I towered over the tallest man.

I had no idea how old any of the workmen were. I pegged most for early middle age and was wrong by between ten and twenty years. This was always a problem for me in rural Turkey, where age differences dictate different forms of address. My Turkish friends have speculated that maybe things between me and the local men at Troy worked out the way they did because the workmen misread my age as well, thinking I was much younger, and felt required to protect me. It was years before they found out how old I was. Because of sunblock and a different lifestyle, my twenty-nine years didn't come close to aging me like three decades in the fields would age a village woman. In daily conversation, typically sprinkled with familial honorifics, only the very oldest men ever called me *kızım* (my daughter), and only the very youngest workers called me *abla* (older sister). I rarely even got the polite address *hanım* (madam), which is used for female government representatives and museum officials—and which in rural Turkey implied a subservient, unequal relationship. Instead, most of the workmen settled on simply calling me by my name, the same way they referred to each other.

On that first day, when I pointed to the distant field where we would be working and said "*Gidiyoruz,*" the workmen followed. I was carrying a water bottle that one of the teenagers took from my hand, insisting he would carry it for me. As we walked with a slow, heavy stomp and an occasional loud handclap to waken the morning-sleepy snakes in our path, I asked the workmen their names. Five of my six workmen were named Mehmet. It was a common name, and every trench had at least one Mehmet, but five of six was exceptional. A call to one Mehmet brought them all running. Later in the season, a young Turkish student visiting from İstanbul's Bilkent University tried to interest them in being called Birinci Mehmet, İkinci Mehmet, Fatih Mehmet, and so on (Mehmet the First, Mehmet the Second, Mehmet the Conqueror). The student thought this was quite amusing, since Fatih Mehmet and İkinci Mehmet were the same person in Turkish history, namely Mehmet the Conqueror, and Birinci Mehmet was an earlier Ottoman sultan. The workmen really hated this. They would accept nicknames based on their height, profession, or village of origin, but messing with Mehmet the Conqueror was way out of line. And, they probably thought the student was laughing at them.

Laughing *with* them, however, was another matter. We set to work, and although the supervisor had said these were not good workmen and that they did not know what they were doing, I found them to be quick learners. We were out there together all day, day in, day out, frequently below ground level in a five-by-two-meter trench. They looked to me for every direction, which I communicated through expressive but ungraceful pantomime. The occasional stifled laugh at some particularly elaborate sequence of hops, skips, and hand gestures quickly led to generalized hilarity. Just try to mime something like "Dig down until the hard white floor appears, leave any soft earth where it is, and collect all the painted pottery in a separate container." I'd hear a soft *hee-hee-hee* starting in the back of the trench, and soon the entire team was laughing, covering their mouths with their hands and looking to the sky so as not to laugh at me. Because of the high wheat all around it, our trench was difficult to see, but the site photographer informed me he could always locate us by the sound of laughter.

Turkish government representatives visited even more seldom than the site director. One of them must have pointed out that I should not be alone with five guys named Mehmet (plus one İsmail), and so the occasional young Turkish college student would arrive to assist me. Most of them were good-natured and, like the "Fatih Mehmet" student, tried to help in some way. One student was a horror though, taking over and shouting orders at the men like the Turkish supervisors did. He ignored every instruction I ever gave him and began doing damage to the site. Physically large, he would try to intimidate me by standing very close when speaking. I was used to working with students and used to getting the bad ones out of the trench, so one day I reprimanded him in stern German, a language we had in common, sharply ordering him not to come back.

Things changed between the workmen and me after that point. They weren't afraid I would dismiss them, and they certainly had nothing in particular against the student in question—as poor villagers, they were quite used to being shouted at by their social superiors, so they didn't take it personally. But word of the incident spread to other workmen, who from then on went out of their way to greet me and treat me with respect—which, as a new excavator at Troy, I suppose I had to earn. I could tell that my workmen respected my archaeological skills. Many of them had spent several seasons at Troy and could gauge our skill level very well. But it was only after I had dismissed the student that I became a serious person in their eyes. My gender receded into the background of our everyday life together in the trenches. I had stopped being female at that moment.

Near the end of that first season, I actually did make a pretty dramatic find—a deep trench cut into the bedrock for a palisade in an area where nothing like it had been suspected. With three days left to excavate, I had very little time to record it, and since the wheat field had not yet been purchased, anything left in the ground might be destroyed. It was late August, so hot and dry that if anyone spit—and between the constant dust and tobacco consumption, everyone did—a hoard of insects would descend on the spot, desperate for moisture. "Maureen, çok sıcak," a Mehmet would say, warning me against working too hard in the heat. They seemed tireless, but in fact they knew how to pace themselves, which is what they were trying to teach me. Was this an example of the paternal behavior my urban Turkish friends referred to? More likely they were just trying to prevent a foreigner from behaving like an idiot.

Years later, after living year-round in İstanbul and working at Troy for three months every summer, my Turkish became very good. Freely able to converse with my workmen, I became aware of restrictions on my behavior that had not been clear before. Because of my genderless status, I could talk and joke with the men about a number of topics, including the work we were doing, the site director, other trench supervisors, politics, and football. But I had to be careful not to broach female subjects. This was fine, since I had no female topics to discuss. I never knew what to talk about with the village women who worked for the excavation as cooks and laundresses. We had nothing in common. But I made mistakes. I once asked my workmen the meaning of a traditional Turkish song, one that was apparently considered to be a woman's song for its salacious rhythm. My best workman and the one I was closest to looked away and gruffly explained, without explicitly stating it, that the ululating in the song was perceived as orgasmic.

Asking about children was acceptable, asking the younger workmen about their mothers was fine, referring to anyone's wife in conversation was not. But I would be invited to village fetes where, to my embarrassment, I would be treated like a queen, with small children kissing my hand and grandmothers handing me sacks of home-cured black olives. I met everyone's mother and wife and sister at these communal occasions, liminal situations in the anthropological sense, where constraints of normal life are cast off in celebration of transitional life cycle events. I could interact with both the wives and husbands during a wedding or *sünnet* (circumcision ritual), when all manner of unusual behavior could be expected.

This was not the case when I moved to the village full-time during the excavation season. After seven seasons, I had simply had enough of the noise and gossip in the archaeologists' camp. A married archaeologist couple was moving into a village house and offered me the extra room. The house had thick walls and an interior courtyard, and the small room I occupied had two windows across a corner, giving cross-ventilation. I was physically more comfortable there than I had ever been in the camp. But as for escaping noise . . . well, a Turkish village is not the place to go for peace and quiet. The livestock next door, across the road, and being driven between courtyards were constantly in full bleat and bellow. As for gossip, I would come home after a fourteen-hour day in the trenches and find my female neighbors squatting at the gate waiting for me. Trying to be friendly, they would adjust my headband so that it looked more like a head scarf and would talk about village-woman topics. Though married, I did not yet have children and didn't know where to begin with a conversation about them. Gossip about who would marry whom and what gifts the bride would receive seemed dull compared to the complex, larger-world conversations I was having with their sons and husbands and uncles in the trenches.

When in the village, I could not speak to any of my married workmen. The very old men might hail me from the porch of the teahouse, but I could not approach and chat, and the younger ones could not greet me at all. My gender returned once I started living in the village. The relationships I had with my workmen while on the site, while not completely denied, could not be acknowledged. New issues had to be resolved. Living in the village meant I had to walk one mile to Troy in total darkness in order to get to the site before dawn. The village was treacherous in the dark, the rough roads unpaved and sometimes running with raw sewage. More threatening were the Anatolian sheepdogs—enormous, vicious animals left to run free when not working alongside the shepherds in the fields. The first morning I set out, I opened my gate to find a teenage Troy workman, not one of mine, asleep against the post. His mother, a neighbor across the road, had sent him to accompany me every day for the rest of the summer.

She was doing more than protecting me from the dogs and the darkness. Perhaps she was worried that a passing traveler would mistake me for a *nataşa*, the term used for foreign prostitutes. There was a bordello near the village— most villages have access to one—and light-haired women from the former Soviet Republics and the Balkans worked there. Most of all, my neighbor was claiming me as a family member to let the rest of the village know I was being looked after. By sending me her paradigm of a beloved son, a boy over whom she would weep with pride whenever she spoke of him, my neighbor offered me a social context within the village. This was necessary for my acceptance as a member of this rural community. For what I really was—the Western woman with whom the village men spent a large part of their day, working but also laughing and arguing—could not exist in a Turkish village. On this point, the simple villagers and my sophisticated İstanbul friends, worlds apart otherwise, would agree completely.

Orienting Express

BY JENNIFER EATON GÖKMEN

"*J*en, I think that policeman wants us to pull over," said Mom in that sunny summer of 1997. We weren't even a hundred kilometers outside of İstanbul and already we were having a run-in with the law.

"It's probably your seatbelt," I said. I had warned her to wear it when we'd bid farewell to my husband, Bilgehan, and set off on this three-week cross-country adventure, but used to locking horns with me, the headstrong fifty-four-year-old artist had blown me off saying, "Which one of us is the mother here?"

"Let me do all the talking," I said as I steered the rental car to the highway shoulder, washed in a tide of red poppies.

"That's the whole idea, isn't it?" she quipped. "To see if you can do all the talking? Handle everything yourself?" She stowed her contraband crackers and peanut butter, creature comforts brought from Michigan in case she didn't find any Turkish food to her liking.

Yes, that was the idea. To be in control. Up until that point, my third year in the country, I hadn't handled much of anything. Like many of my expatriate female friends, I felt as if my wings were clipped by living in unfamiliar territory. But unlike me, an often rash twenty-six-year-old, none of them would have attempted to travel Turkey without male companions.

"Are you sure it's something that's normally done?" my mother had asked me when I invited her to join me on this road trip—a seventeen-hundred-kilometer round-trip journey from my home in İstanbul, trailing along the turquoise Aegean coast to the resort town of Marmaris, on the southwestern Mediterranean shore. Mid-June, the wildflowers would be in bloom, the sweet black Napoleon cherries ripe, and the sunshine bright enough to obliterate my troubles. Or so I hoped.

Was it normal for two American women with minimal language skills to traipse alone through a Muslim country? "Of course! Don't be silly," I lied. Whether or not Mom believed me, she agreed, recognizing my need for self-defined boundaries, a trait that ran strong in the women of our family. The willful daughter of working-class Hungarian immigrants, Mom was the first in her family to go to a university, incited by her father's quip that women didn't need higher education to learn diaper changing. Mom knew that this trip was something I simply had to do, my baptism by fire, and even if our relationship was a constant tug-of-war, I needed someone with her brass riding shotgun.

Three cows grazed and meandered a few yards ahead at the edge of an off-ramp as the highway patrol officer approached in the rear-view mirror. I wondered how much a fine would be, if it was payable immediately in cash, or whether it would mean penalty points on the Turkish driving license I didn't yet have. My Michigan license was supposed to suffice, but would the officer accept it? My palms were sweating. I didn't want Mom to think I couldn't handle it. I had talked my way out of tickets in the U.S. before, but what if the Turkish officer didn't buy my "confused pretty woman" act? What if we were being pulled over for something that required a trip to the police station? I had never seen my Turkish relatives try to fast-talk a cop. Still, the unknown alternative was more daunting.

"*Ruhsat lütfen*," (Registration please) he requested.

Ironically, although this trip was to test my Turkish, to avoid a ticket I was now going to pretend I couldn't speak the language, which played out like bad vaudeville. "No speak Turkish. *Türkçe* no."

"*Ruhsat. Ruuh-saat,*" he said, opening and folding his hands like a book.

"Ohhh. Yes, yes. *Evet,*" I said loudly, as I grabbed my passport. To Mom I said, "I'm going to keep handing him the wrong documents on purpose." I expected her to be cross, prone as we were to criticizing each other for the slightest thing, but she surprised me by covering a smirk with her hand. Amazingly, the rule bender in her was on my side this time. I wondered why she had imposed so many rules on me when I was growing up, given her own penchant for defiance. Ignoring the officer, she leaned out her window to take a photo of the cows.

Though my college graduation, wedding, and move to the other side of the world had been a two-week whirlwind, settling into a Turkish marriage had been a breeze. I had a large, outgoing, extended family in Ankara who offered constant support and praise, as well as a job I loved—lecturing in communications at Middle East Technical University. But during my second year in Turkey, my husband and I had to leave the comfortable capital city. That's when it stopped being easy. The inflation rate had soared to 300 percent, and Bilgehan simply couldn't afford to remain in the finance ministry, so we relocated to İstanbul, to better-paying jobs in the private sector. In unfamiliar surroundings and without Bilgehan's family to rely on, İstanbul's maelstrom of twelve million people was a terrifying prospect.

Unsure of my burgeoning Turkish, I begged my single sister-in-law, Pelin, to come live with us, and before long I was completely dependent on her. Though now the office manager for a large multinational, I still felt disempowered. My position didn't require advanced Turkish, so my language skills atrophied until I needed Pelin's help with everything, from the grocery shopping and going to the hairdresser to veterinarian visits for our cats. I was utterly helpless. I began to resent my life.

Sighing, the policeman took the proffered document, examined it carefully, and handed it back, the beaming June sun making him squint even through his dark sunglasses. *"Bunu ruhsatınız değil. Ruhsat lazım. Ruuuh-saaat."* (This isn't your registration. I need your registration. Registraaaation.) I handed him my Michigan driver's license. Mom sniggered into a tissue and I shot her a warning glare.

After a cursory glance, the officer reached in, flipped down the driver's side visor, where most Turks keep the vehicle paperwork, and took the registration out himself. Whatever information he was hoping to glean about us, the rental car documents didn't reveal it. He handed it back.

∞

By the third year in the country, I was depressed and hostile, prone to crying jags and picking fights with Pelin. Once so self-reliant in America, I needed this road trip. It would reveal whether, if forced to, I could live self-sufficiently in Turkey. If I couldn't, Bilgehan and I would have to consider moving back to America.

Mom's joining me was crucial. A paragon of determination, I wanted her to bear witness to my quest for self, knowing her own bravado would egg me on if my fortitude wavered. Most importantly, as the person with whom I'd always struggled for control, the tables would be turned and Mom would be in my charge as I performed something even she could not: a trip through a foreign country in the local language. In proving to Turkey that I didn't require any more hand-holding, I would prove my autonomy to my mother as well.

"Arkadaşın emniyet kemerini takmıyor. Emniyet kemeri." (Your friend was not wearing her seatbelt. Seatbelt.) The policeman made a slashing motion across his chest.

"Yes. I always wear it. I know," I answered earnestly.

He tugged on my secured belt then pointed at Mom. *"O takması lazım. Önemli. Tehlikeli."* (*She* must wear it. Important. Dangerous.)

"Oh *her?* Okay. She'll wear it." I turned to her. "Finally do you believe me?" She put her belt on, and the officer waved us away.

"Yeah, yeah. You've made your point," she grumbled. I pulled back onto the highway.

We rode in silence. I popped in a cassette of Turkish folksinger Şükriye Tutkun. I sang along to my bittersweet favorite, *"Arda Boyları,"* about a girl who drowns herself rather than marry the boy her mother chose for her.

As the city turned to lush green countryside and squares of farmland, our mood lightened, and Mom recounted her own wanderlust in her 1960s university days, when she survived a trip from Buffalo to Las Vegas on crackers scrounged from restaurants.

"So now that you're wise to the ways of the road, you've brought your peanut butter and crackers with you?" We laughed. This was Mom's second visit to Turkey, and she'd gained a taste for the culture, even if she couldn't leave her snacks behind.

"Always have a contingency plan," she smiled. It felt like years since we'd laughed together.

I pointed to perfect rows of tall, straight poplars. "You see how they're staggered in size? Bilgehan says each time a new baby is born, the farmer plants thirty or forty saplings, and by the time the child is grown and ready to marry, the trees have matured and will bring a good price as lumber."

"An agrarian trust fund?"

"Exactly."

When Mom and I set out, I gave Bilgehan a copy of the detailed itinerary I'd started months earlier, estimating our daily schedule down to the hour. It included our route, the time and mileage to each destination, a historic sites checklist, museum times and telephone numbers, regional specialties for souvenir ideas, and all of our hotel contact information. The process of collecting the data gave me a sense of command over my fate and comforted Bilgehan, assuring him that little was left to chance. As we left İstanbul, he stood on the roadside yelling *"İyi yolculuklar!"* (Happy travels!) and threw a bucketful of water toward the back of our departing car—the Turkish custom for heralding a speedy return: "May you come and go like water."

Since our move to Turkey, Bilgehan was sympathetic to my quest to reempower myself. His friends told him he was crazy to allow me to take this trip, but he knew how competent I was. He met me at the height of my abilities, when I was vice president of the university's judo club. Having witnessed me capable of things most girls didn't usually do—rapelling, driving motorcycles, handling firearms—he understood how it broke my spirit to be unable to complete the most menial task without assistance.

Mom snapped photos out of her open window, tickled with the novelty of

Turkey's rustic everyday scenes: shepherds leading sheep and long-haired goats down steeply terraced olive groves; squat village women each shouldering massive bundles of kindling twice as high as themselves; donkeys trotting reluctantly, carrying men dressed to rural standards—flat cap, wool sport jacket, sweater vest, oxford shirt, and undershirt, paired with baggy *şalvar* trousers. "How can they stand such warm clothing?" Mom asked, herself overheated in capri pants, a t-shirt, and bare feet.

Three cities later and five hours south of İstanbul, our first stop, in the cement-producing town of Balıkesir, was a mere hurried walk through the crowded streets. A city more than five thousand years old, it deserved more attention, but traffic and difficulty parking had thrown us off our tight schedule. With my stilted Turkish, we quickly procured directions to the Zagnos Paşa Mosque from some elderly men playing backgammon on the sidewalk, squatting on low stools over a knee-high table.

"'The scrupulously preserved 15th-century complex was built by Mehmet the Conqueror's Grand Vizier,'" Mom read from the guidebook as I maneuvered her through thronged streets, but the ethereal strains of the call to prayer told us the mosque would soon be filled with worshippers, thus inaccessible to tourists. We headed back to the car, with no time to stop at the 14th-century mausoleum of the rulers of the Türkmen Karası Dynasty.

"Can't we just pop in?" she asked.

"No. We have to be in Bergama by nightfall."

"So much for the itinerary." I felt our camaraderie wither. Did she really care about the mausoleum or was this a dig at my overzealous planning? When we had pulled into Balıkesir she had seemed more interested in the McDonald's she spotted than trudging twenty sweaty blocks to the mosque.

"If we waste time, the front desk will be closed." We might be left with no place to sleep!

Having successfully executed the complicated directions to the mosque, I decided my Turkish was better than I'd given myself credit for, so on the way out of Balıkesir, I asked a man on the roadside for a shortcut to Bergama—the spa and medical hotspot of Hellenic times. Since I hadn't managed to properly orchestrate the first stop, I'd have to make sure we made it to the next stop in time. My ego demanded it.

After his convoluted description, I boldly turned off the main road. Before long we found ourselves on a winding, muddy country lane in the dark. No streetlights, no civilization—only fields and farmland.

"Well, this is the way he said to go," I offered defiantly.

"Doubling back would take too long. I'm sure we'll be fine." Mom was fascinated by the mist rising from the meadows. Squinting at the darkness, she was memorizing the scene for later reconstitution on canvas.

We should have felt wary and unnerved, control-freaks adrift on an uncharted path. Or even more so as two foreign women alone at night, deep in the Turkish hinterlands. Instead we were giddy rule breakers. My stomach trembled with adrenaline.

"You used to hate getting lost," she mused.

Oh, how I dreaded random drives with her when I was nine or ten. With no sense of direction, she would easily get lost, and I would panic, unable to assist and terrified we would never make it back.

I shuddered.

Unlike Mom, when I began navigating myself through life, I was fortunate to have gained an internal compass that rarely failed. I learned to navigate the sprawl of İstanbul more quickly than Bilgehan or Pelin, even without language competency. Usually this radar deftly guided my life decisions as well, and under normal conditions, it gave me a confidence that bordered on arrogance. But moving to İstanbul had scrambled my ability to guide my life. My confidence was dashed. This trip would put my self-assurance back on par with my physical sense of place . . . and if I hadn't yet reclaimed my confidence, for the time being, I was willing to fake it. "The difference is, I chose this road. We aren't lost. We're untethered."

She laughed. "From the day you were born you were doing things your own way. You wouldn't even let anyone cuddle you." Perhaps she wasn't as controlling as I'd thought. Perhaps most of our struggle came down to *my* obstinacy, not hers.

∽

We made it to the *pansiyon* just before the front desk closed for the night. In the bright light of morning, Bergama was overwhelming. Known in antiquity as Pergamum, its well-preserved archaeological sites include the Asclepeium, the most popular health resort from the 4th to 3rd century BC.

"They used to do meditation and music therapy even back then!" Mom read from the guidebook as I rushed through the pension's savory Mediterranean breakfast of olives, cheese, and tomatoes. She had already finished her granola bars from her smuggled snack stash and was ready to go.

After a few winding kilometers up and around a hill skirted by a placid reservoir, we parked the car and trudged over smooth, massive paving stones to the complex that once housed the Altar of Zeus. Its few remaining columns towered over us. Next to the acropolis we sat atop an empty amphitheater built into a steep hillside. Lizards chased each other over tumbled marble pediments. Daisies and purple borage burst through cracks in the carved capitals that littered the ground. We went through rolls of film and took turns narrating each antiquity with our guidebooks. I recognized the names and events mentioned in the guidebook from history class and from Robert Graves's *I, Claudius*, giving me a context for my surroundings. Turns out I knew this place long before arriving.

Feeling more at ease, we chatted in Turkish with the shopkeeper of a copper and carpet store, drinking tea as we talked—an act of protocol and hospitality. I proudly served as interpreter for Mom—my first time in such a role. We were both impressed by the depth of my comprehension.

"He says this one is called a *cicim,* a *kilim* that's been top-embroidered. Those small square patterns are typical of the Bergama region."

Pleased by a Turkish-speaking American well-versed in the cultural norm of small talk, the shopkeeper was eager to chat and happy we didn't hurry a transaction. In Ankara, I had witnessed my mother-in-law, Yüksel, bargaining as part of daily commerce. She often used my foreignness to our advantage, exclaiming, "She's not a foreigner, she's our bride!" Showing my relation to the culture always ensured against getting the tourist rate and often garnered prices lower than the local rate—perhaps a token for having chosen a Turkish life.

I'd never haggled, but knowing social interaction entertained merchants, I told the shopkeeper how much I loved life here, as if my struggle of the past year hadn't happened. Mom perused ornately wrought antique copper kettles and intricately etched pewter trays as I spoke. In mid-spiel I was shocked to find I was telling the truth. I did love this country. Only twenty-four hours into our journey, the obstacles to enjoying myself in Turkey were evaporating. As reward for the pleasure of idle conversation, the shopkeeper let me bargain down the price of two *cicim* wool saddlebags to half their price, saving me $150!

By the time we left the shop, my confidence was flooding back, bolstered by a Turkish proverb the shopkeeper used to bid us goodbye: *"Bir fincan kahvenin kırk yıl hatırı vardır"* (One cup of coffee is remembered for forty years), indicating the ease with which the bonds of friendship can be formed in Turkey—perfect grammar or not.

The concerns I had about my communication skills now seemed silly. It was even easier talking to strangers than to family; they didn't know my Turkish should be more advanced. There was no need to apologize for my paltry vocabulary when the people I stopped for directions repeatedly congratulated my Turkish. Each encounter became an ego boost and an encouragement to speak more.

With our boldness increasing, we swapped the safety net of our itinerary for the authenticity of interacting with the culture. We opted for off-the-path course changes, deciding on routes south only as we met with forks in the road, stopping at every village for Mom's newfound favorite Turkish food, *gözleme*, pancakes filled with potato puree or feta cheese.

At one roadside oasis, we kneeled on *kilim* carpets in front of two women. One woman rolled out the thin *yufka* dough into large circles on a low table, filling the dough with cheese and parsley and then folding it into a square. The other woman sat at a three-foot-round concave iron griddle balanced over a low fire, slapping squares of *gözleme* onto the sizzling, greased surface. She rolled a toasted pancake into a napkin and handed it to Mom.

Choosing a spot under the shade of some cherry trees, she settled down onto a cushion and admitted, "I never meant to be a rigid mother, Jen. I thought that without order, you and your brother wouldn't learn to handle life."

"I'm sure I didn't make it very easy for you. We both know how stubborn I am."

She took a bite of her *gözleme* and added, "When we started this trip, I was worried you would be boxing me into your way of doing things, but so far I think our boxes are actually the same shape! It's not as hard as I thought it would be to let you take over."

I took her confession in stride, trying to hide my pleasure. I taught her the Turkish for different things around us—tree, cherry, grass, pillow—but "*gözleme*" was the only word she could retain. We plucked sweet cherries from the trees as dessert before heading back on the road.

In the long stretches between cities, the Turkish heartland opened in front of us, changing from deciduous green mountain ranges to evergreen foothills and eventually to semiarid chaparral and craggy buttes. We left modern times behind. Long stretches of scrub, plains, and mesas lent no clue to the decade or century, drawing us back to ancient days under the same blazing sun. Over the heat-warped horizon, we imagined galloping hordes of tribal Göktürks or the earlier Huns, millennium-old nomads, cresting the distant hills on decorated steeds. We passed rural villages of fieldstone and wooden houses where plainly dressed women winnowed wheat with crude wooden implements, tossing it to the air to separate chaff from grain, as their ancestors had for centuries.

"This is exactly what I imagined when my father used to talk about 'The Old Country.' I can see why he missed it," Mom said, wistfully watching the countryside slip by.

Now unwilling to stop talking in Turkish, we started asking questions about everything, encouraged by the friendliness of shopkeepers, waiters, and even people on the street. If there was an attraction or an activity in town, we followed the trail—or were led by obliging townsfolk. Having lost our way in seaside Çeşme, we asked directions from a gallant gentleman in a suit and tie who hopped in our car to show us to our hotel in a hidden cove of the Aegean.

Upon his advice, we went early the next day to the town square near the old castle ramparts. There, we were delighted by schoolchildren in bright traditional Aegean costumes performing the Zeybek region's folkdances accompanied by festive drums and a howling, oboe-like *zurna*.

So excited by the visceral effect of the folk music, we bought a cassette of it at a nearby shop and listened to it the whole way to Selçuk, our next stop.

Once there, I found my Turkish was also strong enough to court confrontation. At the house of the Virgin Mary, a place of pilgrimage, I couldn't resist scolding the souvenir shop manager as he cursed his young assistant in foul Turkish slang.

"*Ne ayıp! Tövbe tövbe, terbiyesiz!*" (How disgraceful! How rude!), I reprimanded. "This is a place of worship!" I warned in Turkish. I wasn't a practicing Christian, but the sight of nuns singing in the amphitheater behind us compelled me. Turkish tourists glared at him, silently supporting me.

The next morning in Kuşadası, I woke late for breakfast to find Mom chatting in the hotel restaurant with an old man who had sat down at her table to keep her company. Or perhaps to flirt.

"Mustafa was telling me we should go horseback riding! Let's go today!" Mom said excitedly.

The dapper white-haired senior stood to introduce himself, launching into the standard conversation, asking my name, my husband's name and profession, and whether we had children. I was used to the protocol, and as we were childless by choice—a grievous taboo in this child-loving country—I distracted Mustafa with my Turkish family's pedigree: Bilgehan's father was a well-known former parliamentarian. As if I'd uttered some secret password, Mustafa's attitude toward us became effusive. With courteous introductions, he announced us to the mayor of Kuşadası, Engin Berberoğlu, who was sitting at the next table and who had known my father-in-law since his parliament days. Suddenly, waiters delivered steaming plates of complimentary food to our table as I played my role, plying Mustafa and the mayor with my Turkish, Mom beaming.

Though establishing my family credentials would seem like snobbish name-dropping in my own culture, Turks like to identify mutual affiliations to derive some kind of kinship with new acquaintances, however tenuous, as if being a "friend of a friend" were as good as being family.

Buoyed by our instant acceptance, Mom and I felt like we owned the town, and we started scouring the seaside main road, asking every passerby for the agency that arranged horseback riding. Before long we were riding with a guide through the forested hills and down on the beach, right into the water as the sun set—like a scene out of a romance novel.

"This is the best trip I've ever taken," Mom confessed, back at the hotel. Then, in the next breath, "My rear looks like hamburger meat!"

"Eight hours in an English saddle will take its toll," I commiserated as we traded back rubs.

When we arrived in fig-famous Aydın in the Büyükmenderes River valley the next morning, we were challenged by the coquettishly inconsistent signs to the attractions: the local museum and the ruins of the ancient city of Tralleis from 300 BC. A few kilometers past the last-spotted sign, we found ourselves on a unique course change as we wound through a fragrant orchard.

"This isn't a road anymore. These are just tire tracks."

"Keep going a little farther. There must be something up here," Mom said, confident by now that any risk in Turkey would yield something interesting.

That it did. We soon found ourselves amidst a platoon of shirtless soldiers doing God knows what kind of fieldwork. To their disbelief, we continued down the road in first gear, halving the platoon like Moses parting the Red Sea. As soon as we passed them, the orchard opened up before us onto the most glorious rolling field of vermilion poppies in bloom.

"This is a Monet painting come to life!" Mom crooned as we squinted against color so intense it burned static spots into our vision.

We rounded the curve, and the road ended with massive, two-thousand-year-old stone arches towering above us. The site was surrounded by high razor-wire fencing. We stopped next to a guardhouse, from which a tiny man appeared, sternly cautioning that the site was off limits.

"He says we've breached a military zone," I called to Mom as she meandered back behind the guardhouse to get more pictures of the vibrant poppy fields.

"You have to see this!"

"He says it's an active archaeological excavation vulnerable to looters and scavengers. Apparently the soldiers should have stopped us."

"Hold on, this is a great shot." Was it her faith in me or her obliviousness? Damn this blind bravado! We had just trespassed a closed government site, and as Americans, we might well be thought spies—especially with cameras in hand—but she went on snapping her poppies.

"Don't go too far!" I called out, trying to sound casual. But then I realized my stupidity. If she, a visiting foreigner with no knowledge of the culture, wasn't intimidated, why should I be? Putting my language skills to task, I immediately launched into my Turkish plea. "We've come from so far . . . my mother is visiting all the way from America . . . Can't we please just . . ." I told the diminutive guard how impressed we were by the kindness of Turks, reminding him of a trait Turks are proud to claim. He eventually smiled at the ground and shrugged. Yes!

Unlocking the gates, he helped us up the steep embankment and toured us around the monument for an hour, giving a detailed account of the ruins in Turkish. From working so closely with the archaeologists of the dig, the guard was able to tell us much, whereas our guidebooks could only give us the name and date of the ruin.

For the next week we continued on our way, 350 kilometers through Pamukkale, Fethiye, and Marmaris, testing our abilities and looking for adventure. Just to be able to say that we did it, we stopped by a field between the villages of Kuruçay and Karamanlı to pick one or two shoulder-high white poppies—the opium-producing kind—from a government-controlled medicinal crop (according to the No TRESPASSING sign fronting the unfenced roadside plot). Having no idea what to do with the massive white blooms, they wilted on the dashboard while we continued to Fethiye, imagining ourselves daredevils.

By the time we arrived to Fethiye's windy Çalış Beach, my vision of Turkey and my place in it had changed dramatically. I had gained Turkish citizenship when I married Bilgehan, but this was the first time I felt at home.

"Do you realize you know enough Turkish to avoid traffic tickets, scold louts, ask directions, bargain for carpets, and shoot the breeze with shopkeepers?" Mom marveled as we sipped cocktails and watched the sun setting on the Mediterranean, the Taurus Mountains fading into the horizon.

"And don't forget penetrating military bases!" I laughed.

But it's so much more than that, I thought. No longer an outsider wondering how to engage local life and culture, I realized I was already in the picture. I knew what people expected of me whether they were vendors eager for friendly conversation or new acquaintances searching for kinship by association. I knew what to expect of them as well, relying on the kindness of strangers, like the man in Çeşme helping us to our hotel. Even recognizing inappropriate behavior and finding the voice to challenge it was a claim to belonging in this country.

I was able to run my own life within the new context of Turkey, in a new language and according to the dictates of my personality. I had conquered Turkey. I had reempowered myself.

Starting back on the long road to İstanbul, Mom riding shotgun with her seatbelt fastened, I chucked my feelings of dependency to the side of the highway, cumbersome luggage that could no longer slow me down.

Hello, I Love You

BY AMANDA COFFIN

*W*henever I heard or read a foreign woman's contemporary account of being harassed by men while traveling alone through Turkey, I would shake my head, bewildered. In my nineteen years of living in and traveling through the country, Turkish men had always treated me respectfully, without hassle. But then, I had never traveled to the east.

I returned home to Bursa from a three-week loop through Eastern Turkey with my smugness smashed and served to me on a platter. I wonder now: Had I simply been lucky before? Or is behavior toward women characteristically different in the easternmost part of the country?

Two years earlier, after having traveled in Turkey as often as I could manage it, I decided to live there for a time. I arrived without any specific destination in mind, and serendipity set me down in Bursa. Four hours south of İstanbul and across the Sea of Marmara, it's a modern city in 14th-century attire. The history attracted me first—Bursa was the first capital of the Ottoman Empire and a key stop on the Silk Road—but it's also a diverse city with abundant character.

I always avoided the classic tourist destinations when I traveled, and I quickly discovered that Turks' openness to visitors extends far off the beaten path. In Silifke, a small city near the eastern Mediterranean coast, a woman rushed out of her garden to give me an apronful of fresh tomatoes. In Kütahya, a western Anatolian town known for its tile work—even the walls of the bus terminal are covered in painted ceramics—a barber noticed me standing in the courtyard of a locked mosque and bustled across the street with the keys. When I came out, he sent me on my way with a sack of apricots he'd picked in the mosque's courtyard.

Over the course of seven trips, the ubiquity of gestures like these made me feel more welcome in Turkey than anywhere else. Almost every Turk seemed compelled to act as an ambassador to a traveler passing through. I would come to learn that such genuine hospitality stems from the conviction that a visitor is something to be treasured.

A week before my three-week trip to the eastern part of the country, I mentioned my plans to Mahmut, a shopkeeper in the Koza Han, a 15th-century *kervansaray* that remains Bursa's silk market. Whenever I'm in the neighborhood, I stop for a glass of tea with Mahmut. We might talk about the silk cocoon auctions; the Iraq war; the history of the traditional Turkish Karagöz shadow puppets; the latest novel by Orhan Pamuk, Turkey's most celebrated novelist; and Mahmut's neighbor, who reminds him of a goat. I enjoy these meandering, cordial conversations. They are an essential component of the legendary, gracious Turkish hospitality that has relentlessly drawn me back to this country.

I told Mahmut about my planned itinerary, a sweeping circuit from Turkey's southeastern border with Syria to its northeastern border with Armenia, including the cities of Şanlıurfa, Mardin, Hasankeyf, Diyarbakır, Tatvan, Van, Doğubeyazıt, and Kars.

"Don't go—not alone," he warned me. "The men will assume you are a prostitute." I asked what parts of Eastern Turkey he had visited. "I've never gone east of Ankara," he confessed. "But I hear things. It's different there."

Well, of course it is—that's why I wanted to go. And I couldn't believe that any man in his right mind would mistake me for a prostitute. I'm in my early forties. Only a man enamored of teenage boys would turn his head to look at my body. My close-cropped salt-and-pepper hair elicits, "Why don't you color that?" from Turkish men. Add a backpack, long-sleeved linen shirts over ankle-length skirts, and the result is someone who most decidedly does not look like a hooker in my book. Mahmut, for example, had never made such an outlandish assumption. Why should anyone else?

It was only when I got back from the east that I realized I'd missed his point altogether, had taken him much too literally. When Mahmut said "prostitute," he actually meant "a woman who is amenable to having sex with anyone, anywhere, at any time, for pay, or just as a hobby." Nothing—not my one-step-short-of-a-chador clothing, not my pointedly aloof demeanor, nor the fictitious husband and children that I acquired along the way—nothing worked to vitiate the assumption that a foreign woman traveling alone in Eastern Turkey is wanton. And nothing could have prepared me for the boldness and tenacity of the men inspired by that image.

Urfa was my first destination, but at twelve hundred kilometers to the east, that made for one god-awful long bus trip from Bursa. I decided to rest for a day in Antalya: It would afford me the luxury of a last swim in the turquoise Mediterranean before heading into the arid, land-locked east. In the early morning, I staggered off an overnight bus and paused at the terminal to investigate the Urfa timetables. A young bus company employee showed me the schedule and handed me a glass of tea. "Do you have a place to stay here?" he asked in English.

"Yes," I replied, telling him about my favorite *pansiyon* in Antalya's old city. I thought nothing of disclosing this—it was merely a snippet of casual conversation, the affable chitchat that I'd become so accustomed to.

"My name is Erkan," he continued, writing it with his cell phone number on a scrap of paper. "I am from the city of Batman. Do you know Batman? I would like to show you Batman. You are very beautiful," Erkan volunteered.

"Well, that's very nice, and thank you for your help, but now I need to go to the *pansiyon* and rest," I babbled, not wanting to offend the young man by flatly refusing a guided tour from a total stranger of his petroleum-processing hometown.

A couple of hours later came a knock on my door. The *pansiyon* owner announced that I had a visitor. "I don't know anyone here," I mumbled, half-awake. In the lobby stood Erkan, holding a bag containing a towel and swim trunks, my host watching him like a hawk.

"I can take you to the beach," he offered.

"Oh, thank you, but it's not necessary," I dodged, grasping for a polite way to decline his offer.

"I'm going now to the nicest beach," he persisted. "Please come with me. It took me a long time to find this *pansiyon*." The combination of guilt and my actual desire to swim was too much. I relented. It was possible, I reasoned, that he was just being a gracious guide who was pleased to show a visitor around Antalya.

Erkan was twenty-five at the most, I figured, and tall and lanky. The difference in our ages eased my suspicions about his motives until he took my hand a block from the *pansiyon*. I took it back.

"Why?" he demanded, brows furrowing.

"We are strangers," I reminded him.

Another block farther on, he put his arm around my waist. I removed it. "Don't you like me?" he asked.

"We are strangers!" I repeated, more emphatically. Besides, it just looked and felt preposterous. We walked on, each of us clearly mystified by the behavior of the other. Maybe I had misjudged his age. Maybe he was only fourteen.

"How old are you?" I asked him.

"Thirty-three," he replied. "Why don't you like me?"

We were nearly at the beach, and the sea was beckoning. I consoled myself that once under water, I would be spared these silly advances. At the beach, however, Erkan confessed his inability to swim. Wading out until he was neck deep, he suggested, "We can just stand here." I felt his hands on my waist under the water. "Kiss me," he enjoined. I pulled away from him and stalked out of the water, tossing a goodbye over my shoulder. "Come see me at the bus station," he called after me. "I want to show you Batman!"

I reviewed the whole mess as I made my way back to the *pansiyon*. Let's see. I'd asked about bus schedules, made a bit of small talk, and mentioned that I enjoy swimming: all things that I've done routinely in Turkey with no untoward effect. Antalya is a Western tourist mecca, full of women dressed far more provocatively than I. The people here should be used to dealing with travelers. Then I remembered that Erkan was not from Antalya. He was from Batman, about one hundred kilometers from the Syrian and Iraqi borders. I recalled, too, Mahmut's warning, "The men will assume . . ." But how could a man assume anything from such an innocuous bit of chatter in a bus terminal? Erkan was just immature, I concluded.

The next day, I scurried through the terminal fifteen minutes before my bus was to leave. It's hard to be surreptitious with a full-sized backpack, but I ducked into my seat undetected. My relief was short lived. Two minutes before departure time, Erkan flew up the aisle. "You didn't come see me!" he exclaimed. "I was going to show you Batman—you've broken my heart!" Other passengers stared at the brewing spectacle. Before I could lamely protest that I'd only met the kid the day before, the attendant wrestled Erkan off the bus, and we were on the road to Urfa.

After another all-nighter on the bus, I toppled out onto an Urfa sidewalk. I flipped to a city map in my guidebook, trying to get my bearings. "Do you need help?" asked a man who had just gotten off the same bus.

"No, I have a map, thank you."

The pudgy, fortyish, mustachioed man introduced himself as Fuad Durmaz. He'd just come home after a holiday in Antalya, and he could guide me to a good hotel. Oh, why not? I was still skittish after the fiasco with Erkan, but I wasn't prepared to shun all contact with Turkish men based on one misunderstanding. Indeed, we arrived at a gorgeous place with marble porticoes and more than reasonable rates. The room wasn't ready so early, though; the receptionist suggested I leave my pack and come back in a few hours.

"No problem!" said Fuad. "We can walk together." I was wary, but what was the harm in strolling around the religious sites in this pilgrimage city with an Urfa native? We clambered up to the scant remains of the fortress atop a high hill, which afforded us a panoramic view of the city. Fuad pointed out two pillars known as the remains of King Nimrod's throne. It was here that the megalomaniac king tried to immolate the Prophet Abraham, but as the story goes, God thwarted his plans by changing the fire into water and the coals into fish. In the tranquil, shady park at the foot of the cliff, we fed the sacred carp in the Prophet's fish pools.

We visited Fuad's spice shop in the covered market and drank Turkish coffee with some of his neighboring shopkeepers. Then I felt it was time to return to my hotel. Fuad invited me to join him for dinner. I declined. He asked me for my cell phone number, just in case I changed my mind. He had been a considerate guide, and I didn't want to offend him by appearing suspicious. Tired, tired, tired, and foolishly believing he would never call, I gave him the number.

Later in the day, I explored Urfa on my own, making my own pilgrimage to the Prophet Abraham's birth cave and admiring the stunning periwinkle blue scarves that seem to be unique to Urfa's markets. When I returned to the hotel at dusk, Fuad was waiting for me, angry. He'd been calling my cell phone repeatedly, but I'd left it in the room. He wanted to have dinner in the hotel. I told him I was tired and not hungry, but he had already asked the hotel staff to prepare food. I looked over at the two young employees, who shrugged help-lessly as they stood there with platters of *kebap*. Seeming to understand my aversion to the whole situation, they thoughtfully seated us at a table in the busy courtyard, right next to the reception desk, ignoring Fuad's requests to sit somewhere more private.

Over the next three hours, the effort to remain polite became more strenu-ous, and my patience eroded into irritation. Since he had been alone on the bus from Antalya, I had wrongly assumed Fuad to be single. Oh, no—he had a wife and two sons, but he didn't really like his wife all that much, he casually reported. I was too stunned to respond.

Where was his wife when he was in Antalya for two weeks? Or when he was playing the role of my gallant tour guide? It was now clear, he was simply another seducer who had identified me as fair game. As I seethed, he called someone on his cell phone and received a return call shortly after. He delight-edly announced that he would borrow his cousin's car and drive me out to look at a dam, part of the GAP irrigation project. Completely fed up, I was not about to go look at a dam in the dark.

Fuad was furious. He had gone to the trouble of arranging this tour, and now I wouldn't go? Didn't I like him? Weren't we friends? I observed his indig-nant tirade with disbelief. I had met Fuad for the first time a mere ten hours ago. At what point, exactly, had he decided that he could make proprietary claims on my time? Oh, god, here we go again. How had accepting directions to a hotel come to this? No longer even feigning politeness, I wished him an icy goodnight and went to my room. I could hear him in the lobby, griping to the hotel staff.

In the morning, the receptionist came to my room to say that Fuad was in the lobby. I refused to see him. I crept out of Urfa a couple of hours later, taking back streets to the bus station. I went to ancient Harran, fifty kilometers south of Urfa, also famous for its associations with Abraham, but perhaps more so for its ancient mud-and-thatch beehive houses. My cell phone buzzed all day; I ignored it. By evening, the phone reported that I'd missed forty-nine calls.

I was on the bus from Harran to Mardin, another two hundred kilometers and three hours to the east, when the first text message arrived on my cell phone: "You have very much broken my heart. Why don't you answer my calls?" Later, "You are very stubborn. Write me." And later still, "So this is what your love is worth. I give you ten minutes to answer my message." I turned the phone off.

I switched it back on late that evening when I was preparing for bed in my Mardin hotel room. Soon it was all but smoldering on the bedside table, complaining that it had no more room for text messages. The first one stopped me in my tracks: "I am downstairs in your hotel. I am waiting for you in the restaurant." I vaguely remembered—and now hugely regretted—discussing my itinerary with Fuad when we first met. Now, incredibly, he'd made the three-hour trip from Urfa, and since Mardin has few hotels, it wasn't hard to find me. Had countless unanswered calls and messages told him nothing? Was he just dense, or was he dangerous? I locked my door, turned the phone off, and slept badly.

Earlier that day, I'd been in one of Mardin's Syrian Orthodox churches, admiring an enormous, musty, leather-covered, liturgical text written in Aramaic. I met a Finnish photographer there; he was staying in the same hotel. Mark and I had agreed to meet for breakfast on the hotel's veranda the next morning.

"Who is that man waving at you?" Mark asked me as we ate. I looked over to see Fuad, leaning against the side of a car in front of the hotel, waving and smiling obliviously.

"That," I replied, "is a man whose surname, coincidentally, translates literally as 'Does not stop.' It's a handy reminder for the obsessive-compulsive." I gave Mark a synopsis of my ordeal with Fuad, sheepishly admitting to the gaffe of sharing my phone number.

"Well, yes, that was mistake number one," said Mark, "but you shouldn't have told him you were single, or that you were coming to Mardin, either."

"I was just making conversation!" I protested. I'd never before felt the need to be deceitful to fend off such sloppy, adolescent come-ons.

"You've never been in Eastern Turkey," Mark replied. "It's different here," he said, echoing Mahmut. Unlike Mahmut, though, Mark had traveled extensively throughout the east. He had seen for himself what Mahmut had only heard second-hand.

I resisted his advice, protesting, "I don't want to close myself off. It's not my nature! Why can't I carry on normal conversations with these men?" This was proving to be the biggest case of culture clash I had confronted in my nineteen years of traveling in Turkey. I could not understand what made these men tick. "Hello, where are you from?" is a friendly and polite greeting in Bursa. In the east, it's the beginning of the end.

Fuad stood waiting to intercept me at the *dolmuş* (minibus) stop opposite the hotel.

"*Defol!*" (Get lost!) I screamed at him.

Two hours later, I wandered through Mardin's labyrinthine markets, waiting for the bus to Hasankeyf, a village three hours northwest of Mardin and built upon the banks of a Tigris River gorge. My phone buzzed with a new message: "I am waiting for you by the monastery. Come here now."

Thankfully, Mark was also on his way to Hasankeyf, so we boarded the bus together. The bus attendant struck up a conversation as he came around with coffee and tea, asking right off the bat about my marital status. Defeated, I pointed to Mark and claimed to be married with, uh . . . two children, yes, a boy and a girl. Confident that I'd finally erected an adequate firewall with my "husband" sitting next to me, I proceeded to answer the attendant's subsequent questions honestly. Suspecting that Mark didn't speak Turkish, the attendant carried on, undaunted: "Oh!" he said, "Give me your phone number and address! I will come visit you when I'm on a bus to Bursa." I was dumbfounded.

"You might not want to admit to living in Bursa, either," Mark said, smiling and sipping his Nescafé.

And so it went, all through the east. I loved the severe landscapes. The Işak Paşa Sarayı was an image straight from my childhood flying-carpet daydreams—its melange of turrets, minarets, and domes spiking up from a remote mountainside ledge, its windows giving long views of Mount Ararat and Iran beyond it. Swimming in the Tigris between Hasankeyf's canyon walls at dusk was a taste of the sublime. The ornate and abandoned Armenian church on Akdamar Island still haunts me, as does the vast Selçuk cemetery at Ahlat, with its Stonehenge-like tombstones standing rigid in a sloping field of blowing grass. I will always remember the tall, black, basalt walls enclosing Diyarbakır's centuries of secrets and grief.

Despite such vibrant memories of the place, I came away with only the most fleeting sense of the people. In all my previous travel in Turkey—and throughout my life in Bursa—the openness and genuine hospitality of the Turks delighted me. The residents of the east seemed by contrast totally impenetrable.

I had animated conversations with only a few women there—particularly younger ones—on the rare occasions when I came into contact with them. Sezen, for example, was washing wool in the river at Hoşap. She claimed to have only two years of formal education, but her face and speech betrayed an innate energy, curiosity, and intelligence that startled me in that harsh place. The older women working with her avoided my eyes. Their own expressions seemed hopeless, numb, resigned. Possibly they, too, perceived me as a loose woman and shunned me for it. I had one civil conversation with a man, a restaurant owner in Doğubeyazıt, at the base of Mount Ararat. We talked about the decline in Iranian tourism. Apart from that, I struggled with mixed success to fend off the absurd, clumsy, persistent advances of numerous other men, trying to ignore their angry recriminations when they felt unjustly deprived of something to which they felt entitled.

I stopped at Mahmut's silk shop shortly after coming home to Bursa. When he asked about any problems I encountered, I said only, "It was a bit difficult sometimes." He nodded.

"The people there, they are very closed," he said, drawing his hands downward in front of his face.

With few words and a slight gesture, Mahmut hit the nail on the head. A respectable Eastern Turkish woman would not be roaming around from place to place. She might go to another city to see family, but only with her husband and children—her numerous children—in tow. My body language was at issue, too. She would never make eye contact with a man, nor be looking around at the scenery; her movements would be altogether more restrained than mine. I could never pass as someone's wife from Diyarbakır, and in the men's eyes, a woman who is not thus closed is open. Wide open.

In a different way, the Eastern men's culture is also closed: They are very far removed from the more tolerant, liberal attitudes of the West. İstanbul has one of its feet in Europe; Van sits at the doorstep of the Islamic Republic of Iran.

If the east is so insular, I asked myself, then where do the men get their impression that all foreign women are whores?

From the sky. Even the humblest beehive house in Harran has a satellite dish protruding from its side.

TWO

Last Stop on the Orient Express

*Called "Asia Minor" by the Romans and
the "Near East" by modern cartographers,
Turkey is the last country in Europe and the first
in Asia. It naturally commits a storyteller to a
state of limbo, caught in the ever-shifting flux
between Occident and Orient.*

The Painting or the Boy

BY EVELINE ZOUTENDIJK

"*T*his picture is against Islam!"

It was a random day in October 2003 as I unsuspectingly came walking down the stairs into the lobby of the hotel I own in İstanbul and found my desk clerk Halim awaiting me in a fury.

I was late for an appointment, and it's at such awkward moments that my staff ask me things I can't immediately answer. Suddenly they'll run me the list of daily guest arrivals, start discussing vacation days, or seek my advice on the most trivial issues. This time, however, the subject was something else.

"This picture is against Islam!" declared the otherwise good-hearted boy in an ominous tone, pointing at the small reproduction of an Osman Hamdi painting that I had hung on the lobby wall in one of my earlier decoration efforts. As the housekeeper was dusting its frame that day, Halim had decided to study the image a bit closer and was shocked by what he saw. Rushing out, I didn't pay too much attention to his comment, figuring it was a misunderstanding bound to blow over.

But the next day he came up to my office to heroically announce that it was either him or the painting. Something had to go.

"The painting isn't going anywhere," I replied, trying my best to be calm. "There's nothing wrong with it, and besides, it's been hanging right in front of you for more than a year already."

Painted by Osman Hamdi, an Ottoman court painter (1842–1910) who studied in Paris with the well-known Orientalist Jean-Léon Gérôme, the image features a woman sitting on the open arms of a giant wooden bookstand, richly inlaid with mother-of-pearl. Due to its height, her feet barely touch the ground, thus elevating her slightly above the multitude of books scattered about the floor. I was instantly won over when I saw it at an art gallery in Eminönü, on a little street behind the Spice Bazaar. The woman's yellow dress made a striking contrast against the dark, greenish-blue niche behind her. From a modest décolleté to the classic Ottoman three-layered skirt, her dress oozed with femininity, and her voluptuous curves seemed to simply flow off the painting. She exuded an aura of mystery and peacefulness, with a tiny hint of triumph. Most importantly though, the painting seemed the perfect match for my lobby's carefully chosen yellow/green color scheme.

When I took over the Sarnıç Hotel in the historical Sultanahmet area in May 2002, I was eager to tackle the redecoration of the sixteen-room establishment, as my taste and priorities differed widely from those of the previous owners.

I started by removing their metal-colored three-dimensional version of a Sultanahmet skyline from the lobby's wall and painting over an icy, mint green color. I got rid of the eternally snowy TV in the corner, and I did away with the fake yellow flower wreaths under the glass top of the coffee table, deciding that real red chili peppers looked a whole lot better there. I placed a little candy dish with Turkish delight in each room, filled the previously empty minibars to the brim, and added washcloths to the bathrooms—which, although pleasantly modern, lacked amenities.

Basically, I did everything to make my rooms resemble those of the sumptuous St. Regis in Manhattan, where I had spent six years of my hotel management career. Inspired perhaps by the feminine forces evaporating from our 5th-century Byzantine cistern below, I did my best to add a woman's touch above ground. Now and then, a male Turkish colleague would smile up from his tiny glass of tea, remarking that I was making a big mistake by losing myself in details.

But to me, details were everything. They were the only way to differentiate my hotel from the myriad others in this heavily touristed neighborhood. So I went even further, painting some tulips here, placing a few shells there—little things that give a hotel its distinct character and homey feel. And each time I walked past my Osman Hamdi reproduction, the perfectionist in me praised herself on how stunning it looked in its matching lobby surroundings.

In the three years I've lived in Turkey, I have discovered that my choices and opinions do not always match those of the Turks around me. Although during my first visit, in 1997, I was pleasantly surprised by how tolerant the Turks were of other people's lifestyles and religions, I began to realize over the years that this applies mostly to tourists and the upper reaches of society, and that daily life, as it is lived among regular people, is ruled by a more rigid set of mores.

I was born and raised in the Netherlands. Although my native country is not always as tolerant and liberal as it likes to market itself, and although religion is just as omnipresent there as in any other country, I was brought up with an open mind and without any form of religion. For me, art is an important way to express myself, and freedom is paramount. So when my desk clerk confronted me in the lobby, and in the office later, my instinctive response was to think, *Since when is my staff telling me what I may or may not hang on my walls? Are we running a Muslim hotel here or what? Who's the boss in this place?*

"The painting has to go—in fact, the sooner the better," said Halim, a friendly and honest boy, most of my guests' favorite. He was impulsive, but he clearly took his religion very seriously to make a demand like this. He explained his reasoning: The lady was blasphemously sitting on a Koran stand, and one of the books at her feet looked very much like the holy Koran. I countered with what Ottoman history I knew.

"Osman Hamdi was a much celebrated painter of the court," I said. "Had there been anything blasphemous about his painting, surely the sultan would never have tolerated it. Besides, all books were read on a bookstand like that in the Ottoman days, and an Arabic book doesn't necessarily have to be the Koran, since all books were written in Arabic then."

The boy persisted, claiming that the lady was sitting in the mosque's holy prayer niche, a sacred area where only the imam, or Muslim preacher, is allowed. He was quite certain about this, since he'd been going to the mosque each Friday for as long as he could remember. "Maybe the picture was never shown while the painter was still alive," he volunteered. I had no ready answer. I tried a different tack.

"It will be easy for me to replace you," I lied bravely. "But before you throw away your career for a silly painting, let's research the facts and see whether there really is anything disrespectful about this picture."

After a bit of hesitation, he accepted, on the condition that we would find a solution before the holy month of Ramazan.

"We will," I promised. For him this meant the removal of the picture; for me it meant finding proof that there was nothing wrong with it. And we had a whole month to resolve the issue.

If there was truly something offensive about the painting, I wanted to be culturally sensitive. Even though many of my other staff members told me they didn't really care one way or another, I could feel that they had slowly started to wonder whether the picture was acceptable and whether I was being purposefully disrespectful to their religion by insisting on keeping it where it was.

I started searching on the Internet for more information on Osman Hamdi *Bey*. In Turkish, *bey* means "sir" and expresses respect in lieu of last names, which Turks didn't use until Atatürk instituted the practice in 1934. For men, *bey* or *efendi* were used as titles, and for women, *hanım*.

I found out that the court painter had been a much-respected statesman, artist, and modernist, and that he founded the Archaeological Museum of İstanbul and then became its director. While looking for his artworks though, I was confronted with the strange fact that all I was able to find were perfectly pious pictures of the Koran being read by religious teachers. The painting I had in the lobby was never even mentioned.

The problem became even more complex when I started to ask the opinion of others. Turkish colleagues, fellow hotel owners, told me they had never heard anything so ridiculous in their life, and that by all means I should keep the picture exactly where it was. After all, they said, art is art, and Osman Hamdi was a religious man. But the opinions of my friends, both Turkish and non-Turkish, were surprisingly varied.

Many Turks were instantly irritated by Halim's behavior. "That's what's wrong with our country," they sighed. "What sort of people do you have working for you? You should fire that boy at once."

Others were amazed at my attachment to the painting. "What's so special about this silly reproduction?" asked a French friend as we debated the situation over dinner. "If it bothers the boy, why don't you just get rid of it?"

"If you remove it you lose power; you've got to show them who's the boss," insisted another Turk.

"But religion is important to people, it gives them hope. If your staff feels uncomfortable, you need to respect that," the Frenchman came back.

Finally, yet another friend, a Turk of German descent, suggested I not only remove the picture, but fire the boy as well!

A few days later I returned to the shop where I'd bought the painting in question. The shop owner smiled sympathetically upon hearing the story, as if he'd been through a similar situation before. I felt instantly relieved, for I hadn't the slightest intention of taking the picture off the wall; nor had I any desire to lose my beloved receptionist. We talked for an entire hour, and soon it felt as if we'd known each other for years.

He explained how some Muslims object to this particular picture because it challenges their traditional views about women.

"What Osman Hamdi tried to convey was merely the importance of women," said the art dealer. "No matter how much you read or study, the woman remains the core of existence. She is more valuable than all the wisdom in the world. She's the foundation of life, she is the earth." He added that people afraid of female power turned themselves against this picture. And my desk clerk? Well, he was just a kid, he didn't know any better. He finished by saying that the alleged book at her feet was definitely not the Koran. Exactly what I wanted to hear!

But how was I going to prove this to my receptionist? The shop owner offered to call Halim to relate this information.

As could have been expected, they disliked each other from the very start. Through the phone, I could hear Halim insisting to the shop owner that the lady was seated in the holy prayer niche of a mosque. The shop owner must have realized soon enough that it was a lost cause trying to convey the deeper meaning of this artwork to a boy this devout and determined. Only feelings of frustration were transmitted over the phone line, and they hung up sooner than I'd expected. The dealer told me he'd tried his best. The month of Ramazan was coming awfully close, and the matter hadn't been settled yet.

All this time I'd found the clerk's assertion about the prayer niche easy enough to deny, both to him and to myself. But then, after weeks of futile searching in various shops for books on the subject, I finally found a book about Osman Hamdi at an English-language bookstore on İstiklal Caddesi, Independence Avenue. The shop attendant had to climb up to the highest rung of the ladder to get it for me. The heavy volume disappointed me by having no explanatory text at all, but it did picture the artist's entire repertoire, with each title clearly labeled. Nervously flipping the pages, I located mine. It was called *Mihrab*, the Ottoman Turkish word for a mosque's holy prayer niche (*mihrap* is the modern spelling). My heart sank. *Why hadn't the shop owner told me this?* Still, I wasn't ready to give up.

Halim was being admirably patient most of the time, considering the picture was hanging right in front of him, day in, day out. Eager to find a verdict himself, he sought the opinion of a prominent Islamic religion professor and had a hard time understanding why the professor's rejection of the painting wasn't sufficient to me. I figured that any devout Muslim would find a lady sitting in the *mihrap* unacceptable, but that still didn't mean there wasn't a valid explanation to be found in the painting's defense. Weeks went by as I searched for a more suitable person to give us a final, trustworthy verdict, preferably in my favor. Friends told me I should contact the former director of the Museum of Turkish and Islamic Arts in İstanbul, but it turned out to be difficult to reach her.

Every now and then though, Halim would suddenly lose his patience and step into my office to ask what I had decided to do. "Why is this picture so important to you?" he wanted to know. But how could I explain to him that it was *because* of all this recent turmoil that its value had increased all the more to me? It suddenly represented so many things that I find important: freedom of opinion, the challenge of religious dogmatism, the value and appreciation of womankind. And besides, it fit so well there in my lobby—perfect in size, shape, style, and color. Taking it away at this point would feel like removing a piece of me.

In fact, in a way, the woman reminded me a lot of myself. Just as Hamdi exalted her above all wisdom of their age, I felt similarly distanced from my surroundings, being a single foreign woman running a business by myself in a country as culturally different from my own as Turkey. The woman in the painting seemed to be a positive example for me, overlooking the hotel from her bookstand throne in a calm and determined manner quite different from the sometimes nervous and indecisive style I applied from my upstairs office.

Even though he was making my life difficult, I didn't want to lose Halim. He had come to the hotel through an ad in the paper a few months after I took over. I knew nothing about him, but I liked him from the very start. He hardly had any hotel experience, yet he spoke English and German well, and his good looks and friendly manner melted many a guest's heart. He was popular with the rest of the staff as well. He had started out as a rather clumsy waiter, and eventually, I moved him to the front desk. His occasional mistakes cost me more money than I cared to tally, but his lovely character was invaluable. Despite age and social and cultural differences, there was an unspoken understanding between us. It became clear over time that we were raised with the same morals. Although I got on well with most of my staff, I felt on the same level with Halim in particular when it came to honesty, fairness, loyalty, and fighting for our beliefs. He took his religion in its purest form, just as I took my nonreligion in its purest form. We were two different types of fundamentalist, and both painfully stubborn.

A few days later, I received a phone call from a friend who'd finally gotten hold of the former lady museum expert.

"I'm afraid you'll have to take it down," she sighed.

As it turned out, the expert told her, there had always been a lot of controversy about the painting. One story had it that the lady in the portrait was Osman Hamdi's mistress, and that he was so madly in love with her that he decided to paint her in the holiest of places. The oil-on-canvas original, painted in 1901, was probably never shown while the artist was still alive. For years after his death, it was in the hands of a certain Çiğdem *Hanım*, but then she decided to get rid of it as well—it was too controversial. She sold it for a hefty price to a bank that was taken over by the government for insolvency in the 2001 financial crisis.

"Since then, no one knows where the original is," my friend concluded.

I thanked her for her effort, not sure whether to be content or disappointed with the outcome. By now the issue wasn't really about whether or not the picture was against Islam, but whether it was okay to hang something in my lobby that made my staff feel uncomfortable.

Once I found the title of the painting, it had become a lot easier to find information on the Internet. As was to be expected, the opinions were quite varied, but there were three things every scholar and art historian agreed on. First was that the lady was indeed sitting on a *rahle,* the type of bookstand a *hoca,* or teacher, would use for heavy religious books. Next was that the woman's back was to the *kible,* the holy niche indicating the direction of Mecca. Last was that the books below her were most likely religious ones. Osman Hamdi *Bey* was known as the pioneer of the female figure, elevating and exalting woman above what was commonly accepted, giving her back her wisdom and thus rejecting the cliché of the Oriental woman as sex object. He seemed to me a feminist of his time.

There was little mention of a mistress though. As may have been the case in *Mihrab,* he generally used his French wife, Naile *Hanım,* as his model. One website, however, claimed the lady in *Mihrab* was his Armenian lover.

Hamdi's paintings contrasted sharply with those of his teacher, Gérôme, who liked to portray Islam as something exotic, fanatical, and sometimes even violent. Hamdi presented Islam as a religion that encouraged intellectual curiosity and discussion. *But how did Hamdi get away with his feminism?* I wondered. I learned that just as the features of women were veiled, female portraits were also hidden at the time, even from the gaze of male servants. So any painting depicting a woman—however conventional her portrayal—either stayed in a dark closet or was draped by curtains fastened to the frame.

After all we'd been through, neither of those options seemed a suitable solution to me. I took the painting down that very same day. During Ramazan, I managed to find a fitting replacement piece of artwork for my lobby—another reproduction from the same shop, depicting a harem girl serving coffee to a sultan. It was much too submissive for my taste but was clearly a lot "safer." And the colors were just as perfect as the *Mihrab*.

I couldn't help but feel slightly defeated when carrying my controversial painting out of the hotel, but I was consoled by the fact that Halim hadn't the slightest victorious air about him. He came up to my office the next day to thank me, and it was clear that he meant it. In fact, he began to treat me with even more respect. As a token of his appreciation, he gave me a rather religious book, called *Miracles of the Koran*. He expected me to put it into the hotel's library, but I never did. I have my limits, after all.

Conversion in Erzurum

BY SUSAN FLEMING HOLM

*J*f I had been less naive or more observant—or better yet, both—I might have wondered why many of the women were wearing either the *çarşaf*—a black, cotton sheet made to cover the entire, already clothed body—or the *ehram*, a similar but warmer covering made of woven, unbleached wool.

But the anomaly of Muslim women wearing their outer coverings inside a home when men were absent was not on my radar. Nor did I notice that the women's faces were not yet covered; the *çarşaf* or *ehram* hung loosely from their head or shoulders. As we sat and chatted, I was outwardly polite, responding amiably to questions, but in reality I was totally absorbed in myself, fighting my irritation at the change in plans, which had surprised and mystified me.

When a hush fell upon the group, I looked up to see the imam enter. Each woman wearing a *çarşaf* or *ehram* picked up a corner of the garment and covered her face, but those nursing their babies continued to do so openly. The Muslim cleric was introduced to me, the only *yabancı* (foreigner) in the group, and he spoke the polite Turkish expression I found so poetic, *"Hoş geldiniz."* (Pleasantly you came.)

I offered the response, *"Hoş bulduk."* (We have found it pleasant.)

He sat down. The women looked at him, quietly expectant. He closed his eyes and began to recite from memory. I had heard that the music and rhythm of Koranic Arabic was beautiful, and listening to it, I knew it to be so. All the women around me slowly began swaying to the rhythm, and eventually I began to sway too. But even through the sudden pleasure of this experience, I pondered the irony of women covering their faces (some of them holding the edge of the *çarşaf* or *ehram* in their teeth) while continuing to nurse their children. *A covered face and a bare breast? What a contradiction! I will never understand this culture!* This experience defied all logic in my mind.

I appreciated the healthy custom of breastfeeding and planned to follow that practice when I had children. But I had thought the culture of Eastern Turkey to be much more conservative, much more restrictive than my own American culture with regard to the bodies and the clothing of women. Seeing some women covered face to feet on the streets of Erzurum, where I lived, only underscored that opinion. So when I observed women openly breastfeeding their babies during a religious service, while taking care to cover their faces, I was completely nonplussed.

But this was only one of several surprises confronting me that winter day in Erzurum. The first had been my arrival at the Sevgis' home. When Gülserin, Yurda, and Saliha Sevgi—three teenage sisters a few years younger than I—had come by our apartment to pick me up that morning, I had thought our plan was to go to the *hamam*, the Turkish bath. We had linked arms in the Turkish custom (women with women, men with men) as we trudged up the frozen Erzurum street. I was startled by our arrival at the Sevgis' home, on a narrow, dusty street that had a frozen trickle down the center. "We'll go to the *hamam* a little later," Gülserin explained to me.

My husband, Jim, and I had met the three girls through their father, Ömer Sevgi, who had befriended us during our first weeks of Peace Corps service in Erzurum. Ömer Bey—Mr. Ömer—was a foreman at an outlet for a flour factory, and his place of work was a storefront right beneath our apartment. He had invited us frequently to his home, and his wife and six daughters made us feel warm and welcome, sometimes sending their one young son, Erdoğan, running out to the corner pastry shop for cookies to accompany our many tiny glasses of hot tea. The Sevgi daughters also brought us wool socks and fruit when we were sick, and their mother taught me how to use bulgur and *yoğurt*, foods that were unfamiliar to me in the States.

On the day of the surprise visit to the Sevgis' home, fifteen or so other women were already sitting in a circle on the layers of carpets when we arrived. The small room was warmly heated by a coal stove and by the women's friendly smiles. As soon as I sat down, the comments started, and I smiled politely, struggling to understand new words and expressions, recognizing many familiar comments. I, as the *yabancı*, was the center of attention and the topic of conversation.

"*Aman Allah!*" (She's so thin!)

"Don't you miss your mother?" (This was an oft-repeated question to both Jim and me.)

"How pretty!"

"How sweet!"

"My sweet daughter!"(With so much positive attention, I hoped the *nazar*, the evil eye, wouldn't fall upon me.)

"Does she know Turkish?"

"Do you know Turkish?" (This question was directed at me in a louder voice to help me understand.)

"She knows Turkish!" (This comment in a protesting voice from one of my hostesses.)

"Ah, she knows Turkish! Now she can stay here!"

"You can be one of us."

"You can be a Muslim!"

"She will be a Muslim!"

This was another familiar refrain—I could speak Turkish (an exaggeration, since we had been there only three months), so therefore I could make Turkey my home for life, and become one of them. The imam's arrival, however, was a new experience, and I wondered who had invited an imam to spend time with a group of women, and why. I was pleased with the opportunity to listen to a recitation from the Koran, but I wondered about the intention behind his presence. I leapt privately into defensive mode. *I will* not *be a Muslim!* I thought to myself.

The imam's recitation flowed to its finish, and we all commented on its beauty. He took his leave. Nothing further was said to me regarding becoming "one of us." The other women departed, and Gülserin, Yurda, Saliha, and I, arms again linked, started on our way to the *hamam*. There the girls initiated me into the rituals of scrubbing, soaking, drinking tea, and gossiping with women during a long, steamy afternoon. I was shocked and amused by the lack of inhibition and the sense of humor the women in the *hamam* showed with regard to their bodies—most of them completely nude, a few with towels wrapped around their waists. There was much friendly teasing as they compared body sizes, shapes, and degree of sag. Later I showed my hosts how American women shaved their legs, and they lowered their eyes as if embarrassed. I wondered if I had been unwise to share this custom with them.

When I finally arrived home, late in the afternoon, I was irritated that my time had not gone as I'd planned it. I wished the Turks would learn to be more efficient and more respectful of schedules. And in the back of my mind I was still incredulous that women who habitually covered their faces in the presence of men could openly bare their breasts and nurse their babies in front of a man who was not only not a family member but who was a religious figure.

My consternation in the face of this puzzle became an underground seed in my imagination. In time I could see that it was indeed the beginning of a conversion—not the conversion I had feared and silently protested, but a conversion nonetheless. This seed was germinating and growing within the greater journey of my Peace Corps experience in Erzurum—a city whose history, civilization, and citizens had processed many conversions over thousands of years.

Jim and I arrived in Turkey on a cold, rainy September afternoon in 1966. In our 1960s idealism, strengthened and emboldened by the tragic assassination of President John F. Kennedy, we had joined the Peace Corps. Part of a generation of change, we had marched for equal rights for African Americans; we were beginning to question the war in Vietnam, where those dying on both sides were disproportionately poor; the lives of women were changing dramatically with the advent of the birth control pill and expanded job opportunities.

Now my husband of three months and I were launched on our particular investment in change. We were learning to live in and know another culture while teaching English to students in medicine, engineering, agriculture, and other disciplines at Atatürk University in Erzurum, a city situated at the far eastern reaches of Turkey in a windswept valley high in the Palandöken Mountains.

During the thirty-hour train trip to Erzurum from Ankara, it was as if we had traveled through Anatolian history, with its constants and its changes. We had crossed and recrossed the headwaters of the Euphrates River, called the Fırat in Turkish. We had stopped at Kayseri, which had long ago been given the name Caesarea by the Roman emperor Tiberius Caesar Augustus (AD 14–37) after he conquered it.

We had stopped at Sivas, where in 1919 the Sivas Congress was held under the leadership of *Gazi* Mustafa Kemal Paşa, marking the beginning of the National Struggle against the occupying forces. This war of independence, initiated by the congress, saved the moribund Ottoman Empire from being dismembered by the Allies and began the nation's transformation from defeated empire into the modern republic of Turkey. Later, Mustafa Kemal was given the surname Atatürk (Father of the Turks) by the Turkish Parliament.

From Sivas we had journeyed to Erzincan, a city rebuilt from the 1939 earthquake that had killed thirty thousand people in a matter of seconds.

In between these cities, our train pulled into villages that were so isolated the local children ran to greet the train, yelling *"Gazete! Gazete!"* Not understanding, we had watched the more knowledgeable passengers toss their newspapers to these boys. At one village, a tiny child, running up behind the larger boys, stretched his small arms in the apparently impossible hope of being the one who got the paper. A Turkish gentleman two windows down from ours signaled with his folded newspaper to the small boy and waved the bigger ones out of the way. When the big boys understood, they backed off, and the gentleman on the train tossed the newspaper directly into the tiny hands. The child, his face lit with triumphant surprise, ran like the wind back into the village, bearing news from distant lands.

These scenes were new and amazing to us—even to my husband, who had already lived with a Turkish family for a summer in Denizli, a textile town in Western Turkey. It was because of Jim's very happy experience with his Turkish family that we had requested Turkey when we applied for the Peace Corps. Prior to our departure, many friends and acquaintances in the States had communicated uncertainty about our placement, their expressions ranging from the diplomatic "We'll pray for your safety" to the much more direct "Aren't you afraid of going to the Middle East? They're always fighting over there!"

When we first arrived in Ankara, we were delighted to learn we had been assigned to a university, only to discover that many Turks from the capital and the western part of the country considered Erzurum a cultural backwater and a hardship post.

"Erzurum?" responded waiters in restaurants, cab drivers, the lady who cleaned our hotel room, the representative of the ministry of education— all with raised eyebrows and looks of alarm. "Ooooh. Erzurum! *Soğuk! Çok kar var!*" (Cold! Lots of snow!) I immediately bought a pair of boots from a volunteer who had just been assigned to the more temperate İzmir, on the Aegean coast.

Erzurum's climate was indeed cold, because of its location on the side of a more-than-mile-high mountain plateau. That September afternoon that we arrived, it was raining, chilly, and gray. Around us, the mountains, which dominated the city with monumental and embracing outlines, were brown, sodden, treeless, and furrowed with erosion—the sagging breasts of an old mother who had suckled too many children. Soon, however, we were to discover that for most of the year, snow converted the mountains into softened, rounded forms, their whiteness dancing and dazzling the eye.

Both years that we lived there, light snow fell even into the first days of June. During the long winter months, the streets were packed solid with icy snow, and walking could be a challenge. The horses pulling the *fayton-lar*, horse-drawn phaeton carriages functioning as the taxis of the city, would struggle going uphill or downhill on the slippery streets. On frigid winter mornings, as a *fayton* moved up Mumcu Caddesi (the Street of the Candle Makers) or down Hastaneler Caddesi (the Street of the Hospitals), little birds would follow, settling on the newly dropped piles of horse dung, still steaming from the heat of the animal's body, to pick out the undigested grain. On the cold winter nights, the *faytonlar* would line up outside the *çayhanelar* (teahouses). For the horses, the only protection against the bitter cold was offered by the wool feed bag on each animal's nose and the small wool blanket over its back. Inside the *çayhane,* the drivers would sit around the coal stove, talking and keeping an eye out for fares.

The climate was harsh, but the city, whose citizens were Turks, Kurds, and Armenians, was a wealth of diversity and culture. Erzurum had been for millennia both the crossroads and the site of human civilizations, in one conversion after another—Urartus, Cimmerians and Scyths, Medes, Persians and Parthes, Arabs, Mongols, and Selçuk and Ottoman Turks. It had been an outpost of the Romans—the name Erzurum means "arsenal of the Romans." Parts of the old city were still surrounded by deteriorating Byzantine walls, which peasants were now converting, stone by stone, into their dwellings. In some cases the ancient Byzantine structure served as the fourth wall of the house. Selçuk architectural gems still stood in many places of the city: A *medrese* complex with twin minarets anchored one end of Cumhuriyet Caddesi (the Street of the Republic), and the location of an old Selçuk tomb caused that avenue to waver at one point in its steady path through the center of the city.

War had converted Erzurum to a Russian city three times in the 19th and early 20th centuries, and later, after World War II, U.S./NATO powers had placed a nuclear missile outside the city, facing the nearby border with the Soviet Union. Although the U.S. announced they'd removed that weapon following the Cuban Missile Crisis, every third or fourth man on the street in Erzurum, once he learned we were Americans, would step conspiratorially closer, look around, and then whisper, one hand next to mouth, the other pointing to the outskirts of the city, "There's a missile. Do you know? A missile!"

Compared with the millennia of the city's history, the university where we taught was very new and sat outside the city, comprising in some ways a separate community.

We lived in town, however, as did the ten or twelve other Peace Corps volunteers and some of the British teachers. Some other faculty and staff members were residents in the city proper as well. But whether they lived in the city or separate from it, whether they were natives or foreigners, employees of the university and its hospital introduced change into the daily life of Erzurum.

The Turkish female physicians from İzmir, as well as one very petite German woman, wore miniskirts on the street, standing out against those who wore the *çarşaf* or the more-typical-to-Erzurum *ehram*, and even contrasting with those who wore plain, below-the-knee winter coats and head scarves. Restaurants and grocers brought in foreign foods. I asked one merchant to order peanut butter for me, and some months later, noticing that he was still stocking it, I thanked him. "Oh, even the Turks like it," he exclaimed. The university hospital made contraception available to any woman who sought it. Significant or unremarkable, progressive or questionable, personal or universal, all the changes contributed to yet another cultural conversion in Erzurum.

Both Jim and I unwittingly participated in this process as the objects of curious questions and long stares on the streets of Erzurum. My short, light hair called attention to us, as did Jim's slender six-foot, four-inch frame (once, he was called a "walking minaret"). In spite of my idealistic desire to plant seeds of change, to be an agent of understanding between my country and Turkey, I found it irritating to be so noticeable and so noticed.

It mattered little that I tried to remain inconspicuous. Following the style of my Turkish female colleagues in the English department at the university, I never wore slacks on the street in Erzurum, and over my sweaters and skirts, I usually wore a dark winter coat or a dark blue raincoat, and sometimes a head scarf. Still, schoolboys frequently shouted out, *"Turist, turist,"* as we walked to or from the bus stop. On one occasion I suggested to my husband that I wanted to wear an *ehram* so that I could go unnoticed down the street. He looked up from the Turkish newspaper he was reading, thought for a moment, and replied, "It wouldn't do any good. You walk too fast." He was right.

But some of the attention was endearing, like when perfect strangers would address me as *abla* (big sister) and Jim as *ağabey* (big brother).

Lack of anonymity on the streets of Erzurum never did cease to annoy me, but by our second year, I was aware of a greater degree of comfort in our life. I could converse with more skill and nuance in Turkish. I had learned how to make Turkish coffee, properly *köpüklü* (with foam). *Yoğurt* was a staple in our diet. The call to prayer from a minaret, Turkish music, and Turkish news on the radio were markers in our days.

From Erzurum, we "watched" the 1967 Six Day War and the 1967 Cyprus crisis, including a student demonstration in front of the Erzurum city post office demanding that Turkish troops be sent to Cyprus. In 1968, two months before we left Erzurum, we learned of the death of Martin Luther King, Jr., and then, just before we departed, Bobby Kennedy was shot. Turkish friends begged us to stay and be safe with them, not to go home, where Detroit was in flames, where poor people were marching on Washington, D.C., and where our best leaders were being picked off one at a time.

"Aren't you afraid?" they asked when it was clear that we would leave Turkey, and then, "We'll pray for your safety."

In spite of the fears of our friends, in spite of the chaos in the States, I was happy to be going home. I was hungry for a BLT. I wanted a tall glass of cold, pasteurized milk. I missed my family! My sister was going to be married, and I was to be her matron of honor.

Nonetheless, living again in my own culture against the backdrop of my experiences in Turkey soon became like the slow-motion developing of a photo negative, revealing black as white and white as black. I was amazed by the shock of defamiliarization.

Back in the States, I taught in the public schools of Montgomery County, Maryland, one of the most progressive school systems in the United States, where the dress code for professional women nevertheless disallowed pants. We were permitted to wear only dresses or skirts, including miniskirts, still very much in style. During my first pregnancy, finding a maternity skirt or dress long enough to allow me to sit down in front of my class became impossible, so I stood during each class session—up until a week before my first son arrived.

I breastfed that son, as well as the second one, who was born two years later in Kansas. In our own home I was able to breastfeed without incident, but in public places—in the presence of persons other than close friends and family, in a church, in a Laundromat—I felt pressured to leave my breasts covered and feed my babies with a bottle.

Now, thirty-eight years after I watched mothers nursing their babies during a religious service in Erzurum, a small change has taken place in my own country in the matter of breastfeeding children. In 2004, my state of Illinois passed a law allowing women to breastfeed in public without being accused of indecency or lewd behavior. An exception exists, however: "a mother considering whether to breastfeed her baby in a place of worship shall comport her behavior with the norms appropriate in that place of worship" [Public Act 093-0942, SB3211, Section 10]. The female body in the act of mothering is still subject to regulation by the government and by religious tradition in the United States.

These many years later I revisit, in my memory, in my storytelling, the afternoon spent in the Sevgis' warm home. I see all the young wives smiling at me, and I recognize in each exposed breast an innocent, nurturing, and loving connection between mother and child—not, as I had learned in my culture, a sex symbol.

It was my own culture, as much as Turkish culture, that I didn't understand then. Now I perceive the similarity between our cultural traditions—Turkish and American, Islamic and Judeo/Christian—that make sex symbols out of female body parts, assign guilt to sexuality, and use clothing to discourage, or to license, temptation.

But beyond that, I can see that my wish for the Turks to become more like Americans—efficient, organized, scheduled—was the same hope that they held for me. My Turkish friends wanted me to stay with them, participate in their lives, and learn to value what they esteemed: a delight in meeting strangers, whom they know as guests; spontaneous hospitality warmed by hot tea; the beauty of a recitation from the Koran; guests converted into friends. Even face to face, however, each of us remained too strange for the other to imagine; each tried to translate the other into her own reality.

I have never known whether a conversion was the intent of the religious service in the Sevgis' home, but that ceased to matter long ago. What does matter is that the experience continues to be a conversion, challenging me to remove the veil of my own cultural perceptions whenever I meet new experiences, new cultures, new people.

The Beat of a Different Drummer

BY PAT YALE

*C*oming to live in Turkey, I very much wanted to fit in with local customs whenever possible. Of course if I'd chosen to settle in the anonymity of a big city like İstanbul, I could have lived a life more like the one I had left behind in Bristol, England. But I had lost my heart to the small Cappadocian village of Göreme in Central Turkey, and in Cappadocian villages, most women still lead lives far more traditional than their city-born sisters. There was no doubt that I was going to have to adapt my normal ways of doing things if I wanted to be accepted there.

In 1998 I had rented an old stone house in Göreme. It had not been the most obvious career move for a town-born professional travel writer, but my work for the Lonely Planet guide to Turkey had brought me back to the village time and again, and over a period of ten years, I had picked up many friends amongst the English-speaking hoteliers and the foreigners already resident there. One day I was joking to friends at home that I had a better social life in Göreme than in England—then gulped and realized it was true.

That set me thinking. Wouldn't it be fun to go and live there for a year? Rent a house and live like the villagers? Celebrate Ramazan, the Muslim month of fasting, and Kurban Bayramı, the Feast of Sacrifice, instead of Christmas and Easter? Watch the snow settle over the fairy chimneys? Find out what it was like for women to live in a place where the tourist industry had freed the men from the drudgery of fieldwork to run the pensions, but where their wives were still expected to stay home to cook, clean, and look after the children?

Much of my infatuation with Cappadocia came from a love of its crazy landscape—a whipped-up confection of deep-cut gorges and soaring rock cones ("fairy chimneys") created by the force of wind and rain beating down on the volcanic tuff over long centuries. But of course I was also fascinated by the extraordinary history of this part of Turkey, which seems to have a medieval frescoed church lurking around every corner. What's more, as someone blessed with a curious nature, I was intrigued to find out how a small remote Anatolian village was responding to the pressures of fast-changing modern life.

If you stick a pin in the middle of a map of Turkey, you might well hit the dot marked Göreme. Visitors flock here from all over the world to exclaim at the astonishing rock-cut churches and the soaring fairy chimneys; then they fold themselves in half and squeeze along the tunnels of the amazing underground cities carved out of the rock—placcs of refuge for the early Christians when enemy invaders streamed in. But behind the facade of modern hotels and restaurants full of visitors downing the local wine with their meals, dressed exactly as they would be back home, there exists a traditional Anatolian village with its back firmly turned on the paraphernalia of tourism.

That old part of the village had worked its way under my skin—the part that lurked on a hill behind the hotels, ignored by tourists. Strolling up the hill, anyone could admire the lovely honey-colored stone, the graceful doorways, the pretty paired windows of the crumbling houses. But at the same time those houses played coy with their real charm, which was the way that every one of them was not just built from stone but also carved into the rock itself. For behind the deceptively normal facades lay a labyrinth of cave stables and storerooms still in use, housing cows and horses and storing mountains of sultanas and plateaux of *yufka,* a paper-thin bread made in vast quantities to last families through the harsh Anatolian winter.

In falling for the magical architecture of the old village, I had fallen for just that part of Göreme where no respectable woman ever touched alcohol and where almost all my new neighbors-to-be walked around in the heat of summer wearing more layers of clothing—thick pullovers, cardigans, baggy trousers, tights and socks—than I would put on in winter. And yet it was those same overdressed women—the ones I had seen but never spoken to—that I was most eager to get to know now.

Traveling in Turkey, I had always found it easy to make male friends, especially through my work. But meeting women had proved trickier, mostly because fewer women knew any English, and my Turkish was yet to pass first base. I knew that to be accepted by the matrons of old Göreme I would need to make whatever adjustments were required to be seen as respectable: to become the sort of foreign woman who could be invited into village houses without embarrassment; the sort of woman who could be relied on to observe customary modesty, who would not arrive wearing a low-cut top and plonk herself down beside somebody's husband or sprawl in an unseemly fashion on the sofa. It was the decision of a moment to cross the local bars off my list of visiting places and to resolve to keep my arms and legs (if not my head) covered at all times. I even went back to eating meat so that I wouldn't have to risk offending my hosts by querying the contents of every meal placed in front of me. These were, after all, small changes to make for the rich reward of being welcomed into my neighbors' homes.

Finding a home to rent had not been easy, since I had set my heart on living in precisely the part of Göreme with the fewest empty yet habitable houses. For me the cave-houses had all the allure of novelty, and I was itching to try out life inside one of them. But those who had been born to the troglodyte lifestyle saw things differently. While I was oohing and aahing over how cleverly the houses reflected the local lifestyle—that great niche for trampling grapes to make *pekmez* (grape syrup); that hole-in-the-ground *tandır* oven for making bread!—pragmatic locals would be pointing to the rising damp and descending dust. Satellite television beamed images of life in İstanbul into their homes every day, and the nearby provincial capital of Nevşehir, with its myriad desirable apartments, was only a short bus ride away. So now many of the cave-houses were falling down as those who made good abandoned them in favor of brand-new homes with everything fitted, polished, and dust-free in Göreme's newer neighborhoods.

But eventually I struck gold. Right at the top of the hill, where the old village slowly trickled out into a track, I found the perfect place to rent: a room in a grand house with fetching stone roses carved beneath its window ledges and a steep pedimental roof to keep off the snow. The house was around eighty years old and had been built for a village bigwig who had risen to become a parliamentarian. For less than a hundred dollars a month, my landlord was happy to rent me a capacious room with soaring wooden ceiling. Skirting the walls was a *sedir* (bench seat), on which I could recline during the day then sleep at night, packing my bedding away into a niche in the stone wall as had been the custom since Ottoman times. It had a wood- and coal-burning stove, which would supply me not just with heat but with a constant supply of hot water and a means of drying my clothes in the winter. But best of all, the house had a panoramic view—and who needs an oven, fridge, television, or washing machine when they can have a view to die for instead? Day after day I would throw open the gate and step onto a terrace that felt like a stage overlooking the fairy chimneys. Night after night, more stars than I knew existed would blaze down on me. It was a tiny piece of heaven.

My choice of house came with an added bonus. Living downstairs was a wonderful local family who took me under their wing. With them I learned to eat Anatolian-style, sitting on the floor around a low table with a communal cloth spread over all our knees to collect the crumbs. With them I learned to snack on roasted pumpkin seeds, crunching them between my teeth and swallowing only the seed and not the shell. And through them I got to know my other neighbors, because whenever her friends came for tea, Ayşe, the wife, would rush upstairs and invite me down to join them.

At first these tea parties were agony. Before settling in Göreme, I had attended a month-long intensive Turkish course, but that had proved less than adequate preparation for understanding my neighbors. My teachers had taught me to say *"Nasılsın?"* for "How are you?" but *"Nörüyon?"* was what they asked me here, because the people of Göreme spoke an ancient dialect of Turkish as different from the İstanbul version as Geordie English is from the BBC variety or the Texas drawl from clipped Bostonian. Added to my failings on the linguistic front had to be my failings on the domestic one. A modern career woman who had never thought of making her own clothes, let alone those of her family, I would sit in smiling silence, my hands useless in my lap, while all around me the other women knitted, sewed, and embroidered for their daughters' *sandık,* or dowry chest. But over time and with their help, I learned, if not to sew, at least to speak their dialect.

However, the test of how far anyone can assimilate to another culture really occurs when they encounter local customs that clash head-on with their own most deeply held beliefs. That crunch came for me when a neighbor suggested that I should sacrifice a sheep to show my gratitude at having acquired a village house.

After six months of renting I was so settled into the quieter, slower rhythms of Göreme that I had started to question why anyone would want to return to the hurly-burly of life in overregulated Britain. I had already inspected an empty cave-house with a scary crack running down its facade like the scar from a particularly gruesome operation. A real estate agent would have had problems with a prospectus for this house, which lacked a toilet, running water, electricity, or plumbing. Nor did it have much of a roof—or even stairs to access the top floor. But what it did have, at least as far as I was concerned, was potential by the bucketload. Eight rooms spread across three floors, six of them in caves. Built-in stone alcoves for the age-old tradition of fermenting wine. Floor-cut *tandır* ovens, where previous owners had baked their bread. Rock-cut mangers for sheep and cows. Two terraces overlooking the fairy chimneys. And two courtyards that my imagination quickly planted with roses and geraniums and a grapevine pergola. The view was so splendid that it made me want to weep. It was a place where I knew I could be inspired to write. So when I heard myself putting in an offer for the house, it felt like *kısmet.* And it was in return for my good fortune in acquiring that property that I was now expected to slaughter an unfortunate sheep.

My neighbor assured me that the sacrifice was the normal way of doing things in Göreme; I could divide up the meat to give to the poor and so let other people share in my good fortune. But however much I wanted to do what the locals saw as right, this was a custom that was impossible to reconcile with my own great and very British love of animals. I'd watched sheep being killed to celebrate Kurban Bayramı, the festival that commemorates İbrahim's near sacrifice of his son İsmael. I'd even witnessed a ram being slaughtered to kick off an election campaign. I knew that my neighbors saw the deaths as worthy—Turks thought that the dead animal's spirit would carry the soul of the sacrificer to heaven—and that they believed that sharing the meat served to consolidate a sense of community. But kill a sheep to celebrate my own good fortune? I'd as soon have slit the throat of my best friend! And so I began to consider alternative ways to show my gratitude.

The first idea that sprang to mind was to donate something to the local school, whose headmaster was always bemoaning the patches of damp on the walls and holes in the roof. So I tracked down the representative of the Göreme equivalent of the Parent–Teachers Association. "I'd like to give something to the school for about the value of a sheep, around $165," I told Mustafa, and he agreed to find out what would be appropriate.

A few days passed. Then: "You could buy the school its coal for the winter," he suggested.

That wasn't quite what I had had in mind. I wanted something tangible, something lasting, not something that would literally go up in smoke, let alone something which, frankly, it had to be the government's responsibility to provide.

I was ready to forget the whole thing, knowing that no one really expected a *yabancı* (foreigner) to comply with customs that not even all the locals observed. But then an image flashed through my mind. The house I had bought lay in a conservation area, and before I could start work on restoring it, I had to discuss with the town planner what alterations were allowed. Down in the bowels of the *belediye* (town hall) building, the planner kept a vast zoning map indicating what was and wasn't permitted in every village house. While he was trying to pinpoint my property, my attention wandered, and across the corridor I spotted a pile of drums. The Ramazan drums. The drums that were used to wake people up before dawn during the month of fasting. The drums that urged people to tuck into a hearty breakfast before the start of the long day's deprivation.

During my first few months in the village, I'd joined in the fast myself, keen to experience everything that my neighbors went through. Never before had I felt such a strong sense of what the word "community" really meant as then, when I was struggling, along with everyone else, to resist a quick glass of tea until the *ezan* (call to prayer) rang out and I could break my fast in unison with the whole village.

By chance, in that particular year, the Gregorian New Year coincided with Ramazan. After celebrating the birth of 1999 in a hotel in the less visited Cappadocian village of Güzelyurt, I'd crept out into the chilly early morning back streets and, in a spellbinding moment of revelation, glimpsed an elderly couple arousing Güzelyurt's inhabitants for their predawn feast, the man beating time on a sturdy, upright drum while his wife rapped on each gate in turn.

Back in Göreme it was a different matter. After long years of use, the skins on the Göreme drums had split, and they had been abandoned. Nowadays the village was woken up by poorer members of the community battering on the sides of huge, empty olive oil tins—just as effective maybe, but nowhere near as romantic, at least in my opinion.

At once an idea began to take shape. I would get the drums repaired. They were a part of Turkey's heritage, so in repairing them, I would be substituting one cultural tradition for another. Instead of sacrificing an animal I would try to revive another ancient custom. Perfect! I loved the idea.

That is, I loved it until I tried to turn it into reality. Back in my house-hunting days, potential properties for rent had developed a nasty habit of turning into shimmering mirages, forever just out of reach. Now too, conversations would kick off on a wave of Turkish optimism, only to fade out again in an equally Turkish mood of fatalism. "Do you know where I can get drums repaired?" I would ask, and people would smile and mention the toy drum shop in neighboring Nevşehir or the Gypsies they had once seen repairing instruments in nearby Ürgüp bus station. But when pressed as to whether the shop sold real drums or whether the Gypsies were still in Ürgüp, faces would fall, and a shrug or upward toss of the head—the ubiquitous Turkish gesture that signifies "no"—would crush my hopes.

However, one thing I'd learned during my time in Göreme was that when it came to shopping, all paths led eventually to Kayseri, an hour away from us by bus. Once the capital of the Roman province of Cappadocia, modern

Kayseri is an Anatolian boomtown, the sort of place where you can pick up the latest computer software or the most up-to-the-minute mobile phone. At the same time, it's an ancient city that clings to the old ways of doing things. Behind the black basalt walls of its citadel lurk markets that still exude something of the Orient from the days when Kayseri was an important stop on the Silk Road. And down the back streets inquisitive shoppers like me still stumble upon people selling all manner of oddities.

It was down one of these back streets that I spied trees that looked from a distance to be sprouting giant watermelons but which turned out on closer inspection to be hung with drums. Real drums. Big beige drums with roped-up sides and reverberant skins. Ramazan drums of the sort I'd seen being beaten by the old man in Güzelyurt.

I stepped through the door of what resembled the reception of a down-at-heel London minicab company and found it occupied by a pimpled youth who stared at me as if he had never seen a foreigner before.

"Drums," I managed to stutter in Turkish. "I want to talk to someone about drums."

He shot up and shot out, returning minutes later with a slip of a man, greasy-haired and obsequious. Was I married, he wanted to know. Did I have children? Only with those vital enquiries out of the way could we get down to business. I explained about the Göreme drums, about Ramazan being only weeks away, about wanting to get them repaired—a monologue complicated by the fact that I had no idea of the Turkish word for "drum skins." But it was easy to point, and the man appeared to understand me, beaming and pouring out a stream of heavily accented Kayseri Turkish, the gist of which appeared to be that, yes, he could repair the drums for around the cost of a sheep.

We came, I thought, to an agreement and I trotted off happily to inspect some second-hand iron railings that could be trimmed to fit the staircase of my new house. Back in Göreme, I outlined the story to Ali, an English-speaking friend and neighbor. The look of amusement on his face betrayed precisely what a harebrained scheme he thought this one likely to be, but it was winter again and there was little enough to entertain us in Göreme. The drum project did at least have the advantage of novelty, so whatever misgivings he had, he kept them to himself, and the next morning we visited the *belediye* building to pick up the drums. There was just one small snag, which was that the man with the key to the drum cupboard had gone to help with the digging of a new well.

"Have a tea and come back later," an official advised us.

Two hours and many teas later, we returned to the *belediye* building. Still there was no sign of the key holder. "Let's go and pick it up," suggested Ali, who had better things to do with his day than hang about in the town hall.

Some miles down the road, we came across a group of men gathered around a pump that was being installed to bring more water to Göreme. Every year, as hoteliers installed en suite bathrooms and swimming pools for their guests, the water supply came under greater strain, until the breaking point had finally been reached and the pressure had become too weak to push water up to the old part of the village. Worse still, even the *çeşme* (fountain) that we used to fall back on when the taps ran dry had seized up. So now the mayor was looking farther afield in an effort to ensure enough water for the future.

We found the key holder, who looked completely taken aback by our mission—because, of course, the keys he was carrying were not the ones to the drum cupboard. Those were back in the *belediye* building. Back we went to the town hall, where a key was tried in the lock, the cupboard doors were opened, and the drums were extracted—a whole half-day after we had first tried to retrieve them.

By now we had been joined by the very same Mustafa who had originally tried to interest me in the school's coal supply but who had now decided that the drum scheme sounded far more fun. It was easy enough to find the Kayseri street with the trees sprouting drums. It was easy too to find the man with whom I'd discussed repairs. But now I could smell the alcohol on his breath. No sooner had I stepped from the van than he rushed over and tried to insinuate an arm around my waist, all the while calling me sister as if that could somehow excuse such overfamiliarity.

Ali and Mustafa stepped quickly in between us.

"Where did you find this guy, Pat?" Ali whispered, a question to which I could only respond with a sheepish shrug.

We pulled the drums out of the van, and mighty sad they looked when exposed to the sunlight, especially beneath the brand-new models hanging down from the branches above. I could feel my enthusiasm ebbing again, but it was too late to back out now.

Ali started to recap what it was that we wanted done with the drums while the man stood staring at them with a curled lip. Still, eventually he nodded and shook hands with Ali and instructed the pimpled youth to carry them into the shop. Then we clambered back into our van and started back to Göreme. All the way there, Ali and Mustafa chuckled together, no doubt contrasting my effrontery in trying to organize new drums without their help with the sensible way in which their traditional wives would have left them to manage everything. Meanwhile I languished in the back of the van, licking my wounds and concluding that I should perhaps have taken their advice rather than jumping in with both feet trying to sort things out for myself in the usual independent way of Western women.

With Ramazan still a week away, I returned to England, leaving Ali to pick up the newly repaired drums on his next shopping trip to Kayseri. It was January before I came back to Turkey. Ali was in İstanbul on business, so he picked me up from my hotel there, and we drove back to Göreme over Mount Bolu with snow swirling around us. We had a lot of catching up to do—who had married, who had died, whose baby had been born, what had happened with the building work on my house—but eventually the conversation swiveled around to the subject of the drums.

Ali's face lit up at once. "You and your crazy ideas!" he laughed. "When I went to pick them up, that guy had sold them for scrap. He was furious with me—'if you hadn't come along,' he said, 'I was going to charge that *yabancı* a fortune for them.'"

This was not the first time that Ali had run up against the surprising assumption that in any transaction between a Turk and a foreigner he would be expected to side with the Turk, however much closer a friend the foreigner might be. We exchanged warm smiles that reassured each other just how silly an idea we thought this was, and Ali pressed on with the story.

"Then he said that we'd have to buy new drums and asked for a lot more money. I threatened to call the police but in the end what could I do? The old ones were gone. So now instead of three old drums we've got two new ones."

"Well, that's good, isn't it?" I asked, scrabbling around to find the redeeming feature in what was fast turning into a horror story. It was thoroughly disappointing to discover that my plans hadn't worked out as intended, but then they rarely did in Göreme, which was one of the things I was slowly learning to live with. It was frustrating to be thwarted, but at the same time there was a comical side to the plans that came unstuck, and one of the things that had drawn Ali and me together as friends was our mutual ability to laugh at the many minor mishaps that made up our daily life.

"Yes, but heaven knows what they're made from. Dog skin, probably! The van smelled so bad I had to drive back with all the windows open!" Ali concluded.

Creeping back home that evening with my tail between my legs, I cursed myself for having trusted a stranger too readily. At the same time I took some comfort from the fact that we did now have two nice new drums to wake us up for breakfast. Unfortunately, Ramazan was already over so I didn't get to hear the sound of my drums that year. Twelve months later, however, the roof of my house had been replaced, a toilet had been installed, the crack had been repaired, and I had moved into my dream of a new home. Come time for Ramazan and, hearing the low rumble of the drummer marching up the hill, I dragged myself out of the cocoon of my bedclothes and stumbled onto the darkened terrace.

Hugging myself with anticipation, I waited to see my fine new drums in action. Imagine my disappointment when instead of a deep *boom-boom-boom*, what I heard coming toward me was a sharp *rat-a-tat-tat*. I peered suspiciously down the hill, and sure enough the drummer was striding toward me, bashing the hell out of a huge, empty olive oil tin!

Believe it or not, I never did find out what happened to the new drums. They seemed to have disappeared back into some black hole in the *belediye* building basement, and I was left to conclude that the "drummers" had grown used to the oil tins and saw no need to go back to carrying something bulkier. What seemed romantically traditional to me was, for them, mere whimsy; for them, the tin cans had become the tradition, the real instruments ancient history.

I asked Ayşe what she thought about my adventure, but she just shrugged and rolled her eyes at me, because of course she would no more have taken off to Kayseri on her own to negotiate a purchase with a strange man than she would have flown to the moon.

Ali, Mustafa, and I occasionally referred to the drum incident in that bonding "Do you remember when . . . ?" way of abiding friendships. For myself, I was left to reflect on the steep learning curve that was part of my new life in Göreme. There was so much I had to learn, so much that I still didn't understand, and it hardly helped that the pace of change was so fast that it left even the locals struggling to keep up with what passed for normality. But for me that was the thrill of living in Cappadocia—the sheer unpredictability of life, the seemingly straightforward projects that morphed into whole great time-consuming dramas. I had discovered that there was something perverse in my character that seemed to thrive on the unexpected. It was why I loved living in Göreme so much and why I knew that I would never tire of the village.

THREE

Hamam

Dynasties of mothers once inspected prospective brides for their sons in the hamam. *The Turkish sauna and scrub remains a complex tradition of beauty practice and female retreat. But far from being cloistered, the impact of women's culture in Turkey is often full and frontal.*

Coming Clean in Kayseri

BY WENDY FOX

*W*hen I arrived in central Anatolia to accept a job at Erciyes University, a conservative public school in the town of Kayseri, I was confronted with a paradox. The place was both old and new. I arrived at night and was driven from the tiny airport by taxicab; at first the city seemed modern, with high-rise apartment blocks and illuminated billboards. Then, as we idled with trucks and buses at a traffic light, a tiny Arabian horse and a driver with a whip pulled up alongside in a hand-painted cart. In the light of day most things appeared old—from a nearby archaeological site dating to 4000 BC to the Hunat *hamam* close to my apartment, relatively younger but still built in the 13th century. Yet despite the obvious age of the environment, everything around me was also new—raucous open-air markets with long tables of wrenches and watches and shoes and teacups in various stages of shining and decay; the sound of *ezan* (the call to prayer) cutting across the open fields; the combined smells of spice and diesel and lemon. I too felt new, as if I were being seen for the first time.

Setting down in Kayseri, my anonymity and the plainness I had cultivated in my life in Spokane, Washington, disappeared like food placed on the table at *iftar,* the evening meal that breaks the holy Ramazan fast. Once, when I bumped into a student at the bus stop, he claimed, "I saw you from a mile away." And this was correct, rather than colloquial: I was taller, whiter, and just simply different. I was as noticeable as a splash of mud across sheets flapping on a line, discordant as the one loose head in a chorus of tightly strung drums.

Uncomfortable conspicuousness aside, I discovered how useful foreignness in small Turkish towns can be: When I walked into the *otogar,* the departure and arrival point for intercity bus companies, and weaved through long counters of ticket sellers and destination billboards, a boisterous bidding war for my business began. In the summer street bustle of shouting and brutal bargain hunting, I could stop to admire the symmetry of a produce seller's perfect meter-high pyramid of strawberries and receive both patient service and personal pleasantries. When I attempted, no matter how unsuccessfully, to say something—*anything*—in Turkish, I would get broad smiles and occasional applause. Going to a bank not yet converted to the take-a-number system, I'd be shuffled to the front of the line. But when I entered a *hamam,* where the thick air is damp and warm as a lover, it was not my idea to attract attention.

The Hunat *hamam,* an old, gray Selçuk-style building in the city center, sports the same polished stone and flaky plaster it has probably always had. Inside, the only decoration is a faded plaque describing the proper way to perform *abdest,* a Muslim's ritual washing before prayer. Here there is no opulent tiling or colored glass, only water, rock, and women.

The first time I went to Hunat it was winter, and I was escorting my visiting six-foot-tall, red-haired friend, Menkin. When we came down the stairs from street level and into the changing room, all conversation stopped. Apprehension growing, I somehow managed to arrange for us to have *kese,* a traditional session of rough, exfoliating body scrubbing. This first visit to a Turkish *hamam* represented more than just a new cultural experience. For me, it was something much larger. I would be confronting the shyness and shame I held around my body like a cloak. For most of my life, I was extremely self-conscious, and I worried especially about my weight and my skin. So I hid inside of baggy t-shirts and men's jeans, wore boxy shoes and shirked the razor. I had been an adolescent who bloomed early, and no matter how my body changed I wanted a different one, and I wanted to conceal the one I had. I wanted to stay a private, unopened package. By college, my desire to lose ten pounds escalated to thirty, then fifty.

Under the collective eye of a dozen *hamam* patrons in the changing room, I began to undress. I removed things so slowly that I likely drew even more attention to myself—delicately unlacing my shoes, gently tugging off my socks, unlooping my belt from my jeans, unhooking the earrings I usually showered in. For a moment, I missed the nosy Kayserian women in the grocery store who inspected my cart to see what foreigners ate; their scrutiny seemed innocuous in comparison. Though half the women were completely naked, I worried that we might be thought immodest when I realized that Menkin was wearing a G-string. For my part, I wished I were drunk, or that my own frumpy cotton panties offered twice the coverage.

Though it is not customary to bring a towel to the bathing rooms, once I finally had the courage to slip off my bra, Menkin and I wrapped ourselves up. Inside the main chamber, there were females of all ages, ranging from chubby toddlers, with perfect skin slippery as melting chocolate, to the very elderly, with bony backs bent into a comma, hair rusty with henna.

Hunat's domed roof arches over the central room, the coolest and largest, and smaller, hotter rooms circle around the center, like the petals of a daisy. Menkin and I chose a side chamber and sat sweating near a low basin. And here, stripped to nothing but skin, when both our physical and cultural differences were starkly obvious, our foreignness, like many things under the pressure of heat and steam, began to dissolve.

Two young adolescents approached, shocked but drawn by Menkin's pierced nipple. Encouraged by Menkin, one reached out and pinched it, which sent them both off into a fit of giggles. Soon they drifted back and introduced us to all the women who were now crowding the small room to investigate us. We were doused with water, given soap and shampoo and dippers, and were generally inspected.

After the *kese* woman—a stout woman with well-defined shoulders—arrived, she lay first Menkin and then me out on a raised marble platform and scrubbed us with a rough woven glove. Softened by the steam and the sweat, layers of dead skin came peeling off; as she washed me, she pushed hard, and I was surprised how much it hurt. When I doused myself, the water stung newly exposed flesh, but I felt a kind of clean I have never been able to duplicate on my own. Fellow bathers loaned Menkin and me colorful hand-knitted washcloths and fed us the spicy, homemade pickle *turşu*. If we had expressed any interest to bathers with unmarried sons, we could have been set up on a date for that night.

In the changing room, I squeezed globs of my American acne cream into the outstretched hands of curious Kayserians—it was all we had to offer—and Menkin and I said our goodbyes. When we finally left, I was dizzy. I had gone in burning with shame and I came out just as pink-faced, but from the warmth of acceptance.

I visited Hunat frequently with my fellow teachers, an Australian and a Japanese, and we were always given space, snacks, and once, herbs to put in the wash water by the same women who would, in town, knock us down for a seat on the bus. Though it no longer has a central role in bride selection, the tradition of frank personal scrutiny endures. In the *hamam,* women commented candidly on the size or quality of my breasts, asked extremely personal questions, disapproved of my pubic hair, and razzed me for having such white skin. But I have found that I can take it. In this setting, there is no locker-room crassness. It is hard, for example, to take anyone or anything seriously while squatting in dripping underwear and eating stuffed peppers and soggy bread as if a massive shower were the obvious place for a picnic.

After my first *hamam* and bolstered by successive visits, I started to have more courage about my body. I had my hair streaked blond, bought new clothes, and shaved my underarms. I felt less like I was conforming to the beauty standards I had rejected and more like I was finally unafraid if people looked at me. As I learned to love my body, my weight dropped. As a gift to myself, during Kurban Bayramı, a religious holiday when a sheep or goat or other ruminant is sacrificed to Allah, I quietly bled into a tissue after having my nose pierced for no better reason than to be different and bring on the stares. In this adamantly male-dominated society, women's spaces are like secrets best kept—shocking and intimate, and profound in the creation of instant camaraderie.

My old skin was ready to be sloughed off by a large woman with incredibly strong arms; apparently I had grown out of it. And I was happy to leave that perpetually embarrassed girl there, swirling down the drain of an ancient *hamam.*

Haze

by Katherine Belliel

*W*arm May sunlight guided us through the narrow alley toward an old, domed building. Bursa, a green mountainous city in northwestern Turkey, had changed little in the two years since my last visit, although everything was now different for me.

I followed Selen through the old, heavy, wooden entry doors of the *hamam* and into the Turkish bath's large central room. Still holding my arm, she asked an attendant for an empty room.

"Selen . . ." I called, my voice breaking.

"Relax first, then we can talk," she said firmly as we passed through one of the ornately carved doors lining the sides of the large changing room. Through the scrollwork of internal doors, we could see glimpses of half-naked women lounging in the dressing room, drinking demitasse cups of coffee and smoking leisurely. Inside, secrets were shared, hearts were opened, and joy and sorrow hung heavy in the air. The intimate, confiding atmosphere beckoned us, as it had done for women for five hundred years since its construction during the Selçuk–Ottoman times. Women of that period used the *hamam* to socialize as well as to cleanse; hidden from view, the baths were a social venue and a meeting place outside of the harem.

Like them, we entered our sanctuary and started to undress. Selen passed me a long, soft, *peştemal*—the traditional red and blue plaid wrap worn as the sole covering within the *hamam*. I mechanically imitated the way she wrapped it around her body and secured it under her arm. She took a large brush from her bag and brushed my hair away from my face, her long firm strokes comforting. Fate had almost made us sisters by marriage, and circumstances had not weakened our bond. She pulled my hair into a tight knot and clipped it before

securing her own blond tresses in a quick French twist. We slid our feet into big
wooden sandals lined along the wall and shuffled to the main chamber.

The steam escaping from the interior of the *hamam* made the thick double
doors stick, and while Selen wrestled with the portal, I admired the intricate
Selçuk-style carvings on the wood, allowing the patterns and balm of history
to soothe my troubled soul. I recalled that the Selçuk Turks, who flourished
in Bursa, had filled the city with buildings in elaborate geometric shapes and
decorated with stars—motifs adopted by the Ottoman Turks after the 14th
century. How many other women of all backgrounds, faiths, and creeds had
stood exactly where I was now, at the threshold of this refuge? What secrets
had these doors hidden from the world outside? Whose tears had been shed
behind this protective shield, and how many other brokenhearted women had
fled to this calm, unchanging sanctuary?

The door finally gave way, and waves of steam enveloped us as we entered
the domed inner sanctum. Naked figures drifted ghostlike on all sides of us,
their movements slow and languid. Steam invaded and burned my eyes, nose,
and lungs, making me choke and gasp. Finding our way across the hexagonal
chamber, we sat on cool, white marble seats jutting from pink-and-white stri-
ated marble walls, next to one of several flowing fountains skirting the *hamam*'s
core. Scalloped marble basins caught water issuing from ornate brass spigots,
the excess a waterfall over the sides. Two large white plastic bowls bobbed and
danced atop the overflowing basin; Selen took one and gave me the other.
She filled it and poured it over her face, hair, and body, baptizing her slender,
graceful figure with the hot, healing waters. I filled my bowl and let the water
run through my hair and down my body, opening my pores as it traveled down
my legs.

"Forgive me Father, for I have sinned. . . ." The water burned as it cleansed,
like confession. I felt guilty for a transgression that would be harshly judged by
others—my family and his—yet the offense was necessary for my redemption.
I hadn't sinned in the flesh, but I was burdened by our illicit meeting today. As
he was now a married man, our emotional and innocent reunion was taboo
according to the morals of his Turkish society and my strict Catholic upbring-

ing. I wanted the water to wash away my unrepentant guilt. Today's encounter with my unforgettable love had eased the ever-present ache since our relationship ended two years earlier.

The steam and the water created an aura of forgiveness and rebirth that the confession chamber in Grand Rapids, Michigan, never had. I gazed around at the relaxing, uninhibited figures around us, free and exposed. I too removed my covering and used it as a cushion from the cool marble. Selen laughed at how quickly I adapted and allowed the comfort of the *hamam* to flow over me. My broken heart seemed to sting in the humid air. That was the purpose of this journey to Turkey—to purify a lingering wound I had never properly treated.

I poured more water over my head, leaned back against the wall, and shut my eyes. Steam muffled the conversations echoing through the domed chamber, and a constant sound of water barricaded us from the outside world, from time and obligation. The memories flowed back.

I had met him four years ago at university in Ohio. It was junior year, and I was at a birthday party for a close friend. I watched with disgust as my date pulled a girl onto his lap. Tired of boorish college parties, I went looking for peace and something besides beer to drink. I rarely drank, but I knew it would be at least an hour until someone could be persuaded to give me a ride home. I rummaged through a kitchen cupboard until I found a clean glass, then poured some diet soda and grabbed a tall bottle of clear liquid to mix with it.

"That's not vodka," said a heavily accented voice behind me.

"Really? Then what is it?" I glanced at the bottle, irritated.

"*Rakı*. I brought it from Turkey," he replied as I turned to look at him. I knew almost everyone at the party, and I vaguely remembered seeing this man around our small campus. Medium height, well dressed, with kind eyes.

"My name is Murat," he said as he took the bottle from me and filled a slender glass halfway with something that smelled strongly of black licorice. He topped it off with water and an ice cube, and the drink swirled white. His warm brown eyes twinkled as he handed me the drink. I defiantly took a sip, gasping and sputtering at its piquant taste. Laughing, he took the glass away.

"I guess you have to get used to it. In my country everyone drinks this. We call it 'lion's milk.'"

Selen nudged me from my reverie, handing me a thin, abrasive mitt while she wrapped another around her own hand. "This is a *kese,*" she said, and proceeded to briskly rub her face and neck. I did likewise, sensitive to the invigorating stimulation as I scrubbed my face harder and harder. Layers peeled off in rolls like eraser shavings, black and dead. The new, pink skin stung from exposure, a pain both rejuvenating and welcome.

Murat and I had smoothly fallen into conversation that night and laughed like old friends, unperturbed that we were from two different hemispheres. When it was time for me to leave, he kissed both of my cheeks gently in the traditional Turkish gesture for greeting and parting, expressing a bond of friendship, respect, and affection. I flushed, and my stomach fluttered, a new and exciting emotion.

We became inseparable. I had finally met a decent and considerate man with whom I could speak easily on topics as far-ranging as politics and matters of the heart. He was a man who seemed to understand my sensitive nature and inherent pull toward the intellectual, and who loved me as much as I loved him. We honored each other's achievements and encouraged each other's goals, even if those goals led us in different directions. I admired that he was in America to improve his English to better serve his family business back in Turkey. He valued and supported my aspirations to continue on to a master's and PhD. Time and distance didn't seem like a deterrent to our union. We recognized each other as soul mates. Unlike the other college men I had known, Murat was clearly a different breed. Unpretentious but dignified, he was unfailingly honest, even at the end, when the truth caused us both such bitter pain.

That semester together was filled with happiness. We laughed in the Ohio sunshine as it filtered through the orange autumn leaves and reflected in our eyes, his shining like bright copper pennies. He said mine reminded him of the blue-green waters of the Mediterranean Sea. But underneath the flood of emotion was an undercurrent of concern: How could it ever work? We were from two different worlds, and Murat had to return to his—more than five thousand miles away—in only three months, when his English program finished. His life was in Bursa, heading the textile company his family had founded a year earlier. We never expected to find each other and now had no idea how to manage our respective cultural and religious obstacles to stay together. The prudent thing would have been to say goodbye when he returned to Turkey, but our hearts wouldn't allow it. We could make no tangible plans until I finished university, but we knew that we wanted to be together. We would have to be thankful for telephone calls, email, and letters until my visit during the next summer holiday. The trip would be a test to see if I could make a future in his country.

Selen startled me as she reached over the fountain and brushed some of the dead skin from my face. "We have lots of layers to take off!" she said. She took my mitt and wrapped it around her hand, rinsing it with basinfuls of hot water. "Let me *kese* your back and afterward you can do mine."

My head lolled forward as she scraped my back. Her firm administrations were imitated from her mother's and grandmother's scrubbing of her own body. It was both painful and relaxing. "I'm glad we met, Katie, even though you and Murat didn't marry."

Her words made tears well in my eyes. In her twenties like me, I felt closer to her than to my own siblings. Her *kese* moved from my neck to my back, across my shoulders and down my backbone. It left me raw and tingling, exposed to the hot, pulling steam.

The day he left I was grief-stricken and torn with the pain of indefinite separation. I had never before cried so inconsolably, and he was absolutely helpless. He held me, kissing my face and hair, trying to calm me but only making me cry harder. Being physically cut in two had to be less painful than being spiritually halved.

"In six months we will see each other," he promised. "You know how much I love you, Katie; we will get through this. Our love gives us courage." We both were clinging to the hope that if our romance could endure this long separation, then it could survive other obstacles the future would bring.

Tears streamed down my cheeks now, mixing with beads of perspiration, masked by the clouds of steam. Selen knew I was crying, my shoulders heaving as she scrubbed my back. Teardrops fell to the pink marble floor before swirling away in the never-ending stream of water. At my ear, Selen whispered something compassionate in Turkish, trying to take away my anguish.

After my return from seeing him that afternoon, she had been waiting with a bag packed and ready to go. "We're going to the *hamam,*" she announced.

"I can't go anywhere, Selen!" I replied as I crumpled to the floor. She caught my arm and pulled me back up.

"Have you ever been to a *hamam* before?" I shook my head. "It will help, I promise."

Selen turned her back to me, rinsed her *kese,* and gave it to me. With clumsy and awkward movements, I rubbed her back. I could feel her ribcage, each rib as I passed over it. The rhythm of the *kese,* the steam, the sound of water hypnotized my senses. *Am I really back in Turkey?* I thought. *After all this, I still came back?*

After he returned home, the six months we were parted had seemed an eternity, made excruciating by the lack of support from my family and friends. Although well intended, sharp criticism from my devoutly Catholic family deeply hurt and shamed me. I felt ostracized by many of my closest friends for falling in love with a Muslim and a foreigner, and they offered little aid when I needed it the most.

Murat and I did our best to address the inflexible attitudes of our families. I continued to try to win the support of his conservative parents, to prove that I was different from the rumors and stories they had heard about loose American women. Murat too was fighting a similar battle with my family in America against their image of a domineering Muslim man. Murat had met my family, and they liked him as an individual but remained suspicious and disapproving of his religion and culture.

I vented my loneliness and frustration by changing my course of study and doubling my classes. I had always suspected that a career in music was not for me, and I finally had the courage to switch to a degree in history. I moved back to my home state of Michigan, transferred to a new university, and planned to finish a four-year program in half the time. I found peace studying Turkey and the modern Middle East and realized that it wasn't only my connection to Murat that drove my passion. Though it was a field in which I had previously known little, I found a deep and instant affinity for the history of the Middle East—a feeling that remained even after Murat and I parted.

Despite my studies of the region, I arrived in Turkey six months later, excited, scared, and completely ignorant. Books had done little to prepare me for Turkey. İstanbul, with its pervasive pulse, was colossal and indomitable. Murat had tried to warn me, knowing that I had always lived in the quiet suburbs of Michigan and Ohio. He knew how intimidated I would be by the sprawling metropolis, and understanding my reaction, he immediately drove us south, toward his home in Bursa. Two hours outside İstanbul, the mountains first appeared on the horizon. The tallest peak, Uludağ, still had snow and was undisturbed by the May sunshine.

One more hour and we were in Bursa. Quiet, majestic, and green, his city felt familiar and immediately implanted itself in me. Murat laughed at how my eyes sparkled, knowing my obsession with mountain ranges—so different from the unintriguing, flat landscape of western Michigan and Ohio, where we met.

He was happy to introduce me to the peaks of his homeland. He pretended to be jealous, saying "I think you are more passionate about the hills than you are for me."

I received a warm welcome from his family, although I sensed a tension that would later tear us apart.

"*Bursa'ya hoş geldiniz*, Katie," said Murat's mother, a short, well-dressed woman with keen eyes, warmly welcoming me to her town and into her home. The house was immaculate and impeccably decorated with modern furniture and Turkish art and antiques, modestly showing off their upper-middle-class standing. Her eyes followed me, friendly but curious about the foreign girl in possession of her eldest son's heart. She clearly wondered what was so special about me that would prompt her son to invite me from America and into their home.

"This is my brother Hasan," Murat said as a longhaired younger man shook my hand. He had kind eyes, like Murat. The same age as I, Hasan quickly assumed the role of brother toward me, acting as my personal chauffeur, tour guide, and translator during trips with his mother, since his university classes in town were primarily at night.

"I am Selen, Hasan's girlfriend," said a tall, comely girl with long fair hair. Selen was stunning. I was immediately intimidated by her thin, elegant features, finely chiseled cheekbones, and chic style. But her warm brown eyes beamed at me as if to say, *Don't be.*

"My father will be home from the factory before dinnertime," Murat said as he showed me to the guest room where I would sleep, his hand on my lower back.

Murat had warned me that his family, although very modern in many regards, still held deeply traditional beliefs. Though I wouldn't be sharing a room with Murat, such a visit by a girlfriend was nevertheless something severely frowned upon within most of Turkish society. At the time, I didn't realize what a decisive statement Murat made by bringing me to his house to stay with his family. It signaled to them his intent to marry me, which truly scared them.

The cultural and religious issues that were unimportant to Murat and me loomed as major deterrents for his family as well as mine. His parents preferred him to be with a girl from their own tradition, culturally predictable and acceptable, just as my family preferred me to be with an American man, preferably Catholic. Objections were voiced by both sides prior to my visit. Our families hoped that we would recognize the gap between our cultures and relinquish the affair after my trip.

I finished scrubbing Selen's back and shoulders and returned her mitt, pouring bowls of hot water over her, one after another. Lost in my thoughts, she eventually stayed my hand, washed the two *kese*, and set me to scrubbing my own arms and legs as she did hers.

The second day of my visit Murat took me up Mount Uludağ. In his green Renault, up and around hairpin curves that left me gasping. We stopped outside a small lodge, nestled snugly in the side of the hill. As we parked, a group of people led by Hasan came to meet us, rising from their places near a large bonfire. Even though it was May, the cool air at that elevation made the warmth from the blaze welcome.

We finished our arms and legs, and Selen gave me a vanilla-scented exfoliating cream. After we rinsed ourselves, she said it was time for a break. I was physically heavy and slow but lightheaded from the heat and barrage of memories.

Despite their reservations, his parents liked me very much, and their worries didn't prevent them from showing me excellent hospitality. I spent much of my visit with Murat's mother and Hasan. Together we took tours of the city and surrounding area, from the enormous Ulu Cami (Grand Mosque) to a Silk

Road cocoon market, the Koza Han. I was dazzled by the scarf shops that filled the Koza Han, the 15th-century *kervansaray* where silk cocoons are still traded each spring. We generally enjoyed each other's company during the long hours that Murat was at work. At their home, I would sit for hours gazing out of the windows of the salon, surveying the mountains and the city spread before me, or standing barefoot on the balcony to admire the view, much to his mother's chagrin—she believed the Turkish superstition that walking barefoot causes infertility.

I tried to show his mother my culture as I also learned about hers. She taught me how to make *mantı*, a meat-filled pasta covered with a garlic-*yoğurt* sauce, and I showed her how to make chocolate-chip cookies. Every night his mother would prepare a unique Turkish dish, asking Murat to translate its history and region. She explained that the Ottoman Turks knew hundreds of ways to prepare eggplant alone, and that recipes had been passed from generation to generation.

Though hospitable toward me, his parents told Murat they feared the problems that a foreign bride would bring to their home. They plagued him with questions, doubts, fears. What religion would our children be? As the eldest, he would be increasingly responsible for the family and the business. What if I lured their eldest son to America? He was obliged to look after his parents in their old age, but would an American wife allow it? How would a Westerner like me learn to accept their small-town, conservative life? They didn't think I could. In fact they were sure of it.

We shuffled back through the heavy doors and returned to our room behind the thin, scrolled doors. The air was cool without the steam, and we wrapped ourselves in thick towels. We each lay on a chaise longue and sipped cool mineral water with slices of lemon brought by an attendant.

Selen turned to me as the attendant closed the door. "Now it's time to talk."

Only a few hours yet a lifetime earlier, she had sat by my side at her house as I called Murat. She had held my hand, bending her head to mine, both our ears at the receiver. "Katie?" he had said, his voice barely audible over the noisy machines at the textile factory. "How are you? I've missed you...," he said, his voice cracking. I had closed my eyes, letting his warm familiar voice flood over me, savoring it.

"I'm in Turkey. In Bursa. At Selen's." I heard him drop the phone, then scramble to pick it up. "I have to see you, Murat; we have to talk. We owe it to ourselves."

"I don't know if I can. I still feel ... I still feel too much ..." he said, struggling to control his voice. My eyes had opened. This was it, my chance to free myself from this miserable vise that kept me prisoner for two years.

"Murat," I had said calmly, in a voice he recognized and knew to heed. "You owe me this, at the very least." Guilt, as a last resort, would make him find the courage to face me.

"I will be there in an hour," he said.

After we hung up, I sat by the window, veiled by the sheer white curtains. I watched the sunshine emerge from behind swiftly moving clouds and race over the mountains, as the *muezzin* from the nearby mosque gave the mournful call to prayer, seeming to verbalize my pain and offer solace.

I knew that according to society—his and mine—this meeting was wrong. Yet I had done everything society had asked of me. I had walked away from the love of my life, and I still had no closure. I had tried to forget about him completely. I dated other men, I changed jobs and locations, but I was restless and unhappy. As I looked out the window, I clutched my rosary beads, but couldn't remember a single prayer. I invented my own, relieved by the physical reminder of my past represented by the beads running through my fingers. Although not devout, I relied on the consolation of the opalescent beads I always carried. God, whether called by the *muezzin* or by my own devotions, knew my heart and soul, knew my intentions to be pure and honest. I sensed that Murat was near and looked down as his car pulled up. Selen hugged me before I ran to the street. I took a deep breath and opened the car door.

This much Selen was witness to. She now listened with bated breath on her chaise as I recounted the details of our tryst.

∞

Murat and I stared at each other, and years and circumstance fell away. I threw my arms around him and put my head in the familiar hollow of his shoulder. He held me and buried his nose in my hair. Within seconds I pulled away, realizing we were on dangerous territory.

Murat composed himself too and turned the car away from Bursa. He clutched the steering wheel tightly, and the gold from his wedding ring glared accusingly in the sunlight. His choice of the forty-five-minute drive to the coastal town of Mudanya was both sentimental and practical—sentimental because it had been a favorite spot of ours during my first visit, and practical because it was well away from the gossiping mouths and knowing eyes that could make trouble for his future. We talked the entire way to Mudanya, the words falling from our lips like waterfalls. We reminisced about mutual friends, places and people and things that made us smile and laugh despite our situation. We were two confidants reunited, knowing that this would be the last time we would see each other. We went to our usual café on the sea. The wind whipped our hair, and the sunshine brought out the bright blue contrast of the sea against the green of the mountains. Our tea arrived, and I plunged in.

"Murat, why?"

He cleared his throat. "To forget. I thought it would help me forget about you, about us. You deserve so much more than this."

It was still a mystery how our affair, which brought us such joy, could bring those around us pain and sadness. During the final fight he had with his parents about us, I was sobbing on the phone while he volleyed back and forth between my pleas and his parents' refusals. I was too far away to properly defend myself against their accusations and concerns, and besides, I had no comprehension of the language. In the middle of the argument, Murat's father suffered a heart attack. My world shattered. It was over. I couldn't fault Murat for his commitment to family, nor did I want to be the wedge that came between them. I cared about him too much to put him through the suffering that our bond caused his family. Selen and I stayed in contact, and it was she who delivered the horrifying news of his marriage only six months after our relationship ended.

"Did it work for you? Were you able to forget?" I asked him at the Mudanya café, trying hard to suppress the waver in my voice. He looked deep into my eyes. New wrinkles marked his face since our last parting, and gray flecked his hair.

"No," he said hoarsely. "I still remember every day."

I couldn't speak, afraid I would lose control. Waves crashed onto mossy rocks lining the shore, tossed by the brisk wind. Cries of nearby fishmongers mixed with those of the ever-present seagulls. I gripped my tea glass and asked quietly, "Are you happy?"

"No," he replied.

"Do you love her?"

He couldn't look at me. He fiddled with his teaspoon and watched the seagulls fly overhead. "She is the mother of my son. But . . ." He left it unfinished.

"Murat, I understand your family's opposition to our engagement. But why did you marry so soon after we broke up? Were you dating her while I was in America?"

Murat withstood my barrage of questions and reached for my hands. "My family liked you, but they were afraid. Traditions are important to them, and they don't think highly of American culture. They know they were wrong. I'm not happy, nor are they; now it's too late. I should have fought them, but I was weak, and you deserve someone who would fight for you. A part of me died when I lost you and let them rush me into this marriage. But I have a son now, and there is no turning back."

"So you will raise your son in misery, that's the best for him?" I said bitterly, pulling my hands away. I couldn't help myself, even though his explanation corroborated what Selen had told me. Murat's family introduced him to his wife after we had broken up. They married quickly and conceived a year later. Those two years had been hell for me, as I stumbled and failed in my own relationships, trying to fill an abyss. I had to properly finish this before I could move forward with my life. As we looked at each other across the table, tears in our eyes, he took my hands once again. Despite everything, I still loved and cared for him. If I could hate him, my life would have been so much easier, but it wasn't in my nature.

His shoulders slumped, and I felt sorry for my hurtful comment. He knew the truth too; indeed, he lived it every day, and there was no benefit in me pointing it out.

"Murat, I will love you forever. Take comfort from that. You changed my life by bringing me to this place," I said, facing the crashing waves instead of him to keep myself from venturing further. I listened to the waves break against the rocks. No more could safely be said. After minutes of silence, we reluctantly headed back to his car, our emotional baggage a little lighter.

I wanted to touch his face, to smooth out the wrinkles stamped there. As we drove back to Bursa, his knuckles were white from clutching the steering wheel, trying to keep his emotions in check. Outside Selen's door, he turned off the motor. We both stared out the windshield, unsure of how we wanted to orchestrate our final goodbye.

"I need you," he whispered. "I need you in my life." I swallowed the lump that had gathered in my throat and dug my nails into my palms.

"The mountains," I said, nodding my head in their general direction. "Go to them when you need to get away, you will sense me there." Our memories were thick on the mountains, our happy ghosts picnicking, walking, and delighting in drives over the peaks.

He smiled through his tears. I kissed my hand and placed it first on one of his cheeks and then the other, the closest imitation of the double-kiss of Turkish fashion that I could dare. "Goodbye," I whispered and opened the door. When I glanced back from Selen's doorway, his forehead was on the steering wheel. With great effort he righted himself and slowly drove away.

Selen wiped her eyes with her free hand, the other she had long since wrapped around my hand here in the *hamam*. Her engagement ring left a small mark on my index finger. We tied dry cloths around our bodies and went back into the steamy womb of the *hamam*. I felt better after sharing my burden. Removing my *peştemal*, I lowered myself into the hexagonal pool in the center of the room. I floated on my back, naked and exposed as my hair swirled around me. The rose-colored dome above glowed faintly from the sunlight streaming through the semitransparent glass, and somehow it made me smile. Buoyant and basking in the radiant glow, I realized my somber mood had lifted.

Selen was watching me carefully as she dangled her feet in the water. "What are you thinking?" she asked.

"I am finally at peace."

She smiled wide, but with cautious eyes. She knew I was vulnerable. She lowered herself into the water and hugged her knees to her chest so that her chin rested barely above water.

We had been at the *hamam* for hours, although time had little relevance here. The steam, the rose-colored light, the warm caress of the water loosened something inside me. Instead of being hopelessly depressed, a crucial bridge had been crossed, and I became enthused about the future. A long suppressed energy had begun to emanate from deep inside.

I remembered looking out of the window on the bus on my way to Bursa from İstanbul only two days previous. A mining company had left huge, gaping wounds on the side of a mountain, exposing the reddish flesh-colored marble underneath. However, as the bus drew closer, I saw multicolored flowers growing out of the cracks of the gash. Soon the scar would be covered with flowers, tempering the injury beneath. Flowers would grow from my wound as well. I was brought here for a reason.

I climbed out of the pool and splashed cold water on my face and body, as I had seen the other women do. The brisk water made me gasp with shock, and my skin tightened in preparation for returning to the outside world. We exited the heavy wooden doors, lighter in flesh and spirit, and quietly returned to the changing room to exchange our wet coverings for our clothes.

We walked out to the car, where Hasan—Murat's brother and Selen's fiancé—was waiting for us. He was a witness to both Murat's and my pain. He looked at me in the rearview mirror with questioning eyes.

"I'm all right, Hasan," I said reassuringly. I realized that I was better, as if an enormous weight had finally been lifted from my shoulders. We drove up the mountain and stopped at the lodge where only two years ago we had all gathered around a bonfire. As we ate fresh bread and drank from a thermos of tea, a crescent moon rose over the mountains in the rosy dusk. The sound of the *muezzin* calling from the minarets echoed throughout the valley and filled me with serenity. I felt absolved by their eternal sound, and reaching into my bag, I touched the cool comfort of my rosary beads.

"Thank you, God," I prayed to myself. A cool breeze washed over the mountain and caressed my fresh, rejuvenated spirit. Light laughter seemed to come from the trees, and I smiled at a treasured memory and the promise of a new beginning.

The Goddess Metamorphosis

BY KAREN-CLAIRE VOSS

*M*y first experience in a *hamam,* a Turkish bath, was a decade ago, when my beloved Recep took me from our home in İstanbul to Kayseri, a city of one million in Central Turkey, to meet his relatives for the first time and attend a family wedding there.

It was December 1994, and heavy snow made traveling difficult, but when we arrived we found that despite the weather, elaborate preparations were underway, not least of which was planning the eve of the wedding. Music, dancing, and libations would punctuate the evening's segregated celebrations, the men at one gathering and the women at another. The women's gathering was to involve painting the hands with henna, a tradition to ensure health, abundance, and fertility. But the big focus for me was an event we would attend earlier that same day. All the women in the wedding party were planning to go to a *gelin hamamı* (bridal bath) in order to prepare the bride for her wedding with a ritualized cleansing.

I'd been in Turkey teaching a few classes at a university, giving language lessons at a *dershane,* a private English-language school, and generally learning how to function as a foreign woman in what was then to me a very strange land. My early experiences had all served to develop my intercultural skills: living in Australia for five years as a young girl; studying and teaching at universities in America; and conducting my doctoral research for two years in France. Turkey, however, had initially proved less accessible. My meeting and subsequent relationship with Recep began to open up new vistas, and by this time I had become entranced and enraptured by all things Turkish, but a trip to the *hamam* was something I had then only dreamed of. Participating in yet another alluring tradition was extremely meaningful, particularly this one.

Turkey itself was imbued with everyday customs, folklore, and myth that spoke to its rich heritage and wove remnants of the past into my daily life. Despite the logistics of adjusting to a new culture, these elements of past ages—from Byzantine churches and Ottoman palaces to the local coppersmith who hammered out rustic treasures—allowed me to suspend the present and wrap myself in a world of exotic antiquity. Now I'd come to the Turkish bath. The ritual of the bridal *hamam* resonated deeply with me, as it both paralleled my studies as a historian of religions and touched my fervent interest in the symbols and images of the divine feminine.

Quite familiar with the many forms of the Great Goddess, I knew that the *hamam* experience could be traced back to the ancient Mother Goddess culture of Anatolia from the Neolithic period, nearly ten thousand years ago. Once a ceremony of sensuality and spirituality inextricably melded together, the modern *hamam* still remains true to its ancient origins. In this contemporary *gelin hamamı*, the bride-to-be would go to the *hamam* to be washed and massaged by her closest female relatives and friends . . . and me. She would anoint herself with perfume and beautify herself with cosmetics, in much the same way that the mythical Sumerian goddess Inanna prepared herself for her conjugal union with the shepherd god, Dumuzi.

The idea of witnessing an event so linked with the past and with the divine feminine aroused deep feelings of my own womanliness. I also knew that even prior to Ottoman times, five centuries ago, the everyday use of the *hamam* enabled women to luxuriate for hours in the company of their friends, talking, trading news and gossip, bringing food to share. They would play instruments and dance. In days gone by, the *hamam* was also an opportunity par excellence for women to select brides for their sons, allowing mothers to thoroughly evaluate prospective brides, since modesty was irrelevant in a room filled with bathing women.

The female intimacy that the bath promised was also something I desired. I wanted this experience to bring me closer to the women in Recep's family, especially his sister Gülçin. Since my Turkish was still in a rather embryonic stage, I realized there would be limits to how much I could participate, but I was counting on eye contact, gestures, and my enthusiasm to allow me to bond with the women there.

I knew that everyone would be nude, and I was prepared to disrobe as well. This didn't bother me. I'd been a hippie in the U.S. in the '60s and '70s, after all! Naked is something I do. The wedding party was made up of perhaps a dozen women and girls of varying ages. We packed ourselves into two cars and drove to the *hamam*, which I was delighted to see was quite massive and made of solid stone, carved in the Selçuk style typical of many historical Kayseri buildings. Going inside, I was directed to a locker and was afforded privacy for disrobing. I left all my clothes except for my *peştemal*—the traditional thin, plaid woven cotton towel used to wrap oneself—and my bag of toiletries. Clutching my little bag, and with the *peştemal* secured around me, I found a pair of wooden clogs from out of a pile that fit, and wended my way toward the main chamber of the bath through a series of undecorated anterooms—private toilets; showers; places to sit quietly; storage spaces for towels, soap, and other paraphernalia—that became progressively hot and steamy.

At last I came to a square and spacious central room completely covered in marble. All around the perimeter were numerous small marble basins, with a hexagonal heated solid slab of marble—the *göbek taşı*—dominating the middle of the room. It was late morning, and light streamed in through the round glass openings in the domed roof, illuminating the architectural detail of the finely carved basins. Once more, Turkey had allowed me to step into the past. There was nothing in this *hamam* to suggest present day; these women and I might well have been the first bathers to grace this Selçuk bathhouse, hundreds of years ago. I instantly felt a part of history and a part of this women's clan.

Special arrangements had been made to rent it just for us, so the place was all ours. Women at the marble basins around the sides of the room were pouring water over themselves, others lying on the center stone, some walking around. Gülçin smiled graciously and bade me to join her. It was a harmonious scene of womanly respite . . . until I dropped my *peştemal* to the *göbek taşı*.

Everyone ceased talking. They all stared at me.

Like me, most of the women had discarded their *peştemal.* That wasn't the reason for their silent ogling. Extremely disconcerted, I panicked. Had I done something wrong? It had been going so well. I wanted them all to like me. What now?

I looked back at them until the reason for their stares hit me like the proverbial ton of bricks. There was one *very* noticeable difference between all those women and me—I had pubic hair; they did not.

This was a cultural idiosyncrasy that had never come up in conversation with my Turkish female friends. Was this a general custom? Or perhaps a grooming ritual reserved for the bridal bath? I was unprepared and certainly didn't know the proper etiquette. Moreover, as someone who prides herself on being able to quickly intuit the right moves in new situations, finding myself in such a quandary was extremely discomfiting.

Gülçin finally came over to me, smiling. Extending a disposable plastic razor, she indicated that I was to go into a side room and use it. A few years younger than I, she had been kind from our first meeting the night before, having led me around, introducing me to everyone and generally making a fuss over me. I gathered now that she was again doing her best to make me comfortable. I also realized that there wasn't going to be a choice here. I would have to simply accept how things were—or rather, how things were supposed to be, and *would be,* once I rid myself of my offending pubic hair.

"Do you have scissors?" I asked in English, miming with my fingers so she would understand.

"No," she shook her head. Sighing, I decided to acquiesce to the inevitable and headed to one of the semiprivate cubicles off to one side of the *hamam.* Unlike stalls in modern women's restrooms, which have their own doors and locks, each of these cubicles was open on one side but angled with some degree of privacy, so that one could perform depilation or intimate washing.

I set to the task, laboriously proceeding to eradicate the one physical difference between me and the rest of the women, an act that would ease their acceptance of me. The illusion of having drifted into a scene of ancient ritual quickly evaporated as I performed unprecedented gyrations to reach absolutely everywhere without cutting myself. Some twenty minutes later, pleased with myself and not a little triumphant, because it had not been easy, I emerged.

Gülçin rushed over to me, examined my work carefully, and nodded, pleased. Then, as if to bestow on me a final seal of approval, she reached down, cupped her hand over my now hairless mons pubis and smiled, announcing, *"Fıstık gibi,"* an idiomatic compliment of beauty, literally meaning "like a nut."

I came close to tears because of the enveloping sense of acceptance her gesture and words indicated—an acceptance that was palpably shared by all the women in the room. At once swept again into a feeling of age-old rite and ceremony, suddenly I felt I belonged, really belonged. There I stood, in a centuries-old *hamam,* in the middle of the prenuptial grooming and anointment of the bride-to-be, when unexpectedly, *I* had become the metaphoric bride! I felt absolutely beautiful, extremely feminine, and unbelievably soft. I had become a veritable goddess.

I embraced Gülçin lovingly. I will never forget the feeling of that moment's connection with those women, with my beloved's family, and beyond that, with this land. Like a bride entering a sacred union, this marked my deep, consummate bonding with Turkey and things Turkish—a bond indistinguishable from my Recep and belonging to him. All connections were characterized by a profound sense of inevitability, that this was simply how things must be, were *meant to be.* I felt my connection with the universe looming, mythic in proportion, and at the center of my consciousness was the Great Goddess.

Gülçin's attentions continued. She sat me down on a bench next to one of the marble basins with their ornate brass spigots and began to pour hot water over me with a copper bowl and wash me with a crocheted washcloth. Like my own lady-in-waiting, she attended to me, raising my arms up and firmly scrubbing. She washed my back, my stomach, between my legs, my feet. She lathered my long burgundy hair. The soap was strong and had a bite, but I kept my eyes closed and enjoyed the sensation. Now completely wet and totally clean, I was warmed by the heat of the hot marble beneath me and by the compassion of Gülçin as she bathed and pampered me and drew me into sisterhood. Then she led me off to the *hamam* attendant, who motioned me to first lie down on my stomach and later turn on my back so she could scrub me with a *kese*. The coarse fibrous cloth removed layers of old skin as she exfoliated me down to pink, tender flesh.

These ministrations were all performed on the heated *göbek taşı* under the central dome. When I lay on my back, my eyes caught the slanting rays of light piercing the steam from the dozens of small windows in the dome, shimmering down like so many luminous heavenly bodies. Closing my eyes, I was lulled by the murmuring voices of the women around me and the sounds of running and splashing water. All of the tensions and strains in my body flowed away with the water being poured over me. I recalled water's healing and purifying properties. Such renewal with water was once an integral part of life, thousands of years ago, when the worship of the Great Goddess was alive and well. As it purified then, so did it now. The process was not only cleansing me physically, but was providing an ablution of the soul, renewing me psychologically, emotionally, and spiritually. Oh, yes. I did indeed feel like a goddess in a modern ritual.

I felt a deep connection with all women, everywhere, but especially with *these* women, from *this* land. This was not the *hamam* experience described by books for tourists in Turkey. No, this was a truly mystical experience— profound and overwhelmingly *real*. Lying there on the hot marble stone that day, I recalled how the Sumerian goddess Inanna rejoiced in her own beauty and womanliness as she prepared to lay with her shepherd Dumuzi. I identi- fied with her, *became* her. After the *hamam* I learned that Gülçin had told Recep—not without some pride—that it was she who had helped to make me beautiful and ready for him. There was little to distinguish us, a modern wed- ding party, from women ages past. The rite, pure and unchanged, united us in time and myth. The myth of the Great Goddess and the ritual of the *hamam* unchanged through the ages connected us with Time itself—Time past, Time present, and Time to come.

What I had done in the *hamam*, what all those women had done, was to reclaim power and energy as Woman. An everyday act for them, it is in fact deep with meaning and innate power. They reveled in their womanhood, embraced it, rejoiced in it, and shared it with each other. Gülçin and the others drew me in immediately and without pretense. My womanhood was touched, literally and symbolically. Like so many things that have happened to me here in Turkey, what began as a simple event turned out to be a profound lesson for my life. This long-ago trip to the *hamam* was a sacred voyage into the depths of my own consciousness of myself as a woman. Although a trip to the *hamam* is now something I do weekly, the utterly and continually meaningful thing about it is that it has never become routine. Instead, the experience feels essential. Every trip to the Turkish bath is a reconnection with the past, with the Anatolian Mother Goddess, with the goddess in me. Always, as a result of that first, formative experience, it is an ongoing source of empowerment that encourages me to celebrate my womanhood and my sexuality in a way that I never before dreamed.

FeminİstanbuI

BY DANA GONZALEZ

s any woman knows, a sustained savage and searing itch in one's female regions is—best-case scenario—a yeast infection. While common and generally considered a minor inconvenience by most of my peers, it's not something I discuss openly. Especially with strangers. And never in Turkish. But this is what I had to do. And fast.

My husband Jim and I had been living in İstanbul for over two years since I'd been recruited in 2001 to run the Turkish subsidiary of a Central Eastern European public relations network. We'd come from Tallinn, Estonia, where we'd worked for three years. Unfortunately tonight Jim was away on business, and while he probably couldn't have helped, it would have been nice to have him around for moral support. Ailing, I would have to fend for myself in a foreign country, something I normally do well, but I didn't relish the idea of having to confide in strangers about my intimate complaint, even to a trained pharmacist.

There are no pharmacy chain stores in İstanbul of the kind I was used to in Chicago, Illinois, my hometown. In the United States, people can buy all kinds of potentially embarrassing products off the shelf—from adult incontinence pads to condoms—without even meeting the eyes of another person, thanks to self-serve bar-code scanning checkouts and a debit card.

Turkish pharmacies are quite the opposite. Like traditional European bakeries or butchers, *eczane* are small, family-owned neighborhood businesses. So despite the fact that İstanbul is a metropolis of twelve million people, it's impossible to be anonymous when buying personal health items. I really didn't want the employees of the pharmacy I passed every day on the way to work to know any more about me. They'd already helped me out in the past with remedies for acid reflux and a severe hangover or two; I thought that was detail enough about my life and bodily malfunctions.

Increasing my apprehension over a trip to the *eczane,* Turkish interactions of all kinds are close and personal, which always causes me serious anxiety. The kissing especially. Which side first? Each encounter is a potential nose-bumping fiasco! Americans might hug when greeting family or close friends, and kissing is appropriate within immediate family but is mostly reserved for babies and small children. We do not kiss strangers, for any reason. However, in Turkey, kissing on each cheek is the standard greeting and farewell, even among new acquaintances. And Turks do it smoothly, without ever putting a nose in an ear. After two years in the country I still close my eyes for the salutatory kiss. What do I think it is, a make-out session? Yet even during the most innocuous transactions, I found that Turks wouldn't let me go without a genial conversation. The last thing I wanted tonight was small talk while trying to obtain a yeast-busting cocktail.

My situation had become more complicated, because by the time I finally conceded that this was no minor allergic reaction to laundry detergent or nylon hosiery, it was after 7 PM. My neighborhood *eczane,* as much as I dreaded it, was closed. I'd have to track down the designated all-night pharmacy in my area if I wanted any relief. As the on-call pharmacy, it was bound to be crowded. A bit of medical "research" was in order. On the Internet, I looked up the names of popular over-the-counter remedies in the U.S. I figured these manufacturers exported their products to Turkey. And finally, hoping for a quick and tidy exchange, I got out my Turkish–English dictionary and looked up "yeast," "mold," "fungus," and "infection." I wrote them down: *maya, küf, mantar, enfeksiyon.* Then I headed out to my closed pharmacy to check the name and address of that evening's all-night *eczane* posted in the window. The place listed was a fifteen-minute, itch-aggravating walk away.

As I set out through the upper-class neighborhood of Nişantaşı, trotting past Versace and Hugo Boss boutiques with my pocketful of potential remedies, I knew the chances of obtaining an antidote *and* escaping unnoticed were slim. There are often more people in the *eczane* than have any clear reason for being there. In addition to the employees and customers, the pharmacist's friends often come to have a chat. Five or six people turn to stare at me instead of just one or two.

One time, I opened the *eczane* door and a guy in a lab coat asked me what I needed before I'd even set foot inside. The owner put down her glass of tea and her patron/friend with whom she'd been chatting stubbed out her cigarette, eyeing me up and down, and all the assistants turned to look. Carefully monitored, I had made my way to the pharmacist and waited until I could tell him, patient-to-expert, what brand of antihistamine I needed. It wasn't an intimate purchase, but that still didn't mean it was for public consumption.

As I don't speak the language well, I'd managed to steer clear of the congenial small talk for which Turkish people are famous. Meaningful conversations weren't possible with my limited vocabulary, so most interactions with strangers were trying and awkward. I couldn't imagine how much more inelegant the conversation would now be, given the very personal topic. How was I going to communicate in my current state? Frantic for relief, I was in no mood to chat, but I knew it would be inevitable.

At the main intersection, I loped past the flower sellers, rotund women in baggy *şalvar* pants and cotton head scarves, smoking cigarettes and sitting on large upturned five-liter olive oil cans amid their colorful flowers. They smiled, waving bouquets in my direction as I slid past.

I was mortified, thinking I'd have to detail in my clumsy Turkish something I didn't even discuss with close friends in my native language. I'd dealt with other feminine discomforts and embarrassing inconveniences in my travels abroad for study in Spain and England, and later, backpacking through Europe and Africa after college, so I wasn't entirely unprepared. The most difficult issue I'd had to contend with was learning, through trial and error, how to use the hole-in-the-floor toilet facilities in Northern Africa. Holding one pant leg up, then pulling the waist down, straddling the hole, losing a pantleg . . . *Where's the paper? Oh, great.* That's *what the woman was selling at the entrance.* I usually ended up soaking my pant bottoms thoroughly. While wet pants might have spoken for themselves, I was the only one who could explain the problem currently at hand—in bad Turkish, and likely with more people than really needed to know.

I continued on past gaudy furniture stores gleaming with overwrought, gilded living room suites, and past mangy stray dogs keeping watchful guard over neighborhood children.

I hadn't been able to glean much from the Turks themselves about intimate topics. Confounded by the coexistence of religious conservatism and big city liberalism around me, I was unable to categorize Turks, and this made me agonize even more about discussing my ailing genitals with any of them. Upon entering a pharmacy for a genital disorder, would people spit out their tea in horror, or would my request be par for the course? Was it something they discussed, or would I be pelted with glares for broaching a taboo topic?

In all of my travels, I had discovered that it isn't easy to ascertain how a culture handles medical issues before the necessity of treatment occurs. In Tallinn, I found that Eastern Europeans tend to be naturalists, possibly because commercial pharmaceuticals have always been prohibitively expensive. For me, however, flower petals and sea salt positioned on the counter next to an abacus—which was actually still used to calculate purchases—did not inspire confidence.

On tonight's quest, the only thing I knew about Turkish medicine was that I could buy most drugs without a prescription. If the pharmacist recognized any of my listed American remedies, I might be out the door before ever finding out what Turks thought of a woman waltzing in with a yeast infection. But what if they misunderstood? What if they thought I was describing a sexually transmitted disease? Had other American women, loose or otherwise, trod similarly uncomfortable routes toward healing in İstanbul? And if so, could they have paved my way for a neutral commercial transaction? Or had they cemented my fate to be a symbol, before a store full of strangers, of things gone wrong in the West? As I turned left up a steep residential side street, I spotted two middle-aged Turkish women standing before a stunning sequined gown in a store window. One woman, speaking and gesturing, began to smooth her hands over the other woman's breasts, down over her waist and then her hips, completing an hourglass motion. The tactile description of how the dress might fit didn't cause the woman being touched to flinch; rather, she nodded in agreement as she eyed the glittering gown and mimicked her friend's caress over her own bust and midriff.

It reminded me that European women seem more comfortable in their bodies than the women of my culture. In Estonia I'd observed hefty older women struggling to hoist themselves up the steps of a tram. The man or woman waiting to board behind her would place their palms on her ample buttocks and give her a helpful shove up. Those women didn't seem to mind having their bottoms touched by strangers, and yet here I was terrified at the prospect of talking about a rebellious bit of my anatomy with a trained professional.

Another thing that surprised me in Estonia was the common practice of enjoying a sauna naked with family, friends, and colleagues of both sexes. When I expressed my shock, an Estonian colleague said, "Dana, I think you have issues."

Perhaps she was right. As part of the lifestyle, many countries and cultures have public baths, a place where one routinely cleanses and relaxes with friends. Albeit gender-segregated, public baths, called *hamam*, were a Turkish tradition as well. If ladies in Turkey bathed naked together, what was I getting so worked up about? Here I was, a woman in my thirties with considerable life experience, yet the genital equivalent of a bad headache had caused me to lose all perspective.

Checking my directions, I took the next right while rehearsing the very direct, muted exchange I would have with the pharmacist: "I need something for 'female mold.'"

"But of course," she would say and come back with my relief in a tube.

As I slalomed past other evening shoppers, a horse-drawn cart rolled by, carrying fresh farm-grown garlic and leeks for sale. It seems a modern city like İstanbul can be totally progressive and cosmopolitan while abiding in relative harmony with age-old tradition. The cart plodded along, slowing traffic as the driver called out to people living in apartments above Dolce & Gabbana,

Donna Karan, and Thierry Mugler boutiques. Frustrated drivers of Mercedes Benzes, BMWs, and all varieties of obese SUVs honked their horns. I could have been strolling through the center of Paris or New York—places where I'd have to do much more than mention my crotch to get anyone to pay attention to me. Could the people of this chaotic city be just as difficult to impress, frighten, offend?

I considered the possibility that the taboo was of my own manufacture. Americans have developed a vast vocabulary of euphemisms for human genitalia. Even in adulthood, we refer to the genital area as "down river," "privates," or "unmentionables." My parents talked to my sister and me about everything gender-related openly and honestly, though, and we weren't shamed by nudity, as we'd seen our parents in all stages of undress. As a kid, my upbringing hadn't taught me to be repressed or overly body-conscious, but it seems that somewhere along the way, I've become exceedingly modest about certain things.

At least in the U.S., however, I know I have lots of company. People are portrayed in advertisements discussing intimate topics with friends, spouses, mothers, and sisters, as if American women seize every chance to discuss "not-so-fresh" feelings; yet it's telling that feminine-hygiene commercials don't reference genitalia by name.

If we don't mention our unmentionables in my supposedly liberal country, what indeed was the protocol in a country where some women cover their heads out of religious custom? To some extent, I was a victim of the foreign media's portrayal of all Muslim cultures as repressed, conservative, inflexible, and intolerant. Which side of this culture was I about to confront? The puritanically devout, or the other one?

Turkish culture is a contradiction. Just like the juxtaposition of horse carts and haute couture, head scarves and halter tops, the extremely conservative exists with the incredibly tolerant. A couple of months prior, I'd been indignant when a male Turkish friend revealed another side of this paradox while explaining his Nipple Theory. According to him, visible nipples—those protruding through clothing—are offensive in Turkey. The idea did explain the generally rigid appearance of many Turkish women's breasts—their brassieres seem to have more padding than a bulletproof vest! Yet, while erect nipples may be a no-no, trendy Turks happily join the rest of the world in exposing their pelvic bones in low-riding pants, and their crop tops reveal belly button rings, tattoos, and a whole lot of flesh. But even though every shop window displays mannequins with erect nipples, none of the women I saw, no matter how they were dressed, ever sported protruding nipples. Last month, after deciding the Nipple Theory might be true, I ended up buying a new bra.

This evening I was wearing my specially padded bra. It was hard-won. Acquiring it had highlighted gender issues in Turkey as well as my own. I'd gone to the Beşiktaş bazaar, one of many outdoor markets held daily in different neighborhoods, where one can buy everything from clothing and shoes to fresh fish and produce at rock-bottom prices. That day, I had been both bewildered and entertained by the pandemonium of merchants barking out their wares and prices from every direction. There were dozens of stalls full of strappy bargains, but no female vendors. Some of the peddlers wore bras on their heads while tossing handfuls of G-strings into the air! I'd laughed at the whimsy, until, without any affectation of subtlety, one retailer eyeballed my bosom and suggested a 36 B-cup.

More shocking was that everyone else—women in *kara çarşaf* (the head-to-toe black covering of conservative Muslim females), those in miniskirts, and every kind of Turkish lady in between—were buying intimate apparel from these men in a nonchalant manner akin to selecting ripe tomatoes or fresh cheese. The salesmen treated us all the same—as customers with money to spend. But we weren't the same. I had never in my life purchased a bra from a man, and I felt weird doing so. Talk about old-fashioned!

Finally, I'd arrived at the extended-hours *eczane*. I counted a dozen people inside; thankfully, the one in the lab coat was an attractive young woman with bright pink lipstick. Others appeared to be employees, but there were also a handful of teenage boys standing about aimlessly until, to my dismay, one of them asked how he could help. I *so* didn't want to be helped by a young man! I ignored him and tried to wait until the pharmacist was available. She wasn't free, but she noted my entrance and shouted across the small crowd to me:

"Buyurun!" (May I help you?) I clutched my list of Turkish words and treatment names but was not about to shout back.

I "tssked" the colloquial Turkish "no thanks" to everyone else who approached until the pharmacist was free. Her crisp lab coat eased my panicked mind, as did her French manicured nails and high heels. I started asking for American product names, but none were familiar to her, so I referred to my list of all things embarrassing and began to croak them out in uncertain Turkish: "Female mold?" "Women's yeast?" "Girl fungus?" She showed no glimmer of recognition. To my horror, she gestured to the seventeen-year-old who'd tried to help me on the way in. He looked at my list of synonyms, then conferred with her and began throwing out words to me in Turkish. I didn't understand any of them.

"İşte, anladım!" (Here, I understand!) After much fruitless guessing, the ailment I'd been trying to describe was finally clear to the pharmacist, who was eager to prove her comprehension. While my heart tried to beat its way out of my body, this woman began miming a frantic crotch-scratching session, enhanced by some dramatic and spot-on facial expressions of simultaneous agony and ecstasy.

My worst nightmare came to life, as customers, shoppers, and teenage delivery boys turned to focus on the sweaty foreigner trying to buy medication— or, more likely, to observe their boss, who could have earned an Oscar for her stellar performance as Young Woman with Itch.

I quickly yelled, *"Evet!"* (Yes!) to affirm her correct assessment of the problem—but more importantly, to get her to stop scratching.

I examined the tube she handed me, thankfully recognizing the polysyllabic active ingredient. I turned to the teenage cashier as I fumbled for my money, relieved the pharmacist had guessed my ailment correctly, rather than handing me a shampoo for pubic lice or ointment for herpes. Mercifully, the end of this ordeal was near. Or so I thought.

"How did you get it?" came a voice from behind me. Incredulous, I turned to look at a fellow customer who'd witnessed the entire exchange. When I didn't respond, she conceded that she gets yeast infections after a visit to her summer cottage, where she swims in the sea. Here was a total stranger, talking to me—in a language foreign to her—about a topic I'd deemed unspeakable in my own. I did not have any exotic cause to offer. No cottage, no sea, just me.

I slapped some *lira* bills on the counter, not waiting for change as I slunk past the inquiring woman, mumbling that it just happened, I didn't know how. I was out the door.

Fifteen minutes later, in the cool comfort of my home, medicated in body and spirit by one part clotrimazole cream and several parts gin and tonic, I was tempted to regale some friends with the crazy ordeal I'd just survived. "And there she was, scratching her crotch for all the world to see. . . ."

Yet in the lull brought on by my newfound peace of mind, I realized that it didn't really matter what my health problem was, how Turkish women view their bodies, or how they relate to others about intimate topics.

The only thing I needed to know was the nature of Turkish people. I *did* know it but was overwhelmed by the greater knowledge of my own repressive culture. So worried about what people would think, it didn't even occur to me that ultimately my Turkish neighbors would have cared for me as a person. In the end, even without adequate language skills, I found a professional pharmacist willing to humiliate herself in order to help me in my trauma. I found a teenage boy willing to assist me in a professional manner. What's more, I now realized that, far from prying, the customer asking how I contracted my infection was probably trying to ease my misery by openly joining the league of the beleaguered.

I'd seen the universally accepting character of Turks a million times without recognizing it. The stares inside of a pharmacy might well have been each person's interest in being able to help, should a foreigner like me need assistance. Maybe all those people looking at me and asking me what I wanted were just trying to ensure I felt at home.

As I sat alone in my apartment that evening, I realized that I *didn't* feel at home, not in Estonia and not in Turkey, and maybe it's because I've never felt at home in my own body, much less in my own body in another country.

FOUR

Henna'd Hands

Courting etiquette and marriage rituals can be difficult for a foreigner to comprehend. Yet, navigating the labyrinth of dating and mating—from henna tattooing and traditional village bride bargaining to modern civil services of high society complete with voracious paparazzi—is an exhilarating experience.

Forever After, For Now

BY TANALA OSAYANDE

*H*ope, Avril, and I sip our coffees in a café, moaning about our love lives. I'm having my usual au lait, served French-style in a bowl; Hope, a latte in a tall glass; Avril, filtered black coffee. This is our typical twenty- or thirty-something New York lifestyle, a leisurely Saturday lunch at the spot of the moment.

But this is not New York; it's İstanbul. Transplanted to a dimension superficially similar to our native territory, our personal ceremonies continue. Living, working, and playing in Taksim—a large cosmopolitan area, with chain stores, movie theaters, and discos; with a sizeable expat community and slew of foreign schools for Turks—we are surrounded by a Westernized Turkish populace. We know we have experienced only a fraction of Turkish culture. We're not privy to more private and traditional parts of life in this huge city. But even rooted in familiar comforts and choices, we are confused initiates.

Here we sit, three single American women on the İstanbul dating scene, puzzled by the upending of all our established dating precepts.

"He's insane," Avril declares about Hope's latest guy. "Another man who phones you all the time. What happened to acting cool and standoffish?"

I said the very same thing a month ago, not about Hope's Turkish man but my own. Our years of friendship and support have accustomed us to analyzing men's behavior in girl-talk sessions and advising each other. By now we are veterans in dealing with a distant man who refuses to communicate or one who avoids commitment, but our strategies are useless in this country. The rules of engagement are different.

"I'm starting to get nostalgic for the days when a guy didn't call for three days after a date," retorts Hope, which makes us all laugh. Our Turkish suitors wait only three or four hours. A waiter sidles by to take our order. He knows us, and our three-hour lunches at Ara never raise the expressive Turkish eyebrow. Owned by the famous Turkish photographer Ara Güler, the café's walls are hung with his artistic black-and-white images of local subjects. Popular with up-and-coming artists, young entrepreneurs, and the occasional Turkish pop star, it's starting to fill up with the late lunch crowd.

In modern Western culture, it seems dating is about proving who is more independent, who needs the relationship less. In the dating-as-hunting analogy, both men and women want to be the hunted, and no one wants to be perceived as the hunter. Being desired is most desirable.

However, a year of living and dating in İstanbul has proven to Avril, Hope, and me that the tenets of this theory do not apply here. We consider a first date the beginning of the hunt, finding mystery and elusiveness an enticement to continue the chase. Turkish men, when we agree to meet, consider our acceptance of their company as the capture itself. There is no discovery period of getting to know each other. They're already mounting the trophy of our love on the wall. For an American man, it might take seven or eight months of dating to declare a relationship; here, it takes only one cup of coffee, one movie, one walk in the park.

The waiter clears our drained coffee cups. It's time for our next course—dessert—and we all take fresh looks at the menu. Hope's cell phone rings. She glances at the display. "Yüksel," she says with a grimace, and we all exchange rueful looks. Hope's latest Turkish boyfriend had professed his love three weeks after they met. An engineer by profession and, in our opinion, a stalker by inclination, he had been calling incessantly—begging, yelling, seeking forgiveness—since she'd broken up with him five days earlier. He even resorted to calling Avril and me, imploring us to intervene on his behalf.

"He just wants to understand why it has to be over when—for him—nothing was wrong," I say, knowing that there is no way to explain to a lovesick Turk that what's wrong is that he's too lovesick.

The inequality of emotional investment, we find, is particularly disorienting to our progressive Western consciousness. We're not prepared to encounter a warm-blooded Mediterranean culture that, instead of fleeing from commitment and encouraging individualism, actively embraces a couple culture and interdependency. Instead of sorting through the options to find the "perfect" partner, like Americans do, Turks seem to think the one they go out with is perfect.

Companionship itself is a form of love; for Turks, togetherness brings comfort. Turkish women are rarely seen unescorted—in movies, in cafés, while shopping. If not accompanied by a man, then she is with a friend or relative. In striking contrast to the United States, discos are usually filled with couples; men are not allowed in without a female companion, and Turkish females are never alone.

Being alone is not a favorable idea culturally. The family unit and one's network of friends are tightly knit, interdependent structures. A single female is definitely looked on as an anomaly. What we Westerners view as admirable independence is construed as loneliness, a lack of friendships, a pitiable state of being. Even lone males seem to share this stigma.

Being products of American feminist culture, Avril, Hope, and I resist the idea. "I'm too young for a long-term commitment," says Hope, setting her phone to mute and burying it in her handbag. "Life has too many experiences to offer to settle down right now." Avril and I nod in agreement. Our very presence in İstanbul—traveling, working, and studying—confirms we are capable and independent women out to see the world. We're not looking for the perfect man to fulfill us.

From my mother and her contemporaries who struggled for rights, I learned to guard my independence and equality as a woman. As a child of the '70s, I was raised by an educated, divorced woman in an all-female household. Culturally and politically, as women fought and won important battles for gender equality around me, I naturally internalized the era's social gains. Moreover, I seem to have developed a deeply rooted defense mechanism against anything smacking of male dominance. That attitude worked to my advantage in the U.S., where dating involves opening my own door, calling the man and making the arrangements, getting to and from the date. So it was a shock to discover how much dating in Turkey gives me pleasure in being female, without feeling a loss of self.

One of the first Turkish men I went out with, Turan, was what Avril, Hope, and I would call an "old-fashioned gentleman." He would always defer to what I wanted to do, pick me up, and open the door for me. Going home unescorted was literally unthinkable. The first time I suggested that I see myself home after a date, he was offended, as if I had insulted his manhood. Perhaps I had. As a Turkish man, he was concerned for my safety in a city that's considered dangerous by its citizens merely because of high pickpocketing rates. I found the concept charming, since I come from a country that hosts the murder capital of the world. To me, dangerous means the potential for being physically assaulted, not being relieved of the money in my purse.

The waiter comes to take our dessert orders, and we all say "cheesecake" together, and then laugh. It is a ritual with us, a comfort food in times of crisis. While waiting for our traditional treat, I recall another cheesecake confession, when I admitted how much I appreciated Turan's thoughtful behavior. Avril and Hope laughed that I was becoming a girlie girl.

But in İstanbul, we have all become girlie girls. We have come to expect almost a 1950s standard of dating behavior, eliminating undesirables by rating how well they perform basic tasks of setting dates, picking us up, paying for the check. We have found a headiness in this kind of power, especially since we can indulge the parts of our natures that American self-help books warn will drive away the opposite sex. We feel free to ask questions, to assume that our Turk will want to spend all his free time with us, to offer dress advice, to help stock refrigerators and buy essential household items. Should we so choose, we can hold hands and snuggle into a shoulder whenever we want to, secure in the knowledge that we won't be rejected. Though we express irritation and exasperation with all this love-struck behavior, inwardly the thrill of being so openly wanted nurtures our visions of self.

We do not have to falsely proclaim our indifference to a man's negligent behavior; we don't need to be restrained from calling when a suitor suddenly disappears from our lives without a word. In Turkey, we are free to be codependent. We can phone when we want, and we are always rewarded for showing our interest. Guys here will call to say, "I miss you," or "I just wanted to hear your voice." They don't seem afraid, like American men, that confessing such emotion traps them in a relationship. For Avril, Hope, and me, the novelty has not worn off. Yet neither has it sunk in.

We spend our lunches cataloging the behaviors we see, comparing them to what we have experienced with our own Turkish men. "'Exfoliating wash' at nine o'clock," Avril suddenly whispers behind her napkin, dodging the elbows of the waiter, who is setting down our plates. She's referring to one of our codes for the overeager attentions of Turkish suitors. A mirror hanging to our right facilitates surveillance as both Hope and I watch a man at a nearby table wipe his hand down the face of his girlfriend, who smiles and cuddles closer. Our code also includes the "headlock" and the "24/7 after two," which means wanting to spend every moment together after two minutes of knowing us.

"Ah, memories of Turan," I smile mischievously over a forkful of cheesecake, but a moment of true nostalgia creeps in.

Hope laughs. "Do you remember how irritated you would get when he rubbed off your date face," she asks, referring to how he would suddenly, without warning, pass his hand from my forehead to chin while I was speaking. At first I thought he wanted me to be quiet, but later I realized he was trying to show how much he appreciated me. It was as if he didn't notice I was wearing makeup. He'd finish the move with a *"canım"* (my love) and a tweak to the nose. Then he'd take my hand or throw his arm around my neck. Some form of touching had to occur, be it in the car, at the restaurant, or in a bookstore. Although I am an affectionate person by nature, eventually I was overwhelmed as my sense of personal space was erased.

A couple walks into the restaurant, in full headlock. The man bumps into my chair as he passes, as there is not enough room for two abreast. Avril snickers, "It's the same on the street!" It's a constant source of irritation for us in a city with uneven sidewalks only twelve inches wide: Couples refuse to walk single file.

Hope looks at Avril and asks, "So, have you heard from him?" She's wondering about Raşit. She knows his easy and open affection attracted her, as love given and returned so freely is its own intoxication. We've all admitted that dating a Turk flexes some traditional female muscles that have been allowed to atrophy in our own culture, bringing up new issues. We're wondering how to relate these new experiences to our own sense of female identity.

"No," Avril replied quietly, playing with her fork. Hope and I exchange glances, remembering the dynamic of her relationship with Raşit and how it changed. The protectiveness that we all found so charming in our dates began to seem paternalistic with him. While she enjoyed being prized, the sensation of being dependent began to inhibit her. She told him she was unable to continue seeing him, not because of anything he had done, but because of what she could not do.

This conflict exists for all of us. We have not managed to maintain one dating success story here in İstanbul, and our catalog of failed relationships grows thick. Relationships that began with promise end in anger and confusion. Often the disorientation of culture shock plays a major role. Avril, Hope, and I have found that not replying immediately to a message or phone call is considered extremely rude, whereas if the same thing had happened to us, we would assume that the man was busy or unable to answer. Apparently it is normal in Turkey to tell your suitor all the times you will be available during any given week, so that he can schedule meetings. Our dates expected to be given precedence over any other friendship or nonessential appointment. But for young American women like us, who thrive on a busy social schedule—meeting friends to check out film festivals, coworkers for lunch or for gym visits and drinks after work, girlfriends for shopping expeditions and boat trips—spending all our free time with just one person seems like an impossible enterprise.

"Yeah, well, if you went out with him any longer, you'd have had to tell all your family secrets," joked Hope, referring to the immediate trust that Turks seem to expect from us. Every man we have dated has expected us to reveal the most intimate details about our lives and family, all our deepest fears and desires. None of us are comfortable with that. I have been the recipient of truly intimate information, spoken in confidence because of our new dating status. Being as forthcoming and frank with my own life has been difficult for me, and I have hurt suitors with my reserve, which for them translated into a lack of love. I was unable to surmount the walls that protect me from ridicule and rejection in the United States, while my Turk's fortifications were open wide and welcoming me.

As we finish up our desserts and prepare to leave, I look into the laughing faces of my dear friends, and for a moment I feel sad. These Western inner boundaries both free and inhibit us, I think. We are free to make decisions and choices in a bid for more independence, but it is also possible that we prevent ourselves from making real and lasting connections.

"Why is it always feast or famine?" I say to my two friends, who look at me with tenderness, fellow veterans in love. "Are we saving ourselves from inappropriate relationships, or are we just unable to accept and return unconditional affection?"

They don't answer, because this is a big question, left to hang over our finished lunch like haze on the Bosphorus. I think about all our euphemisms for a relationship we are not yet ready to claim: We are "seeing someone," "dating casually," and "going out." These terms do not apply to the dates we have with Turks. We don't even have words for the idea of committing to a brand-new relationship, exclusively seeing someone we just met—all with the aim of forging a deep and meaningful bond.

The Turkish formula seems more pragmatic, perhaps even more human. Perhaps this culture is teaching us to respect the instinct of emotion, the essential need to be found worthy of love.

On my bedstand at home is a book that describes love that kindles without the testing and interaction that Westerners like my friends and I have come to expect and require. In *My Name Is Red*, by Turkish novelist Orhan Pamuk, a man's youthful love for a woman is born from the sight of her and sustains him for more than a decade. One glimpse of her at a window confirms and reinflames his love, and hers, without a word exchanged. They finally unite, despite lovers and marriage and children, murder and death and tragedy. As the waiter clears our table, I wonder if such a relationship is less real or less meaningful than one put through the rigors that Western standards of communication devise.

It's Avril who breaks the somber moment. "Well, maybe that's what being independent and liberated is about. Making choices based on what life offers us."

Hope and I agree. We are all works in progress. Casting aside internal feminist restrictions, rejecting preconceptions of independence, we may just choose to embrace open emotions like the Turks do, wherever that may take us.

Village Bride

BY EPPIE LUNSFORD

*A*s Zübeyde and I made our bumpy way via a crowded, smoky *dolmuş* (minibus) to her family's village near Çankırı, two and a half hours northeast of Ankara, she explained what to expect from the village weddings we were about to see.

"The night before the wedding, we apply henna paste to the bride's fingers and palms," said Zübeyde, miming the motion of binding the bride's hands to let the henna set. The fifteen-year-old daughter of the doorman in my sister Nancy's apartment, Zübeyde had been Nancy's housekeeper, nanny, and personal guide to Turkey in the past year and a half since my sister relocated from Jakarta, Indonesia, with her husband and young son. Though Nancy and her family were seasoned expatriates, this was my first experience abroad. I was looking forward to accompanying Zübeyde on visits to her aunts and uncles, cousins and friends; it reminded me of trips to the rural town of Lynchburg, Tennessee, where I and my twelve other siblings had lived for six years. I imagined Çankırı would be similar to that rural community of four hundred people—everyone would know or be related to everyone else. The celebrations preceding the wedding ceremonies that Zübeyde described, though, like the *kına gecesi,* or henna night, would bear little resemblance to the kind of rituals we had back home.

Straight out of university, at the age of twenty-one, I had come to Ankara in 1987 for an extended stay to help Nancy. She was heavily pregnant with twins, eager for family to be near, and excited to share all her tales of living abroad. My older sister was also keen to guide my first journey to a foreign land. Unfortunately, she was too pregnant for the role of tour guide, so the task fell to Zübeyde, who was thrilled to share her country with a second Lunsford sister.

In over three months, I had picked up enough Turkish to shop and carry on basic conversations. I was ready to strike out on an adventure to Zübeyde's village.

The jerking, never-ending ride tried my patience. The *dolmuş* was packed with people, chickens, and sacks of vegetables. It was such a relief to finally step out into the open air of Şabanözü, the village where Zübeyde's family lived. Walking along the broken cobbled roads and dirt paths, we greeted the locals, who were carrying *harar* (burlap bags) of beans and other dried goods or were balancing water jugs secured to a pole across their shoulders. Painted cinderblock houses had adjacent fieldstone stables. Outhouses made of wood with scattered hay in and around reminded me of the small smokehouses we had back on the farm in Tennessee. Abandoned or in disuse, we'd used them for storage and games of hide-and-seek. The autumn air in Şabanözü was crisp with the smell of manure, the aroma of food on the stoves, and a slight acrid undertone of burning coal.

As villagers emerged from their houses to welcome us, Zübeyde laughed, "They are always ready to entertain guests and gossip about the other hundred people not present!" Upon arriving, the introductions were endless. The *"hoş geldiniz," "hoş bulduk"* welcoming exchanges were like a community mantra, but of the dozens of introductions, I only caught about five names. Just as in my own hometown, I recognized the importance placed on family and relationships when the villagers asked me where my father's father's father was from. Wanting to foster the instant connection I felt, I mentioned the *Kızılderili* (Native American, literally "redskins") element in my family tree. I explained in broken Turkish that we had common ancestors from the Ice Age—mine had migrated to America, theirs to Anatolia—a theory Atatürk, the father of modern Turkey, even told the Turkish people. The fact that they knew my sister Nancy already—combined with our Indian blood and the knowledge that I came from a large family—seemed to give the villagers instant comfort in our kinship. They welcomed me as part Turk.

After offering the gifts we had brought from Ankara—plastic slippers (to be worn inside the home, politely leaving soiled shoes outside), hand towels, and chocolates—we settled down for an early dinner in the home of Zübeyde's *teyze* (aunt). A husky woman, she looked much older than her age of forty, with deeply wrinkled face and hands and a wide, snaggletoothed smile. She wore the common village attire of loose *şalvar* (the baggy pants of Anatolian women) with long johns peeping from beneath and a long-sleeved, tightly fitting sweater with a hand-knitted vest buttoned up the front. Similar to other older village women, she wore a white cotton kerchief on her head, tied under her chin.

As I had learned in the weeks I'd been in Turkey, being a polite guest entails accepting anything that is offered. This nicety became an unfortunate detriment to keeping my figure and a sound stomach, because at mealtime it translated into consuming heaping portions of the wide variety of dishes prepared. That day we indulged in delicious pasta; peppers stuffed with rice, pine nuts, and currants; and freshly prepared rabbit stew, washed down with copious amounts of the *yoğurt* drink *ayran*. Afterward, we recovered by strolling through the village and drinking endless tiny glasses of tea in every other house as we stopped to chat with neighbors. As the sun set, the nuptial festivities began.

The village was buzzing with activity. Traditional rural weddings can last from two days to a week, depending on the wealth of the families. Both of the weddings we were to attend—one for a girl named Fahriye and the other for Nimet—would last two days.

Because of the traditional segregation of men and women in rural Turkish areas like this one, I knew I could not take part in the men's ceremonies; then again, women aren't generally welcomed at bachelor parties in America either, unless they're the entertainment. Even on the wedding day itself, there were few moments that brought the sexes together in this village. But I was looking forward to joining the women's celebrations. First was henna night, *kına gecesi*.

The eve of the wedding is customarily the time for both men and women to apply *kına*, or henna paste, at their respective parties as a symbolic blessing for maturity and fertility. Spread on the bride's hands and feet, it creates burnt-orange/red markings that last nearly a month and permanently dye the fingernails and toenails orange until they grow out. Brides henna their hair as well for an auburn sheen. In the groom's case, just the hand or finger is dyed, depending on regional custom, Zübeyde had explained on the long minibus ride. Friends and family attending the henna parties dye their hands as well.

Fahriye's *kına gecesi* would soon be starting, so Zübeyde and I set off to a neighbor's house with a small group of girls aged twelve to seventeen. Outside, the entrancing beat of the *davul* drum and the energetic nasal whine of the oboe-like *zurna* were beckoning.

A slow, stately drumbeat heralded the coming fugue of alternating rhythms, echoing through the darkness. The twisting melody and high-pitched screeching notes of the *zurna* seemed to put a mesmerizing seal over the whole community, announcing to everyone within earshot that the festivities of Fahriye's wedding had begun. But the music was not for the women's celebration; it was for the men's. Flames of a distant fire, which the men surrounded, and the wail of the music drew me. I wanted to hear more, see more. I suggested we take the roundabout way to the bride's house, to bring us closer to the men's fireside festivity, but I was overruled with a fit of giggles from my girlish companions. When we arrived at the women's celebration, chastened, I quietly settled into a crowded room with fluorescent lighting and a boom box. After the romanticism of the men's fireside scene, this setting seemed depressing. I thought it was unfair that I and the rest of the women were isolated indoors and under harsh light on such a gorgeous evening.

But soon I was absorbed by the scene around me. A sea of smiling faces stared back at me, eyeing my uncovered shoulder-length hair and very conservative long wool dress with matching shawl. The village women dressed in *şalvar* or in long dresses. All wore head scarves, some made of patterned cotton muslin and some more simple, synthetic ones. The younger women tied them loosely like kerchiefs, while the older women wore ones that were a bit longer, past the shoulder, more tightly wrapped around their heads.

No sooner was a warped cassette of melodramatic arabesque music put into the boom box than a shuffle of cables and the sound of static left it boomless. Thankfully the technical problem allowed us the better fortune of listening to one young girl's cheerful voice leading the crowd in song. Everyone clapped and sang along to the *türküler* folk songs she chose, themed specifically for henna nights. Zübeyde later explained that most of the songs, though upbeat sounding, expressed the sorrow of the bride leaving her mother. "For us, family is everything. It isn't easy for a girl to leave her mother," Zübeyde said.

Then some of the women got up and began village-style belly dancing. The dance was unlike the flashy, sexy moves I had seen on television, or the variety tourists might now witness in a nightclub with floor shows (a *gazino*) in İstanbul. A pair of wooden spoons was passed to one of Zübeyde's aunts, who began clapping them like castanets as she rhythmically lifted her abdomen toward me, slinging her gut upward in quick movements while her torso remained still. I joined her and did whatever I could to keep up. So this was why belly dancing was often called *göbek atması*, throwing the stomach.

When this merriment came to an end, I realized the bride, Fahriye, was not yet in the room. The crowd's chatter died down as one of her cousins began to sing a slow, melodic *türkü*. Although the girl's voice was raspy, it was strong and stirred the audience of forty to respectful attention. Before we could applaud this beautiful performance, there was an abrupt interruption. Giggling women and girls burst through a back door and rushed to the center of the room. Suddenly they began enacting a dramatization of the wedding night. Two of the bride's girlfriends acted as the bride and groom—the taller, huskier girl playing the man. Women all around me chortled as the groom instructed his new bride in the proper way to pray, walloping her on the head when she made a mistake. Then things heated up: time for mock lovemaking! Raucous laughter met the grand finale as the bride began resisting the amorous advances of the groom. The cucumber they were mischievously using for a prop quickly disappeared into the hands of elders when word came that Fahriye was approaching the room. The laughter died down as well. "My family has a bit of Gypsy in them," Zübeyde explained to me in a whisper during the hush that followed. "Everyone expects them to do something unusual," she winked at me. Apparently such ribaldry was allowed only because the bride was not there.

Fahriye made her entrance into the stuffy room, which was now uncomfortably crowded with latecomers and their children. Her face was covered with several veils of thin red muslin edged in *oya*, finely tatted, motif-laden colored lace. An older relative led her by the hand. Her grand entrance was prolonged by her unhappy sniffling and hesitation. It was hard not to notice the stark difference in mood. The hot room was silent, not only because the women were about to witness Fahriye's rite of passage, but also from the guilt of guffawing at the entertainment—a comic look at the young bride's future. Meanwhile Fahriye, nervous and scared, was probably mourning the loss of her childhood and fearing the impending separation from the bosom of her family.

The bride took her place in the middle of the room while another beautiful *türkü* of joyful pain was sung. A large tin plate of green henna paste was carried in and set on the floor. It smelled of drying alfalfa, I thought, remembering the farm in Tennessee. The *kına* was thick, sticky, and very messy. Everyone crowded around the plate. Zübeyde and another girl began applying the *kına* to the bride's feet and hands as other revelers applied it to their own hands as well. I noticed the paste was generously spread in no specific pattern, unlike countries I'd seen featured in *National Geographic*, such as Saudi Arabia or India, where henna is meticulously applied in elaborate symbolic and aesthetic designs. To complete the ritual, a coin was placed in each of Fahriye's palms for luck and prosperity before her hands were wrapped in scarves to let the henna dye set overnight.

Fahriye's marriage was an arranged one to a much older man, a man whom she did not particularly want to wed. "It's natural for a bride to be sad," Zübeyde responded when I showed concern that Fahriye was crying. "She's leaving her family. Why wouldn't she be sad? Some even say it's the sign of a good daughter not to smile on her wedding day." In the years since, I've read that arranged marriages still account for at least half of all marriages in Turkey, particularly in rural areas. Also, contrary to reports from my sister's elite Turkish friends, who were educated abroad, that the process is illegal in Turkey and doesn't happen anymore, there is still a *başlık*, or bride price, applied to young women in many villages, set by the elders of the respective families.

The next morning, I witnessed firsthand the bargaining for a different prospective bride: a young girl named Selma, who happened to be engaged to

Zübeyde's brother Kemal, who stayed in Ankara to work that weekend. The groom's family, now mine by virtue of my closeness with Zübeyde, rode out to a nearby village forty-five minutes away to see the family they hoped to impress with a negotiable price and lots of gifts of jewelry and clothes. Perhaps bringing a foreigner to this occasion was part of impressing the other family. The elders gathered in the corner to receive tea and cakes, served by Selma. Kemal's father had a serious countenance but was a flexible man who did not demand full attention in social settings and was quite relaxed with his wife's abrupt interjections and loud guffaws.

Selma was all smiles but a bit nervous, neatly dressed in a skirt and blouse with a colorful synthetic veil tied in the back. After exchanging pleasantries, the older family members and Zübeyde cajoled me with questions about my family and of course made fun of my accent. After about half an hour, the bride's and groom's parents, the grandparents, and another elderly relative stood up and moved to another room, closing the door behind them. The official bargaining began, and Zübeyde tried to listen and give an occasional bit of overheard information to Selma, who was peeking in from the kitchen. There was laughter among those of us on this side of the door, but heated arguments began on the other side. Bride bargaining seemed to be the women's domain, with the elderly grandmothers shouting their opinions loud enough for everyone to hear. My translator was giggling throughout, but at one point she put her ear closer to the door, then turned around to say, "Oh they want too much." Shortly thereafter, the deciding committee emerged from the boardroom quietly. We said our farewells quickly, sensing the tension. But Selma smiled and winked at me. She seemed confident that her betrothal to Kemal would be approved.

On the drive back to our village for Nimet's wedding, I couldn't follow the discussion, so Zübeyde would turn to me intermittently to relate what Selma's family had requested. "Clothes," "gold," and "not working in Ankara, for Selma's sake." Nothing was settled that day, but groundwork was laid, and the young couple was eventually married the next year in a civil wedding salon in Ankara.

I would have thought the act would be disturbing for all involved, negotiating for a young woman as if she were a commodity. Then it occurred to me—though the custom seemed shocking to me as a Westerner, the dowry system was commonly accepted in my own country until relatively recently, and that system required the bride's family to make a substantial offering to the groom.

The practicality of the Turkish bride-bargaining custom, on the other hand, seemed to be that the family received some financial help to compensate for the loss of a "worker," as the daughter most likely supported her family by working in the fields or tending to the labor- and time-intensive duties of the household, making olive oil, soap, tomato paste, *yoğurt*, butter, cheese, preserves, and most other prepared foodstuffs. "The man's family thinks a good catch is friendly and attractive," Zübeyde described to me. "A hard worker, and a good tea server to the elders," she added. But the price paid for a bride, explained Zübeyde, had more to do with the groom's family wanting to prove they had the means to take care of their future daughter-in-law. So it seemed to me to be a mutual need for the families to bless the union and pledge their support, rather than one party selling off a daughter to the other.

The following day, Zübeyde took me to meet Nimet, the other bride to be married that week. A short fifteen-year-old, she seemed to be a very sweet girl who never stopped smiling. Cheerily she welcomed us into her home, a well-kept and carefully decorated house with carpets and framed photographs of family and a large cabinet in the main living room, complete with color TV and dish set. Nimet laughed at Zübeyde's stories about flirting with the *Bakkal* market boys in Ankara and her tales of escaping her overbearing brothers. Nimet's unabashed joy, and that of her guests and family, surprised me. Nimet was radiant, making eye contact with everyone present. Her liveliness contrasted with poor Fahriye's attitude toward her own impending wedding.

"She's happy because she chose him," Zübeyde told me. Apparently Nimet and her fiancé, also an adolescent, were somehow related. They had renewed their acquaintance at an earlier family wedding and decided on their own to get married, with little parental intervention—unusual for their conventional village. When I'd met them the first day, both of them were all smiles, truly wanting to celebrate their togetherness.

We had stayed for a short while, then left only to see her again a few hours later in one of her relative's houses. Nimet's *kına* ceremony started when she entered the room, dressed in her best skirt and blouse, a long red veil covering her face. Escorted by an older woman singing another *türkü*, Nimet slowly took her place in the center of the room. The singer's voice rose with emotion, silencing the room and bringing me to tears, although I couldn't understand the lyrics. Other women were crying too, wiping their eyes with rough hands.

The scene drew me back to my Appalachian childhood, to something I hadn't thought of in a while. My father was a fiddler, and my three eldest sisters would sing with him every evening. Around them, the rest of us younger siblings would settle in slumber or quiet attention, warmed and comforted by their music. How quickly I had forgotten the beauty of family, I thought, in my years at college, only to regain the reverie in a village in Anatolia! When the singing stopped, henna was applied to Nimet's hands and feet. Her hair had already been henna'd and was now covered by the veil. Most of the other women were already henna'd from Fahriye's ceremony the night before, so they continued on to a prayer. Everyone raised her hands, palms inward, cupped open to the heavens, saying sentences I couldn't follow, then finishing with the one word I did get, *"Amin."* Amen.

I felt close to home here, in this place, in this wedding ceremony. Raised in a large unconventional family in the 1960s, when rituals were being reinterpreted and many kinds of music were used in religious expression, it all seemed oddly familiar and easy to accept. Even the complete absence of men was no longer on my mind. Afterward, the celebrating resumed with music and dancing, and we passed around dishes of roasted nuts and seeds.

As the women and children continued their merrymaking, Zübeyde and a cousin of the bride tapped me on the shoulder and indicated I should follow them. We walked in the darkness, toward the live music that had attracted me the other night during Fahriye's henna night. I realized that, as I was a foreigner and guest in their village, they wanted to show me what had enthralled me; we were to see what was going on around the fire. As we scrambled onto a neighbor lady's roof and crouched down to avoid detection, she and the two girls pointed to the dramatic scene below and grunted in a hushed laugh, *"Erkek kına gecesi!"* (Men's henna night!)

About a hundred men were gathered around the fire, taking their turns chasing the groom and each other around the hot coals. Jumping over the flames, they whooped and hollered, laughed and smoked cigarettes. The drummer relentlessly beat the *davul,* and the *zurna* screamed out a boisterous melody.

We couldn't stop giggling as they pointed out which boys they thought most handsome or sweet, explaining their relation to each one. Cousins were considered suitable husband candidates. Eventually our noise was noticed, and men started shooting glares in our general direction. It was enough to tell us we were overdue for a *çay molası* (tea break) at the farthest house possible!

The next day was Nimet's wedding, done quickly and behind closed doors. After such a rowdy celebration the night before, this was a letdown.

Fahriye's wedding had been less joyful. She didn't crack a smile.

I went to Fahriye's simple home, unadorned and quiet, to pay my respects to Fahriye and wish her happiness. She was seated in the center of the room, dressed in white with a red sash around her waist and a white chiffon veil flowing down her back, holding a bouquet of fake flowers intertwined with silver threads. This was not typical attire, according to Zübeyde. "Usually brides in our village wear a red dress," pointed out Zübeyde, and on top of that, a bedangled headdress of colorful scarves according to the Seymen regional folk tradition.

So Fahriye might not have chosen her husband, but she chose her own gown, I thought, with a little bit of satisfaction. Her long hair was let down for the special occasion. "Normally she wears it tied up and covered with a scarf," Zübeyde explained. In an effort to decorate herself, she was wearing a lot of makeup, rouged cheeks doubly red from her constant weeping. She was seated for everyone to kiss her as she cried. A few times she looked up to smile through the tears, but never long enough for her guests to think she was happy. To her dress, people pinned money or gold coins fitted with a special clasp, as wedding presents. I asked Zübeyde where the groom was while his bride received the good wishes of both men and women from the village. "He's at another house with the elderly men, letting Fahriye have her last goodbyes," she said, pointing out to the street. I never learned whether this was custom or just the preference of a much older husband.

After giving our congratulations to Fahriye, we left the girl's house to wait outside for the procession. As with Nimet's wedding, the actual ceremony was limited to family in the small house, and the wedding audience waited outside. I wasn't able to see the bride and groom together until they emerged from the house with other family members, got into a station wagon loaded with gifts, and drove off. The crowd yelled after them: *Güle, güle!* (So long, farewell!)

Since that week in rural Anatolia in 1987, I've been a resident of Turkey for nineteen years, and I married a Turk myself. I've been to all kinds of Turkish weddings: elaborately celebrated feasts at luxury hotels, with professional dance shows and orchestras; simple wedding salon parties, with intimate conversation and lively dancing; and casual weddings that were held in quaint country restaurants near the sea, very romantic, with Gypsy musicians and the bride and groom dressed like the lovers Julie Christie and Omar Sharif in *Dr. Zhivago*.

My own wedding took place in a hotel in Ankara with three hundred guests. A combination of live and recorded music had both families' extroverts taking the mike to sing along with popular Western tunes like "Summertime" and "Mambo Italiano." The wedding itself was a blur of handshakes and photographs and sore feet for both of us, as we had been celebrating for a whole week with out-of-town guests and local family and friends.

And yet, the village weddings I experienced with Zübeyde are the ones I remember most vividly. Perhaps because I felt then, as I still feel now, that I am an American villager. I relate to an upbringing in small towns where everyone knows each other's business and where a sense of community is fostered. Perhaps I remember these weddings because the general sadness of the bride who leaves her family for married life corresponds to my longing to be closer to the family

I have left. I have lived in İstanbul for the last thirteen years, with a loving and understanding husband raising children in a modern metropolis that is only an hour's drive from its rural edges. In the end, I'm comforted knowing I've married into a culture whose villagers' ways echo my Appalachian country background. And although my feet are no longer rooted in Anatolia, the roots, rites, and customs shared between our cultures have sustained me these last two decades and often make me feel I'm not really too far from home.

A Fine Kettle of Fish

BY TRICI VENOLA

*K*azım would take a cab for one block if he could; I thought he was lazy and grandiose and that may have been true, but later I realized he had only one pair of shoes, and they hurt him. It was 1999 and I was in İstanbul, with about three words of Turkish, following this Dionysian satyr into eternity.

I drew him many times. I drew everything: crumbling Byzantine bricks, swinging Ottoman lanterns, smiling street vendors, domes, boats, and minarets. The Turkish Tourist Office, always glad for good press, had commissioned me to produce pen and ink line drawings of Turkey. After years of building computer art for Disneyland and Silicon Valley, I was drawing by hand again—and from life. I was on fire with creative joy. A whole new life at fifty, all because I had become entranced with both the Turkish culture and with Kazım—who one friend called a careening festival of a human being and another called an alcoholic Kurdish carpet salesman. I called him a catalyst. There was just something about him apart from his beauty, some compulsion to engage with him that made me want to hit or hump him, or dance with him. At thirty-four, he had more life force than anyone I'd ever met. He wasn't nice. But I felt compelled to engage with him, violently, passionately, and we would go for days and nights fighting and making up.

Thank God I met Mona, American with North African roots, smack in the middle of Sultanahmet, the oldest district of one of the oldest cities on earth. Our friendship was my little lamp of comprehension in a dark night of dim bars down twisty cobbled streets, taxis plunging off into mystery, tilting tables in tiny shabby cafés thronged with dark arguing men, all in incomprehensible Turkish.

One night, we had walked down the hill to Kumkapı, once the Sand Gate in the massive seawalls protecting the Byzantines from Marmara Sea invaders, now a long row of fish restaurants with tables set outside on the cobblestones.

Everyone along the way wanted to feed us. Mona has these black Medusa looks; she looks like she stepped off of an ancient vase, and all the men were in love with her. All the restaurant touts were touting, and one said, "Excuse me, but are you not Mister Kazım's friend?" So we ate there. They must have phoned him; he called and asked us to meet him later.

When we arrived at his nearby hangout, Mona muttered, "A fake English pub in a Ramada Inn, for Chrissakes." Kazım was at the dart throw, dark in his pale gold suit, a big fleshy man with his slacks worn high. He paused, dart poised, and looked up at us. That diamond-shaped face. "Ah, Sweet," he projected over the music. "Welcome." Then he threw the dart. He ushered us to a table cluttered with beer steins and carrot sticks in lemon juice and little plates of finger food. I think the Turks invented finger food. There were a lot of them sitting around the table eating and drinking. It was clearly his party.

With Mona he was downright courtly, and demonstrative with me. Soon he was kissing my hand and saying to her, "Ah *love* this woman! An' *you* are like ma sister, because Ma Sweet is like ma *wife!*"

Many were the nights I'd sat drawing Kazım and his friends while the waves of Turkish rolled right over me and he never gave me a glance. When we were alone, sure, but in public . . . "Why won't you *look* at me?" I'd said. I could never look at anything but him.

"Sweet, you mus' know Ah no look at you because you are part of me."

"That sounds romantic as hell, but I still want you to look at me."

That night was different. Like many men, he was at his best and sexiest when there was another woman around to appreciate it. A small boy appeared, loaded with roses. Kazım bought them all and presented them to me, taking one out for Mona. When fruit arrived, drizzled with honey and powdered pistachios, he fed me gently, holding a banana slice speared on the end of a fork, cupping his other hand under it to catch the drips, his eyes slumberous, looking into mine as he sang softly in Kurdish.

Mona and I went to the ladies' room. I got in there and fell backward against the door. My eyes crossed. She said, "*Oh* my *GOD.* He's like a . . . *sultan,* or something."

"Thanks, I'm just getting my breath," I said. "I'm so nuts about him, I just don't trust my perceptions."

"Well, you're not crazy," she said. "He's larger than life. Geez, if he had money and an education there'd be no stopping him."

"He *had* money," I said. "He threw it away." From his first wife, a Belgian attorney, who gave him three million dollars. They opened a hotel and some restaurants; he bought a BMW and gambled the rest away; that was a few years ago. Mona would hear all this from Kazım in the next twenty minutes. He carried his glorious past around with him like a credit card.

When Kazım ordered gin, I knew our time was limited. Soon he would be someone else. I remembered from my own drinking days how I would feel great and keep drinking, and then awaken with no memory from the night before and a vague sense of unease. A black-jowled, flat-eyed goon grinned vacantly from Kazım's place as he toasted us with gin. Mona looked at me in consternation. "What happened to him?" She didn't bother to lower her voice. I pantomimed a drink going down a gullet. She looked at me and her eyes grew enormous. With dawning comprehension, her hands clasped over her heart, she said, "You mean, the only thing that's wrong with him, all the meanness and violence and bad luck, is just that he's *alcoholic?*"

I nodded. "Ohhh," she said, "I *get* it."

Mona left when Kazım announced he wanted to dance. We reeled up onto the floor. He was draped over me as we staggered around to the music, his mouth fastened on my neck. It hurt like hell. I arched my back and threw back my head, and that's when he fell on top of me. We picked ourselves up and I led him, huge and reeling, outside, his feet splayed out, my arm in his. Afraid he would pull me over, I leaned into him, taking his weight on my bruised hip.

We lurched across the tramline to the square in front of Ayasofya, survivor of fifteen centuries of fire, earthquake, conquerors, and the Crusades. It is painted red and lit at night. Glowing rose domes and minarets and arches sprawl below a squabble of lunatic gulls, circling and shrieking. And there under the chestnut trees, across from this magnificence looming up in the warm summer darkness, Kazım went insane. He began to scream about his horrible life, this rotten existence, a roaring, gargling litany of strangled frustration and rage. It was about one-thirty in the morning. I couldn't take him back to the hotel; local mores dictated that you couldn't take a drunk to your hotel and cool him out unless you married him first. Shouting, shaking his fist, he took off into the dewy, pristine tea garden, and I took off after him. We stomped through the wet grass toward the silent fountain, over fences and through the flower beds— one of us in high heels—and collapsed on one of the benches. His arms were flailing. One of them walloped me on the cheekbone. My earrings flew off and skittered on the cobbled path, my ears rang. "You *hit* me!" I said to nobody. It was the first time. I sat stunned, trying to comprehend it—*violence!*—while another part of me, urbane and amused, drawled, *How very Tennessee Williams of you.*

He was crying now, slamming his fist against the bench. I grabbed his ears, put his head in my lap, stroked his hair, and talked to him. He was shuddering, and finally quiet. I bent over him, and that's when the police arrived. Four of them stood us up and quick-marched us back across the wet grass to Ayasofya, Kazım protesting all the while. They twisted his hands behind him and cuffed him. One officer deliberately slapped him, hard, back and forth across the face. I had wanted to do that myself, but it sure wasn't any fun to watch. A cop shoved me hard into the patrol car. We racketed down the bumpy cobbled hill to the police station at the bottom, all in Turkish.

I don't mind being arrested now that I don't drink anymore. I hadn't done anything and I knew it. I assumed we were there because of drunken screaming in the park in the middle of the night. I was wearing black slacks and a long shirt, tied up tight around my waist and low on top. In the dark patrol car, I untied and shifted it so that when I got out, I was in a conservative black tunic.

They hustled us into the station, bleak with yellowish light. They slammed Kazım into a chair next to a battered filing cabinet and pushed me toward another. I sat down carefully with my sketchbook on my knees. All this time I had held it. Stalwart in their straps and buttons and buckles, they talked to Kazım as if he were a child, in the patronizing tone people use with drunks. They were reading his business card, the only ID he had. The cop who had shoved me squinted at me. Nobody spoke English. I heard Kazım saying my name to them, but they shut him up. The cop behind the desk looked over at me contemptuously and said, "Your pass-port." I handed it over. He looked at it and grunted something. The other one said, lip curling, "Your pro-fession." I held up the sketchbook. He came over and got it, an older guy, thick in the middle and bald on top. He walked back around the desk and sat down. Total silence while he looked at every page. Then he got up, walked back over to me, and held out the sketchbook with both hands. He bowed until his eyes looked right into mine. He said distinctly, handing me the sketchbook, "Madam, no problem."

They took the cuffs off Kazım then and offered us cigarettes. He took one. They stood him up and took him out of the room. I started up in alarm. The older cop, very nice now, made calming gestures and pantomimed face washing. He offered tea. I accepted. The one behind the desk lectured me in broken English on my choice of companions. I thanked him. They brought Kazım back in, damp around the hairline and a little more sober, jocularly giving them a hard time. They were a little sheepish. Later Mona told me that we'd been arrested because the police thought I was a *nataşa:*

"A Russian prostitute. When they saw your passport and that sketchbook they must have *shit.* You could really have gotten them into trouble. Yanking an American artist into custody—didn't even ID her first—treating her like a hooker . . ."

"I wonder if stuff like this happened to Hemingway or Gauguin?" I'd asked her.

It was 4 AM when the policeman called us a taxi, and twenty minutes later we were precisely where we had been two hours before when Kazım went crazy, and he was still drunk. At this point, all I wanted was to take him to bed, any bed, a flower bed! And sleep. It was very quiet. I wanted to keep it that way.

But he was hungry. "Ah want fish," he said as I looked up the dark street, ghostly tramlines in the night, thinking: fast food. "Give me thirty millions. Ah buy fish."

Thirty million Turkish *lira* was almost seventy dollars U.S. at the time. I said yes to him for the rollercoaster he provided. I wanted to stay on it, any way at all. It never stopped. His recuperation from dead drunkenness was awesome. When *I* drank that much I'd had to go to a 12-step program and had become so respectable that now I positively craved a little chaos.

So I gave him thirty million and we careened back down the hill past the police station and out onto the highway, Kazım in the front seat with the taxi driver in rapid-fire conversation all the way. I clutched my sketchbook. I wanted to see this seventy-dollar fish. We tooled up the highway in the silent darkness and stopped beside a jetty. He told the driver to wait. There was a strong smell of the sea.

Still in our nightlife clothes, we walked through a gate in a chain-link fence, down a corrugated metal catwalk, along a splintered wooden pier and through an open door in a metal wall. We were suddenly in a noisy cavernous warehouse of metal and scaffolding and spotlights like stars. It was lit up like day and full of shouts and echoes. Trucks were backed up to the open far end. The place was crowded with hundreds of men in rubber boots, ponchos, work shirts, and caps, the wet cement floor covered with boxes of fresh fish, every conceivable kind: shellfish and finny fish and flounder fish. Men walked between the boxes, talking. The air was damp and full of haggling, and I was like a demon, drawing it all. Kazım strolled between the boxes, all shoulders and draped gold suit in contrast to the lumpy plaid and rubber around him. Drawing, I watched him. He walked gracefully, with complete assurance, stopping here, there, to glance down and comment. Men fell in with him like iron filings. They deferred, gestured, smiled. I remembered he'd owned restaurants. I thought, *No wonder people have given this man millions.*

I had gotten what I wanted: a completely new experience, and the drawing to keep it. As the sky paled I saw we were across the highway from the restaurants in Kumkapı. Kazım came back with a white plastic grocery bag dangling heavily from each hand, clearly happy with himself. He was excited about the fish. I would see! He would cook for me! He went over to a little stand and gestured with a sleepy boy who, it turned out, sold vegetables. We rode back up the hill past huge rosy Ayasofya into the Sultanahmet. The sun was coming up.

It was the best fish I ever ate, and he'd made enough to feed an army. After I had eaten myself into a stupor with prawns, he brought in the platters of bluefish, sautéed and lightly breaded, with an enormous platter of chunked fresh vegetables. The suave carpet salesman, the ruined remorseful millionaire, and the drunk were gone. Here was a happy, complete man. He ate voraciously and with joy, pulling out the bones for me.

"*Süt* . . . see?" he said, parting the flaky fish with the fork. "'*Süt*' . . . means milk . . . flesh lak milk." I went back to my hotel glutted with fish, fell into bed, and woke up very happy.

But before, in the dawn, tired and gleeful, with our fish still in the bags, we walked in our rumpled ritzy clothes down the damp silent pale street to the carpet shop, pounded on the metal door, and woke up the guy who lived in the shop and guarded it. The shop had a kitchen about the size of a teakettle, and Kazım wedged himself into it. The wall slanted over the stove, barely clearing the top of the dented double boiler steaming upward into the curling patches of peeling paint. Kazım wielded the knife amid the garlic and the butter, humming a little song. His hair looked like a black pelt and he moved like he was dancing. He was cleaning prawns as big as my hand. I was standing outside the kitchen alcove, drawing him so cheerful after our night of mayhem, when he set down the knife, washed his hands, leaned out the door and kissed me intently, passionately, for a long time, his lips and tongue very strong, with a little scratching of beard, one huge hand wrapped around the nape of my neck and up into my hair. I stood there holding my sketchbook with both hands, kissing him back for all I was worth. When he returned to his cooking, I said, gasping a little, "What was *that?*"

He said, "That was love."

Tying the Knot, Ottoman Princess-Style

BY ANASTASIA M. ASHMAN

I had just fired the young maid for being unable to resist using my makeup and perfume, and now I was doing my own cleaning, much as I had my whole life before my husband and I moved to Turkey two years earlier. *What a sooty, sultry place,* I thought as I wiped down the furniture in our downtown Beyoğlu apartment. *Open the windows on what looks like a fine day, and in comes black dust from the Bosphorus road.* I picked up a silver-framed wedding portrait and studied my upswept hair studded with pearls, my husband's shy smile in his dapper midnight blue suit, the choppy water beyond the marble quay. A fairytale moment in time. We had been married, a few miles from our current home, on an idealized trip to the country, a trip that convinced me my life here could be that of a modern Ottoman princess.

It was official, I was marrying my Turk in August 2001. Somehow my Manhattan manners passed muster during an introductory trip to İstanbul the winter before, as did my physique. Refreshing me in the white and gold boudoir of Aunt Muko's upscale apartment after the long international flight, the smiling, gap-toothed family masseuse had given my hips the childbearing seal of approval. Hers was a modern rendition of the traditional inspection in the *hamam,* the bathhouse that once doubled as meat market for mothers selecting mates for their sons. I misinterpreted her gesticulations, understanding no Turkish.

"She says I have a big rump," I reported to my fiancé, Burç, after what I incorrectly presumed would be a relaxing hour with a professional body-worker, like the many I had known growing up in California. Instead I had endured a flesh-testing session by a family retainer overtly interested in my posterior dimensions. Burç chuckled, saying it would take time to get used to being his bride and the family's gelin, the vaunted position of the daughter-in-law that piques everyone's interest. Though familiar with clan closeness from my own sisters and female cousins, it was a shock to experience the intimate physical observations Turkish women often make to one another. Despite the physical exam, marrying into Turkish culture seemed like the fulfillment of a forgotten wish.

I never consciously imagined tying the knot like an Ottoman princess when I fell in love with İstanbul-born Burç, although since childhood I have been fascinated with ancient civilizations and the capitals of vast empires, which fueled my study of classical and Near Eastern archaeology at Bryn Mawr. It was easy to romanticize the land from which this well-spoken, erudite computer scientist sprung, even before going there. Byzantium. Old Constantinople. İstanbul. Three times a focal point of Mediterranean and world civilization, I knew it was an enchanted city, serving as capital to the Byzantine, Roman, and Ottoman empires. With its hilly, crossroads-of-the-world topography, studded with palaces, fortification ramparts, and soaring minarets, it had a history of inspiring writers. One 19th-century traveling poet mused in *The City of the Sultan* that Shakespeare might have been envisioning an Ottoman garden along the silvery Bosphorus when he wrote the midnight garden scene in *Romeo and Juliet*.

Although my parents named me after a Russian grand duchess, my own upbringing did not support the princess bride fantasy. My Northern California family's style tends toward low-key, nondenominational garden nuptials set to a solo cello amid wildflowers and with quirky, anything-goes dress codes. With that kind of earthy milieu, I wasn't the type of woman who spent much time fantasizing about flashy weddings. I wasn't likely to travel the land, forcing a bridely vision of "tangerine and gold, for two hundred people" onto venues and suppliers, relatives and friends.

A pragmatic thirty-something couple, Burç and I would have been content with a trip to New York City Hall, but we decided to abdicate all responsibility for the wedding. Instead of juggling expectations and managing cultural differences between our families, we figured we'd award it to those whose enthusiasm eclipsed everyone else's: the Turks, a people prone to festivity.

Burç's family missed him in his decade and a half studying and working in Manhattan, making them eager for an effusive display of kinship. Simply being Turkish made his family well suited in social temperament to orchestrate the affair, and they were more celebratory than my distracted family, which has been known to forget a birthday or two. Turks seemed easy to rejoice, judging from my earlier trip to Turkey, when we attended three birthday bashes in the space of a week—parties for near strangers. And Burç's decorative mother, Ayten—whose dining table is littered in porcelain roses tied with satin bows, the salt dispensed by a tiny spoon from a crystal swan with silver wings—was exhilarated at the renewed prospect of throwing a wedding. She'd long given up the idea, with one son a bachelor extraordinaire and the other lost to America. She'd also have a lot of help from her five sisters. We would marry on Turkish soil. My own small family agreed that a summer vacation in the historic capital sounded more enticing than repainting the house for visitors and asking the cellist, my former babysitter, to clear her schedule.

So we handed the wedding reins to Ayten and her resourceful sisters. Muko, the youngest and a public relations veteran, brought her flamboyant expertise in event staging. Like most modern Turks, they began to plan for a civil ceremony, the only type recognized by law, to be followed by a reception. It was usually a ten-minute affair at a government-run wedding salon, but the wedding service the sisters arranged would be held at our reception site, the custom of wealthier Turks.

The family chose the historic setting of Esma Sultan Palace in Ortaköy, a waterside İstanbul village. A colonnaded Ottoman ruin operated by a luxe hotel chain, it was built in the 18th century as the private residence of a daughter of Sultan Abdulhamit I. She was a woman historically noted for her sharp intellect—which I took as a nod to my own cerebral nature, even if it wasn't.

Most details of our wedding adhered to glitzy standards set by the Turkish social elite. With polished Aunt Muko involved, and as Burç's father, Süleyman had had a long European career at NATO, the family—although not technically a prominent one—adopted the glitterati standard. Fancy weddings provide fodder for the country's voracious industry of society magazines and television shows; newspapers are filled with color photos of movers and shakers. The press were invited to our nuptials, and celebrity guests were expected to trail their own paparazzi, assigned to document new love liaisons, the latest fashions, impressive jewels. I took the showy notion in stride, even if it didn't exactly accord with the understated life Burç and I lived. As an occasional extrovert, I do enjoy contained moments in the spotlight.

As the date drew near, my parents started to lose their cultural composure. Besides basic prewedding jitters, a couple of things were to blame: Their research was turning up unfamiliar images of villagers in head scarves, and there was a story in the mainstream U.S. press about İstanbul's black market in kidneys. The muckraking slant of conversations about the region in my parents' Northern California city of cause-conscious Berkeley must have exacerbated the situation. My counterculture father began spouting antimilitary sentiment when he learned that a slew of generals were invited. Then the questions started. "Are Turks Sunnis or Shi'ites?" he quizzed, dismayed I didn't know the majority are Sunni. Burç's family appeared mostly secular; a discussion of the branches of Islam had never come up. Unable to imagine herself in the setting, my mother asked whether she could wear pants in Turkey, whether she'd have to cover her head during the ceremony. What few details I had to offer about the wedding failed to correct my parents' skewed expectations, their responses to me grating. When I mentioned that the dress code would be formal, with Ayten in a full-length gown and her husband a tuxedo, my informal Berkeley mother suspected a prank. "I don't want to be the only one dressed up," was how she put it.

In an afternoon's lark, I vented my frustration with their angst about all things Turkish. I wrote my parents a facetious, never-to-be-mailed letter as if it were penned by my new father-in-law, indulging their worst Orientalist fears. "We are happy our son İsmail the Besot will marry the pulchritudinous Anastasia," the sham Süleyman began, using my husband's Biblical middle name and the epithet of a particularly dissipated sultan who ushered the downfall of the Ottoman Empire. "Her problematic temperament we will cure with age-old Turkish techniques. At the palace, amid sacrificial offerings, dancing girls and great feasting will be held during the new harem girl's circumcision and veiling. Report to the rear gate at dawn to hold the hand of your child for the last time." (I wrote this even though I didn't think sacrifices and mutilation were even remotely Turkish.) Then he invited them to dine on "a roulette of local amoebae" and other Turkish delights. "Soldiers will escort you to the Iranian border, where you will donate your left kidney and navigate your way home. I understand you are well versed in the politics of the region, and no one needs two kidneys anyway," concluded my cruel character, far from the affable blue-eyed Süleyman I knew. The exercise provided me hours of mirth, even if it would do nothing to alleviate my parents' anxiety. At that point, what could I tell them about Turkey—a place I knew only through my husband and his family, my studies, and one trip? Their fears may have been unfounded, but they were real.

Arriving in İstanbul with friends and relatives a few days before the wedding, we lodged with Burç's brother, Bora. Burç served as a translator, since fluent English-speakers among family and vendors were few. We hammered out instructions with the professional disc jockey, selecting tunes to which we'd arrive, dance, and cut the cake. When we met Muko and the stylish wedding coordinator, they pointed to the marble dock behind the palace and suggested I arrive by boat. I imagined the logistical nightmare, brackish Bosphorus staining my dress and frizzing my hair, and then the ungainly hoisting from water to land in front of a crowd. Veto. Burç's father inscribed the names of unmarried men and women on the soles of our wedding shoes, to send the singles our luck in love as each name wore off during the wedding, as per Turkish tradition. In his blocky, careful, accountant's print, Süleyman made a forlorn list of bachelors on Burç's stolid oxfords: his older brother and a decade-older friend, Karaca. A double standard materialized when I contributed the name of a twenty-five-year-old Turkish cousin to fill out the men's list. "What about Cenk?"

Ayten countered, "He's too young," and then instructed Süleyman to add an even younger secretary to my silver platform shoe, a much smaller area that was already overwhelmed with women waiting in the marital wings. After that I asked no further questions.

"I'm an Ottoman princess at the center of a huge marital production, its rituals proscribed by culture and hewed to by a multitude of others!" I said to my sister Monika when she inquired about the proceedings. "I have no clue what is happening!" She laughed, knowing that ignorance was regal bliss to me, a disciplined woman accustomed to shouldering responsibility. I had been a latchkey kid at age twelve, when my mother, a real estate agent, began working full time. I fed and clothed myself and maintained the household with my sisters, and under my parents' scrupulous tutelage, I had been filing my own taxes since the age of fourteen, reporting earnings from housecleaning jobs I performed after school and from secretarial and catering work I did on weekends. Being pampered by Turks who assumed I couldn't or shouldn't do everything by myself was an unexpected and welcome luxury.

"She trusts us," Muko told everyone, pleased that the foreign *gelin* wasn't attempting to micromanage a Turkish affair. I had uncertain moments though. Mother-in-law Ayten mentioned shopping for a veil—a prospect I failed to act excited about, never having worn a veil even when I was a practicing Catholic. The idea was quietly dropped. Another day Ayten asked me to model the wedding gown—a décolletage-boosting costume I had chosen in New York. She and another sister sat close together on the bed in the guest room, expectantly holding hands, as if it were perfectly natural that I should strip naked in their presence. I wrestled into the gown with the help of my sister, embarrassed to appear so undignified in front of my mother-in-law. It was better to imagine the situation as a princess donning royal finery in the presence of admiring attendants.

Attendants were working behind the scenes too. In the days before the wedding, a small army of family retainers—drivers and cooks and administrative assistants—arranged reservations and transportation, prepared and served food, as Burç and I effortlessly hosted private and public gatherings: serenades by Gypsy violinists in bohemian Beyoğlu, rooftop cocktails overlooking the Golden Horn waterway, dinner at classic *kebab* houses.

On the steamy August wedding day, my scraggly, hungover wedding party lined up at an exclusive salon to be groomed to Turkish standard. Eyebrows were plucked and trimmed, nails polished, hair dyed. My sister Monika's curly hair was combed and chignoned to the point of tears, while my friend Andréa's limp perm was bolstered with half a canister of hairspray. My own natural waves were first blown straight and then reconstituted as spirals with a curling iron by an unlikely trio of bronzed young men wearing braided leather chokers and tight t-shirts. I leaned over to Andréa. "Are these diversions for the middle-aged clientele?"

"Gigolos like that Warren Beatty film *Shampoo!*" she quickly answered as the short-cropped owner brushed her out of the way. He began to work me over, palms up and barking for bobby pins and hairspray like a surgeon for scalpel and sponge. As he twirled me around in the chair for the 360-degree view, I gasped at the drama: My hair was a majestic cascade of black tendrils, caught by pins of imitation pearls and diamonds. *Why didn't I always wear my hair this way?* I thought, impressed by the extraordinary transformation. My long neck was now distinctly swanlike.

Next was the makeup artist. The idea of a stranger glamourizing my face for an important life event disconcerted me. Growing up I had little exposure to makeup and nail polish, girlish things my parents discouraged as a waste of time. Even though I subjected myself to a few experiments at cosmetics counters, they invariably left me looking unlike myself and needed to be rubbed off. Having noted the Turkish penchant for piling it on, I requested a natural maquillage from the salon's bespectacled, sensible-looking artist, who nodded and agreed. "*Tabi, tabi*" (of course, of course), she said, whipping out brushes and pots of paint and powder.

I closed my eyes and, playing with fire, added, "My gown is silver." When she swiveled me toward the mirror minutes later, I was a 1960s film star Cleopatra: thick kohl-lined eyes, silver glitter on the lids, lips gooey with metallic gloss, eyelashes five coats thick. My parents would have a heart attack when they saw this cosmetic conversion. I looked like a drag queen. The shock must have shown on my face.

"For the photos," assured press-savvy Aunt Muko, appearing in the mirror behind my chair, her caramel-blond hair blown straight up. "The flash. Otherwise you have no face." Mother-in-law Ayten joined us to take a look, her hair still in curlers, patches of pink rouge high up on her cheeks.

"Don't eat anything," she suggested—I might mess up the silver lipstick. Fueled by adrenaline, I wasn't hungry anyway.

Meanwhile Burç was being shaved, getting a haircut, and having his eyebrows trimmed and his ear fuzz burned off across town at a men's salon with his father and brother. Barbering is just as much a part of Turkish men's lives as hairdressing and beauty treatments are to Turkish women; a weekly visit for at least a shave or trim is average.

Monika confirmed that our artsy architect father cut his own hair for the event, like he always does, with a hand mirror and a pair of straight scissors. "Mom's having her nails done at a salon near the hotel to match her dress," she reported. My mother was never a woman to wear polish, and her small grooming gesture was all the more shocking with her choice of blood-red lacquer.

Disruptive breezes grew, and there was a threat of rain, but Ayten proclaimed, "God is on my side." After twenty years in Europe, apparently she took a religious turn to match her İstanbul friends, embracing a kind of fair-weather faith. Or in this case, a bad-weather faith. No one dared to contradict the matriarch's belief that Allah would provide, so no alternate plans were laid at the palace as florists wrestled with arrangements made unruly by the whipping wind, and attendants optimistically scattered oversized lounging pillows on the wooden deck along the waterfront. I too chose to believe in Ayten. I had already placed myself and this wedding in her hands.

Or rather, in one of her hands, since she had broken an arm that month after tripping on a stone staircase. Now she fretted about how to hide the flesh-colored cast behind her back for photos as we corralled the combined family for a series of shots around the palace grounds, to be taken by a trio of photographers and a videographer. Raindrops were beginning to fall. "Your Ulla Maija gown may be called 'the Whirlwind' because of its draped charmeuse," laughed

Monika as she watched, "but there's a bit of tornado about it now!" She mimed all the swirling tendrils of hair and billowing silk.

Burç was handsome in his Cacharel suit, and my mother, in her satin outfit and black suede sandals studded with rhinestones, never looked better. Muko and Ayten wore custom-made lace dresses by an İstanbul designer. Dapper, white-haired Süleyman was in black tie, minus the tie. It was a mystery how he misplaced it during a five-minute car ride from Bora's house. A familiar sense of resignation washed over me when my nonconformist father showed up sporting a mismatched blue and gray suit with a purple shirt. This could not be the outfit he purchased for the occasion, a salesperson would have surely pointed out its impropriety. Regardless of what happened—to his suit and to my dress-code request—in the eight thousand miles between İstanbul and Berkeley, the rainbow-colored tie seemed purposeful, a hint of my unconventional origins. With that tie my father was saying, *My daughter may be marrying into this family, but I do not belong here.* However, no one seemed concerned, so I may have been the only one to take his garb personally. In fact, the two patriarchs might even have commiserated about apparel lost in transit!

Then, as if Ayten's wish had been granted, the wind stilled, the sky brightened, and guests began to arrive. Burç and I stole away to our dressing room for a stiff drink to quell a sudden onset of stage fright. The videographer documented what we could not see. A parental receiving line formed in the flagstone courtyard, with Ayten and Süleyman introducing besilked and sequined Turks to my culture-shocked parents, who had never approached a receiving line let alone performed in one. Muko presented her distinguished and bejeweled invitees—captains of industry and tawny divas of İstanbul's social stage, all looking like cosmetically enhanced sisters. Burç's brother welcomed his raucous contingent, who were bearing gag gifts in expensive packaging. Most scandalous were the his-and-hers vibrators from naughty Karaca, who handed them over, saying "Use these in good health!" He counted on the Turkish tradition of gifts being opened immediately—and in this case, by older female family members. Roaming photographers captured guests sipping sunset cocktails among the relic-strewn grounds, the royal residence illuminated, vessels large and small churning the strait beyond.

Meanwhile, I was leading a princess's rarified existence in my tower, guarding my five-hour-old makeup, daintily sipping a gin and tonic through a straw and lobbing bits of stale bread past my gooey lips. Burç and I were both ready for the whole thing to be over.

At nightfall we made our spotlit appearance to the reedy 6/8 strains of our favorite Dead Can Dance tune, invoking both medieval tarantella and Middle Eastern processional, its whirling triplets soaring in the summer night. Gripping my hand at a gentlemanly shoulder level, Burç was nervous as he guided me through the crowd. But I bloomed. Smiling toothily like a star, I was suddenly in my element, if not my own culture. I was meant for this! Well-wishers threw coins in the air, and I laughed when a few disappeared down my cleavage. As if recalling a buried dream, I was loving being a princess bride. Blinded by lights from the society television show *Alem*, we mounted a dais adorned with diaphanous white and silver ribbons and were soon joined by the government officiant, in a maroon satin robe, and our two witnesses, Muko and a four-star general—a former chairman of the Turkish Army joint chiefs and a family friend.

A mercifully short civil ceremony ensued in Turkish. I said *"Evet,"* into the microphone, and the crowd of 160 roared—perhaps at my pronunciation of the Turkish for "yes," or the fact that I had no idea what I'd just agreed to. We all signed the officiant's logbook. Kissing to applause, when we spontaneously kissed a second time, it was to laughter. From the general, I accepted our official marriage booklet, the *aile cüzdanı* (family portfolio), which logs future children and serves as a legal record. Then kisses, and more kisses. Everyone had to be kissed the double-cheek kiss of Turks. Flashbulbs exploded in the starry night.

After posing with the family for magazines and newspapers, we commenced dinner al fresco. Impeccably uniformed waiters in collarless black jackets over white shirts attended tables festooned with sprays of eucalyptus and white roses, anchored by flickering hurricane lanterns. Burç and I began to make the rounds, greeting guests and receiving traditional gifts of jewelry and gold coins, or *altın*, pressed into a puffy little satin bag made for this purpose and now hanging from my forearm. We would visit a few tables, return to our own for a glimpse of food, then visit a couple more tables. Queen for the day, a radiant Ayten led the way, whispering names and associations so Burç had half a chance to make appropriate conversation. I did not need to comprehend who anyone was in order to graciously beam, chat, and kiss with regal self-assurance. We greeted a brawny, soft-spoken general's son, whom my new husband had declared in babyhood he would marry one day. I consoled him like an old chum: "No hard feelings, I hope."

Midway through the evening, after the lemon sorbet, the wedding coordinator prompted us to open the dance floor before more people drifted out experimentally like the two-star general and the precocious secretary whose name Ayten had wanted on my shoe. A languid samba cleverly disguised my immobility due to the floor-scraping hem, and Burç was a prince among men, managing to avoid it with every turn. Soon guests young and old negotiated the marble as a gentle breeze set the hanging lamps into motion. Even my mother danced, shyly and for the first night in forty years, with a handsome Turk in a white suit. She and my father then sat whispering at their central table, on their best behavior, swiveling their heads, nervously licking their lips when the videographer shone his light in their direction. I knew they'd eke plenty of mileage from the uncomfortable experience back in Berkeley, whether amusing friends with its excess and exoticism or bolstering their worldly images by association.

It was midnight. The lights dimmed, and a five-layer cake was wheeled out, towering four feet high—the kind of monstrous confection out of which an entertainer usually bursts. The discreet master of ceremonies—a short, middle-aged man in a dark suit who had faded in and out of our consciousness all night, expertly notifying us of our responsibilities seconds before they were to be enacted—handed us a curved scimitar. Laughing at the drama of the huge instrument, together we grasped the handle and attempted to make the first cut. But this mountain trimmed in white roses was just a ceremonial decoy, and the knife glanced off the impenetrable layers. Burç and I were the last to know, oblivious royals. A small section of edible pastry was embedded in the decoy, plated for us by waiters.

We led a wordless champagne toast. There were no speeches—if there were, no one was listening. Instead, the DJ turned up the volume on an infectious Algerian beat, which drew a rambunctious crowd. Soon Turkish men in sweaty summer suits were belly dancing, and my father-in-law, Süleyman, was the instigator. The women—Frenchwomen and Tunisians, Americans and Turks—clasped hands and, raising them, moved in a circle around us, celebrating a well-married couple. Muko popped silver-coated, chocolate-covered almonds into our mouths as she twirled by, calling out a Turkish good luck proverb, *"En kötü günleriniz böyle olsun!"* May your worst days be like this one.

The shimmering Ottoman dream didn't disperse by light of day. No one wanted the party to end, so we took a group honeymoon. An entourage of ten friends accompanied us to a private Aegean resort near Bodrum for a week of dancing, boating, and dining under the stars. Describing a "night of romance and beautiful women," gushing wedding announcements appeared in newspapers and glossy society magazines, the Turkish social equivalents of *Town & Country* magazine and the *New York Times*. Aunt Muko sent us back to America with souvenirs of a modern Ottoman wedding. Burç and I had given the wedding away, but the Turks gave it back to us in the form of an extravagant fantasy. It took weeks for the stardust to settle.

Finished with the dusting, a soft ache had begun in my lower back. Straightening, I looked out the windows to the Bosphorus. It was the green-blue of a late-spring day. In two years' time I'd distinguished the different tones of the strait—the silver of overcast mornings, the deep navy of a summer noontime, the dazzling obsidian with a trail of moonglow on nights of the full moon. Shakespearean nights. *Like the night we married.*

Marrying like a princess in Turkey before I knew the place, I surmised that the unfamiliarity—with my new family, the wedding plans, the culture—made the magic possible. It was a spectacular image drawn on a blank slate. But living in Turkey has only heightened my enchantment. İstanbul's storied panorama, viewed from my living room, is an everyday miracle, a series of 19th-century Ottoman mosques built by imperial architects from the Armenian Balyan family, palaces, a lighthouse, and hillsides covered in pink-flowering Judas trees. Muko and Ayten still blow their hair straight up before a big event, though I rarely do, and they delight when I wear the girlish, trendy clothes they give me as gifts, or the sparkly eye shadow I am now attracted to. I'm still indulged as if in preparation for my special day, pampered and chauffeured when they have any say in the matter, because that is how the family wants me treated. Sometimes the coddling is a refreshing change from my natural tendency to do everything myself; being my parents' daughter, at other times, the attention is decidedly unnecessary. Burç's family accepts my idiosyncratic assimilation, just as they originally welcomed me into their midst, an imaginary highness with an earthy past. My own parents haven't yet been back to Turkey. Although, as they recall the spotlit adrenaline of the reception line, they must understand why the self-reliant girl they named after the daughter of a Russian czar is drawn to the pomp and possibilities of the place.

FIVE

Darbuka *Drumbeat*

An innate part of the Turkish psyche, folkloric
song and dance can erupt at any moment and
overwhelm even the most intrepid expatriate.

Dancing My Way Home

BY DIANE CALDWELL

*I*t was completely unsought, unexpected. Turkey had been a compromise destination negotiated between me and my traveling companion in 1998. Frida had wanted to go to Israel. The Greek Islands had been my choice. But suddenly Turkey was all the rage of travelers of distinction in Seattle, and after viewing a friend's slides of the country, we booked our flight. There were no long-standing fantasies. No daydreams of living in İstanbul. No whispers in the night urging me to come to Turkey.

But as soon as I hit the streets of İstanbul, a strange power and sense of belonging filled me. The city's rhythm beat a perfect accompaniment to my inner syncopation. Turks sang in the streets or around tables at outdoor cafés. Music filled the air, and people erupted into spontaneous dance. As an American woman who had spent a lifetime struggling to bottle my spirit, I immediately adored these people who so passionately let theirs bubble out. Ice cream sellers beat exotic rhythms with metal scoops; schoolgirls sang and danced to folk songs in the park; *kebab* sellers crooned Turkish standards; and men everywhere, arm in arm, danced, leaped, and belted out football chants. It seemed to me that Turks let their emotional energy soar in song and dance. I knew what it meant to be able to let go like that. I had once felt the same way.

It was 1955 in Philadelphia, Pennsylvania, and I was in first grade. Miss Lissy's black-cardigan back was to us, bent over the record player. The glasses that usually hung on the chain around her mottled neck now perched on her birdlike nose. With exacting precision, she placed the needle on the outside groove of the black vinyl disc, awaiting the first notes of Prokofiev's *Peter and the Wolf.* Music filled the classroom and I entered another dimension—the place I went whenever I heard music. My hands unfolded, my feet untwisted from their good-girl ankle lock, and before I knew what was happening I had

151

left my desk and was twirling ecstatically around the classroom, impervious to everything but the music. The scrape of the needle across vinyl abruptly brought me back.

"Just *what* do you think you're doing, young lady!?" said Miss Lissy, white spittle foaming in the corners of her mouth. *Tee-hee*s escaped from the pursed lips of my classmates.

"Sit down and don't you *ever, ever* do a thing like that again!" Miss Lissy hissed at me.

Frozen, I tried to understand what was happening. Music played and I had danced. Nothing could be more right in the universe.

My entire young existence, every gesture and action, was devoted to my mother's daily dictum, "Be a good girl, Diane." But that day in Miss Lissy's classroom, a horrible truth emerged: It was bad to dance. I loved dancing more than anything in the world. Did that make me bad?

Decades passed. My mother died. I moved away to Seattle, Washington, and Miss Lissy's memory faded to a frayed photo. What remained was the knot in my stomach, the clench that gripped my solar plexus the instant music played and my body and mind became two antagonists sparring for ownership of my actions. Decades of struggle were spent trying to repress my most powerful primal urge, my compulsion to dance: The instantaneous bobbing of my head, tapping of my feet, drumming of my hands, and shaking of my shoulders that preceded my body's flight into full motion. Like trying to quell a volcanic eruption, it took all my energy to suppress the innate force that exploded at the call of music. Many times I lost the battle, abandoning myself to music's proddings while trying my best to ignore the disapproving sneers, critical stares, and arched eyebrows of the surrounding people.

Fifty-five years in the United States, and always the sense of living in the wrong place at the wrong time with the wrong people. Then, during a three-week trip to Turkey, for the first time in my life I found home. A place amid İstanbul's cafés, cobbled streets, and glorious chaos. Returning to Seattle, a numbing fog of depression engulfed me. I had been living in the Pacific Northwest for seventeen years, but now I began fantasizing about returning to Turkey. As often happens with fantasies, weeks turned to months and then years. I found myself trying to be a responsible adult, continuing to maintain my psychotherapy practice, tending my garden, being a devoted partner to my beloved Roger. But the taste of dissatisfaction began to coat my tongue—the foul flavor of living the wrong life, the bitter reflux that came from a lifetime of swallowing back self.

Deliverance comes in the most unsought circumstances. Waltzing with an old friend at my usual Monday night dance venue in Seattle—where I attempted to channel my natural inclinations for wild self-expressive dance into socially appropriate partner dance—he said, "This Sarah McLachlan song always reminds me of Uzbekistan." The song was from one of the three CDs he had brought with him the year he spent teaching English in that Central Asian republic. A pregnant seed fell on tilled, fertile soil. All night I lay awake thinking the same thought over and over. *I would teach English in İstanbul!*

Immediately the inquisition began, a flood of questions from friends: "But why do you have to go to Turkey to teach English? Can't you teach refugees in Seattle?"

"Is it wise to leave the country at this time?"

"But Turkey is a Muslim country. Will you be safe?"

"What about your retirement fund?"

My own racing mind scrambled to compute the risks. At fifty-five I had health complications, financial difficulties, safety concerns, an established psychotherapy practice, a family of friends, and a fourteen-year love relationship. Could I give all that up? Could I adapt to a new country? Could I learn to speak Turkish? Could I live on a low salary? Would Turkey give me what I so sorely wanted? Or would I cry myself to sleep every night filled with loneliness and alienation? As a foreigner in a Muslim country, would I be able to dance? I mean *really* dance?

Desire overcame doubts. I walked out of my old life and into my new one. Through friends of friends, I procured a room in a flat shared with a passionate, music-loving Turkish woman whose daughter and niece lived on the next floor. Perched above three cafés in the bohemian quarter of European

İstanbul, I now had a home on Jurnal Sokak, or Diary Street, in Asmalımescit, a neighborhood named after a vine-covered mosque. Four minutes walk away seethed İstiklal Caddesi, or Independence Avenue, a pedestrian walkway like a raging river of humanity cascading through the historic area formally known as Pera. Once the 17th-century home of a multiethnic, non-Muslim population of Levantines, Greeks, Belarusians, and other Europeans, it is still lined with the ornate stone buildings of European consulates. Along with bars, boutiques, and bakeries İstiklal is home to several grand cathedrals, whose clanging bells compete with the mosques' haunting call to prayer.

My two suitcases were unpacked, and I had already obtained an English-teaching job that was just a five-minute walk away from my apartment, so I made my first attempts at surfing the sea of Turkish mayhem that lay just out-side my door—the carnival of *kebab* shops, newsstands, banks, mobile-phone dealerships, bookstores, coffeehouses, turn-of-the-century buildings, and modern office suites. Every block resounded with amplified song tracks boom-ing from music stores: ululations of Turkish divas, quivering quarter notes of male baritones, primal thumping of *darbuka* drums, and piercing wails of the Turkish clarinet. Above it all was the call of parading iron collectors pushing their wooden carts over the uneven cobblestones, bellowing, "*Demir!*" (Iron).

Closed to vehicle traffic except for the historic trolley car, the avenue was a flood of wondrous and mysterious humanity forever swirling along a grand boulevard: Turkish men in their dark suits and heavy mustaches; students in jeans; head-scarved women; fashion victims in pointy-toed, stiletto-heeled shoes; dolled-up transvestites; one-legged men on crutches selling tissues; beret-donning uniformed policemen with bored expressions and automatic weapons; Turkish vendors selling sesame bread rings; lottery-ticket hawkers; street sweep-ers; and bakery delivery men balancing large, pastry-laden trays on their heads, darting through this sea of pedestrians like silver fish.

Overwhelmed every time I returned to my flat, I daily had to force myself to dive back in. Taking deep breaths, talking myself through each step, I repeat-edly swam into this schizophrenic part-European, part-Asian, ex-Ottoman city. Painstakingly, I installed myself as a neighborhood regular, shyly attempting a

"Merhaba!" (Hello!) or *"İyi akşamlar!"* (Good evening!), pointing to recognizable cooked foods in buffets, purchasing small items and allowing shopkeepers to select change from my outstretched palm.

The first Wednesday night in my new home, my Turkish roommate, Kebire, announced, "We're going to Badehane. Very good musicians. You want to come?" Badehane turned out to be a dimly lit, smoke-filled bar three minutes from our apartment with persimmon-colored walls, whirring ceiling fans, and windows steamy with body heat. Just inside its doorway, four Roma—Turkish Gypsy musicians from Thrace—sat around a black table covered with full ashtrays, plates of appetizers, and glasses of *rakı*, the national alcoholic drink made from anise.

From where he was sitting, the clarinetist raised his horn and produced a wail that sent its tendrils into my viscera. Another player picked notes on a *kanun*, a complex lap harp with seventy-five strings. One dark paunchy musician strummed a large, lutelike string instrument called an *ud*, and the drummer's fingers snapped against the goat skin of his ceramic, hourglass *darbuka* in a frenzied exotic beat. Following Kebire to a table of her friends in the back, I sat down. Holding my breath, my stomach muscles clenched and my jaw locked. Around me buzzed the chatter of a strange language, and everywhere people sang to each other along with the music, their hands outstretched and waving in the air. The vocals ended and clapping began to a rhythm I had never before heard. I tried to grasp the beat of the music, the rhythm of the clapping, but to my 4/8-count Western brain, this 9/8 Gypsy music seemed to have no beginning or end to its measures. The song changed to a quicker beat and suddenly everyone was on their feet dancing with each other. Everywhere I saw shoulders shaking, hips swaying, arms waving.

But how did one dance to this impossible beat? My body ached to dance, but nowhere in the music could I find an entry point. I watched, studied my friends' movements, trying to grasp intellectually the pattern of their motions, but the strain of controlling my body was too much. Finally letting go, I allowed the music to pull me from my seat. Joining others, I imitated the women, shaking my shoulders and undulating my hips, allowing myself to be transported by the music. The expected rebuke didn't come. Instead, the henna-haired woman dancing opposite me grinned with smiling eyes. *"Canım!"* (Darling!), she cried. "You are a Turk!" And with that, she pulled me to her large bosom, squeezing me and kissing me on each cheek.

Hours flew by. Kebire's eyes glowed brightly as she watched me, a smile of delighted amazement lighting up her face. The large-bosomed dancer was forever pulling me over to dance with her as her friends joined in the shimmying frenzy, and when the crowd applauded the musicians, I was included in the applause.

First light of morning, I replayed the incidents of the night before. No sneers. No admonishments. No disapproving glares from any Turkish Miss Lissys. I had been embraced and rewarded for following the music and letting my body respond. It had been my first taste of freedom and evidence that there was a place in the world I could feel I truly belonged.

But it was one wonderful, isolated incident. My good-girl instinct crept back and knotted in my stomach to warn me. I couldn't expect that all the time.

Many times, returning home after teaching my evening English class, I would sneak a longing look at the little café directly opposite my house. It was tiny, cozy, its windows fogged and sweaty, and I yearned to join its huddled patrons, who sat in intimate conversation. Yet nightly I would see they were mostly men and would decide it was best to just unlock the massive green iron doors to my apartment building and climb the three flights of stone steps to my flat. Then after one particularly hectic night, I surprised myself by making an abrupt 180-degree turn and instead pushing open the wooden door to Derya's café. Filled with an odd array of mismatched tables and chairs, the place was occupied by four men sipping tea from delicate, tulip-shaped glasses. A song from the soundtrack of the film *Frida* played. As I entered, the men all looked up at me. *This is a huge mistake,* I thought. *Maybe this is a place just for men.*

"Oh, hello," said one midthirties man in near-perfect English, his brittle black hair wrapped in a black bandanna, splotches of paint dappling his jeans and shirt. "I have seen you walking in this street. You are American, yes?"

I nodded, and he invited me to sit and have tea. He told me about himself and his life as a painter in İstanbul. The same song played over and over. He motioned to a tall young man with long black hair hanging halfway down his thin back, sitting at the next table. "He looks like Jesus, no?"

Jesus was sipping tea and talking to another young, long-haired man. The fourth man in the café sat by himself reading a Turkish newspaper. Then a fifth young man, slight as a blackbird, descended the five steps from the cubbyhole of a kitchen and bummed a cigarette from the fourth one reading the paper. After the same song had played a dozen times, my newly acquired artist friend trotted up the stairs, saying, "Wait, I will put on other music." Suddenly the most popular song blasted by the music stores on İstiklal Caddesi filled the room. *İlk Aşk* (First Love) played, from an album by the Turkish folk-fusion group Ezgi'nin Günlüğü (Ezgi's Diary), the plaintive vocal of its female lead singer pleading: *"Gitme. Gitme."* (Don't go. Don't go.)

My body activated. But this wasn't a place where people danced, it was a café where men sipped tea. *Control yourself,* my inner voice warned. *This is a Muslim country. You are the only woman in here. It would be inappropriate. There's no room for dancing, anyway. Don't do anything stupid!* But my incorrigible feet began bouncing, my miscreant shoulders began swaying, and then I was on my feet, dancing in the tight space between the tables and chairs. The song ended, and I sat down, eyes averted from everyone, arduously studying the grain of the wooden table.

My face flushed, sweat suddenly dripped down my sides, and my mind raced. Oh my God, what had I done? And in my own neighborhood too, where word would get around. Out of the corner of my eye, I saw the young man who looked like Jesus walking toward me with the stooped gait of the very tall. I could feel him looming over me, and reluctantly, I raised my eyes, anticipating a stern rebuke for my outlandish behavior. His dark-brown eyes were looking down at me, warm and smiling. "Excuse me, my English is not so good. I am a grunge-rock musician. I see you are dancing very good. Please, you will dance in my rock video?"

I was thunderstruck. My dancing wasn't inappropriate to them. It wasn't misconstrued. They didn't find my wild abandon abhorrent. Instead I was being applauded for it! I was asked for more!

One year in İstanbul, and acceptance everywhere. Letting go of my inhibitions, I experienced repeated rewards. Able to embrace my vivacious spirit and delight in the exuberance around me, living inside the music, I finally found my home. Nothing made that clearer to me than the Friday night of the annual Tünel Spring Arts Festival. That night the narrow paving-stone streets and alleys of Asmalımescit overflowed with Turks and visiting Frenchmen, Italians, and Bulgarians: musicians, artists, dancers, and even circus performers assembled together for this one-week arts festival. This historic corner of İstanbul crackled with electric energy—a mad swirl of art and chaos. On one corner, musicians created magic; on another, locals fist-fought over free festival t-shirts. Şehbender Sokağı, or Foreign Consul Street—a narrow gray lane lined with cafés, restaurants, and music venues—swelled with explosive energy. In one of its brick-walled haunts, a Bulgarian drummer/singer created mad delirious music with other Bulgarians and French Turks—shouting "Dance, dance, dance, dance!" his head swinging side to side, long black hair flying across his sweat-drenched face as two accordions filled the background. A Frenchman on sax, another on the oboe-like *zurna*, the small subterranean café teeming with electricity.

Then, breaking through the melodious din of music came an otherworldly wail. Stepping out of another time, another century, on softly padded feet of sheepskin moccasins entered two musicians costumed in traditional Bulgarian dress: With soft tan leather wrapped around their muscular calves and sheepskin caps upon their heads, they were adorned in rough-woven cotton tunics bound by studded cummerbunds and embroidered sheepskin vests. Cradling grotesque, kidney-shaped animal bladders, they blew into sculpted black pipes, filling the bladders with air and birthing a wail like a child wrenched from its mother, a woman erupting in the cries of sexual passion, God calling us to her paradise embrace. The crowd jumped and writhed, joined hands and danced. My shoulders began to flutter like excited butterflies, my hips swirled in figure-eight patterns, my arms traced graceful pictures in the air, and my hands circled like slow-motion blossoming flowers. The musicians paraded up the steps and out onto the street, frenzied pied pipers with dancers filing after them, sweet mayhem chaos music dance erupting in the narrow cobblestone street. I became a vortex of energy, a contagious smile of ecstasy spreading across my face. People gathered around me—girls and boys, men and women— wanting to dance with me, shimmying their shoulders opposite me, bumping hips together, dancing the Gypsy five-step. They hugged and kissed me, laughed and said I was more Turk than they were. The waiter carrying brimming trays of beer said to me as he passed, "You are one of us!"

It was a fairytale night. Candles set on the outdoor tables flickered wildly as if to the beat of the music. Seagulls circled overhead, underlit by the lights of İstanbul like flying phantoms. The music crescendoed. Young, old, men, women, Turks, foreigners—all danced together exuberantly. It didn't matter who I was or what kind of life I'd left behind. Here and now, on this tiny backstreet of İstanbul, I was living my true self. I recalled the words of Mary Oliver, a British poet I love dearly. Her words I once read with yearning now became my own: "I was a bride married to amazement."

From the Hip

BY SALLY GREEN

*W*hen I think of dance, I think of Turkey, where my arms sway wider, my hips lose their starch, and my fingers tell an alluring story that ebbs and flows like water. I return to a culture where music plays constantly, where the slightest provocation can move the spirit to dance, and anyone nearby will beam approvingly and clap along.

But here in Colorado, under fluorescent lights, before a wall of mirrors, ten other women and I form two lines to twitch our hips in dead earnest, our eyes glued to our reflections. It's 1988, I'm at my belly dance class in the city recreation center, a year since I've moved back from Turkey. I've been to Turkey three times, this last stint spanning three years. The blinds are tightly drawn against the men playing basketball across the hall, a stark contrast from the vibrant, inclusive atmosphere on the dance floors at restaurants and clubs in İstanbul.

We students range in age from eighteen to sixty, most of us in our thirties. Our attention is trained on the mirror, on these moves made tame and instructable, in named, numbered steps and counted-off turns: hip up, hip up; hip drop, drop, drop; camel to the right and camel to the left; grapevine, and shimmy. Our slim, blond instructor—who has no belly—expertly models the moves, identical as clockwork, time after time, robotic. The goal seems to be to duplicate her exactly, but my left arm has a mind of its own. I used to think I was good at this. But here, in this bright white square room, I feel nothing, which doesn't help. I can't lose myself in the sound of the *darbuka* drum, which now comes loud but distorted through the portable stereo on the floor at the front of the room rather than full-bodied and resonant from a bright-eyed, impish drummer tapping out complex 9/8 rhythms on the traditional Turkish belly dance instrument he cradles under one arm. Here no one talks or even smiles; we all seem obsessed with how we look as we struggle to acquire these moves.

I've never belly danced while staring at myself. My reflection in the mirror mocks me—warping, grotesque—as I fight for concentration, chanting the steps. Today I learn there are exactly four distinct ways to figure-eight these hips, memorizing them as if it were mathematics. As I stiffly follow directions and run through each variation, the exuberant Turkish dance floors of my memory shrink ever further away.

During my various stays in Turkey, I prided myself on my acquisition of authentic belly dance style, with its smooth, liquid steps. Bedia, an aunt of Turkish friends, taught me the basics in their İstanbul living room. Laughing, she would agree to give a lesson, stand up, smooth her dress, and then stoop to take one last drag from her cigarette and sip of her tea. Her style came from classical belly dance, called *oryantal,* which includes intricate arm work and tight hip turns. She taught me how to shimmy—not by shaking my breasts, but by controlling the muscles in my back so that my chest moved with subtlety and power. Bedia danced patiently as I followed her lead with tentative moves of my own.

"*Evet, evet*" (yes, yes), she would punctuate our dance, encouraging my fledgling moves. She offered none of the corrections the rec center instructor regularly doles out. As my years in Turkey went on, I spent many memorable evenings in discos and dance clubs, at engagement parties and weddings, learning the fluidity and joy of Turkish dance. Blending in on the dance floor, joining circles of friends that ebbed and flowed into the men and women dancing around them, I learned by observation and response. Everyone I danced with seemed to know the basic moves, though none would refer to them by the names my American instructor did: the body wave, the grapevine, the chest drop. The uncontrollable desire to move drove the dance, rather than some prescribed sequence of steps.

Part of the problem with this class at the rec center is that it is focused on one style, which most Westerners assume all belly dance to be: *rakkass,* the flamboyant dance done in some kind of beaded, glittery bikini top and low-riding, transparent skirt, with seductive hip work and salacious shimmies like the kind performed at tourist cabaret shows in Turkey. As the women stiffly try to mimic the instructor's exaggerated technique, I yearn to tell them about the many styles of serious belly dance from Turkey, Arab countries, and variations originating from the Gypsies.

In my everyday life in Turkey, I saw belly dance moves used in most people's casual dancing, making belly dancing a part of life. At home, in the car when a good song came on the radio, at parties, in nightclubs and discos, on the beach under the moon when someone had a drum (or even if no one did), Turks—with their small children, their teenagers, their parents, friends, or anyone who wanted to join in—would circle their hips, ripple their arms, loosen their ribs, and swirl their wrists. No sequined costume required!

But here, under the stark institutional light, like our instructor, we wear big, poofy harem pants sewn from a pattern she provided, with sequined hip scarves. The thick, stacked bangles some students wear make my few gold ones—a wedding gift from my in-laws—look like toys. *Are the other women here to conjure some past life at the Topkapı Palace, with a storybook sultan and fifty drumming eunuchs? Or just to burn fifty calories in diversion?*

At the first class, we take turns introducing ourselves and explaining our interest in belly dance. Our instructor was a dance major and also teaches jazz and hula, from which her interest in belly dance grew. No one else in the room has traveled to Turkey, the Middle East, or any place where belly dancing is common, though our instructor says she would like to. Most of the students state that they are simply curious. One has a weak lower back that she hopes to strengthen. A couple of them say they want to perform for their boyfriends.

My turn comes, and I take a deep breath.

"My husband is Turkish, and we lived in Turkey for a few years. I really enjoy belly dancing, and I would like to improve. At our İstanbul wedding, we belly danced all night." I smile at the memories: my sister dancing on the table with my husband's cousin; the *lira* notes waved in the air by my new relatives, beckoning me to do a backbend shimmy and straighten up with the money stuck to my forehead, amid much cheering for this flexible and sporting *gelin*, the family's new bride.

"You belly danced at your wedding?" someone asks, dubious.

"Well, of course," I answer, smiling at her encouragingly. "My mother even designed my dress for the purpose of dancing. I wasn't about to just sit there and watch!" I chuckle, picturing the hundred or two guests crowding the dance floor, a sea of arms waving, hands beckoning, people laughing and hugging each other between songs, spectators clapping along, lifting glasses in endless toasting—such broad, unabashed sharing in our happiness.

"What did your husband think of that?" asks a woman who plans to dance for her boyfriend.

"Well, he danced too," I answer, getting impatient. "It's just the way people dance over there, you know, women and men. It's not some cabaret act." The instructor nods impassively, then frowns a little as I pluck at this exaggerated outfit I feel so silly in, bought from her collection of extras so that I would fit in with the class. It's a far cry from the comfortable wedding gown I purposely chose (I wasn't about to be corseted at the best party of my life).

"Everybody likes to dance, especially with the bride," I say, trying to draw a connection between the bacchanalian image they seem to have and something more familiar to them.

"Belly dance with the bride?" one of my older classmates repeats, with a look of distaste on her face.

"I don't think you're picturing what it's really like. Sometimes it's sexy, and other times it isn't," I hear myself begin to talk faster. "Everyone does it—grandmothers, little kids, uncles, friends. You know, it's just *dancing*," I finish, sounding defensive, as some of the women have started fiddling with their hip scarves, while others gaze at me in disbelief. I don't know how they reconcile their vision of Turkey and its neighboring countries (tuneless, drab, and repressive) with their image of belly dance—colorful gyrations performed to wild music by scantily clad women for consumption by the dirty-minded. Perhaps they see the two images as flip sides of the same nasty yet intriguing coin—like my university colleague who, during a large faculty meeting, errone-ously referred to my Turkish belly dancing background as "striptease"!

The instructor mercifully directs us back to the lesson. Staring at the mir-ror, undulating dutifully, my negative inner monologue almost drowns out the bad tape of the drum. *What am I doing here? Why can't there be even one Turkish restaurant in Colorado? How can this be the only place outside of my own living room where I can practice this dance? Couldn't there be a single person in this class who has had some real experience with belly dance culture?*

Stop it, I finally command myself. *What they think doesn't matter. You are here to learn, to improve at what you love.* I close my eyes and try to feel the moves, not just obsess over my jerkiness in the mirror. *Don't judge these women on the basis of their naiveté,* I remind myself. *You may be surprised.* Perhaps they really are here seeking insight through movement, whether they are brave enough to say it or not. Maybe they crave the leap between cultures, West to East, toward union with the unknown. Well, if so . . .

I grin to myself. What we really need to access the truth of Turkish dance is three fingers of *rakı,* the traditional anise-flavored Turkish liqueur; a comfortable dress that swishes around our knees; and the ambience of cigarette smoke, warm perfume, and much softer lighting in a waterfront İstanbul *meyhane* (tavern). Ditch these wall-length mirrors and the ballet bar, replace them with an overwrought chandelier, and bring on a musical ensemble with a really talented drummer. We need obsequious waiters who weave their way past dancing arms to serve us fish, feta-like cheese, roasted eggplant casserole, and a trayload of spicy dishes. We also need friendly strangers at the next table drinking to our health, shouting *"Şerefe!"* with raised glasses, buying roses for each other from persistent street sellers.

When the rapid strains of a song from the Black Sea region begins, a circle of men will form. With their arms intertwined above their heads, they snap their fingers and scissor their steps, shouting out the lyrics. The next song, pure pop with a surging drumbeat, fills the dance floor with revelers while a woman at another table kicks off her shoes, climbs on her chair, and pulls her boyfriend up to the tabletop. As they dance on the table, they're cheered on by her seated parents, who clap along in approval. Lines form for *halay,* a hora-like dance, with friendly strangers grasping each other's raised hands, dancing as they wind through the long lines of tables, out onto the sidewalk, and back in again. Two women do the *mastika,* a popular Gypsy dance. They kneel, facing each other, rippling forward and back, inches apart, as the circle around them claps.

And there is the Bosphorus Strait across the street, its fast waters alluring in the moonlight. Tied to a nearby dock are sleek yachts from sunny southwestern Bodrum, a resort town on the Aegean. Their smooth rounded hulls of unpainted, varnished wood gently rock the people inside to sleep. In their dreams, they hear us shout, buoyed by the sound of our music, and join in the dance. . . .

Though I continued taking belly dancing classes for four years at the recreation center, with different instructors who taught a variety of styles, it remained a largely academic exercise, the soul and spirit of the dance tamed by rote memorization. Wearing the same harem pants and leotard to every class, I learned how to control my pesky left arm, to dance while playing *zil* finger cymbals, to perform a veil dance, and to move my head from side to side while holding my shoulders still. My instructors won my genuine respect for their expertise in the thousand and one techniques of the dance.

Early on I attended a few class dance fests, from which men were strictly banned. They were fun but also made me sad. In Turkey, when we women danced together in the absence of men, it was simply because the occasion evolved that way, not because on some level we believed our movements were too titillating to display in public. What was the point of learning to move so well if we were only allowed to do so behind closed doors? Unlike in Turkey, where everyone danced in joyful expression, my Colorado classmates were ashamed to move their bodies in front of others—perhaps the reason why few friendships I made in class have lasted.

When I went back to visit Turkey, I did indeed amaze and impress my friends and family with my expanded repertoire and improved flexibility.

"Ders aldım" (I took lessons), I explain to my cousin-in-law, a particularly adept dancer, as we quiver, shake, and grin at being back together on the dance floor the first night we go out. She waggles her head from side to side in

a distinctively Turkish gesture that conveys appreciation, bunching together her fingertips like a tulip and giving them two quick, emphatic shakes, which shows me her approval loud and clear over the music. I smile my thanks and shrug modestly before the music pulls me into another fluid series of moves.

The years of fluorescent lighting, mirrored walls, and awkward conversations are all worth it now, and I finally integrate the dissected, drilled steps into their natural setting, in my own personal style. My husband and hers, along with their daughter and son, join us on the floor to raise our arms, spin, undulate, and laugh in vibrant celebration. I wish I could transport the entire rec center class to this spot, if only for five minutes, so they could experience the pure joy of belly dance as Turks know it. Now *that* would be a lesson they'd never forget.

SIX

Kin, Cauldron, and Kısmet

Balancing family bonds with personal boundaries, clan devotion is sealed by the nurturing rituals of repast while place and belonging are often ironically determined by assertion of self over group.

The Language of Family

by Ana Carolina Fletes

"Carolina, tell me about your father's farm in Guatemala," said Serpil, my future mother-in-law, as she set down a tray of delicate porcelain coffee cups and a bottle of cherry liqueur. It was 1994. We were in the living room of the Ataköy, İstanbul, apartment that I shared with her and her son Can. Her two-bedroom flat was cozy, the living room filled with furniture Serpil's father had made—every piece at least forty years old, all crafted with love by the man whose picture sat atop her dresser, his worn carpenter hands wrapped around his wife. I would stare at that picture and wonder what my wedding picture would look like, linking the memories Can had shared about his family with the future we were beginning to trace together.

Serpil's well-intentioned question struck a very soft part of me. At twenty-two, I was just finding my bearings—in life, in my new home, and in my relationship with my future mother-in-law. To answer her simple question was difficult. First, I would have to answer in Turkish. But even more challenging, I would have to broach the threat of loss between mothers and sons when the son has chosen a woman as a mate. I would have to answer Serpil's real question: "Who is this woman?"

Until that moment, I had kept to a tidy, structured path—breakfast in the morning, Turkish classes in the day, taking my turn making dinner in the evening, being careful not to impose too much on Serpil's life and space. I certainly had not spent time considering my own feelings about my father and his death three months earlier—an event that led me to Turkey.

I was now drawn back to the month I spent in Guatemala, preparing the will, meeting with what felt like an endless line of condescending lawyers, and spending near silent evenings alone in my grandmother's house. I walked barefoot through the tiled corridors folding around an outside patio filled with roses she once painstakingly grew, into the light-filled dining room and from there into the kitchen, the heart of the house. This was the home my father loved.

I knew some of the Turkish words. Usually Can was our translator, but he was busy in the bedroom, studying for exams at Bosphorus University. The week before, I had learned the names of a few farm animals: *"tavuk"* for chicken, *"koyun"* for sheep, *"keçi"* for goat. As Serpil and I took a sip of the cherry liqueur, and then another, I assembled vocabulary in my head and wondered how I might describe the four-hour bus ride through rocky terrain that leads to the eastern highland town of Jalapa, my father's hometown. The cherry liqueur quelled my hesitation and Serpil's professional interview demeanor set me at ease, her pursed lips just slightly smiling, her eyebrows raised above bright eyes, expectant. Soon enough we were bumping along a hot and dusty Guatemalan road, along steep mountains filled with small individual plots of black beans and local greens. Once we were past the military checkpoint, the road flattened, and a proud row of junipers, nestled alongside a half-mile dirt road, welcomed visitors to Jalapa.

I wanted to tell her about the milk and cheese for which my father's cows were renowned. He was proud of those cows, and the fact that they were famous in three different counties made me proud of him too. His milk and cheese tasted like soft molasses and freshly harvested wheat—a memory rendered painful by its stark contrast to his irrepressible desire to drink. My dad had a special bond with animals and went to great lengths to keep them well fed and exercised, yet he was careless with his life. I wanted to share with Serpil the one thing that stood out about my father and his farm, a memory of what he loved.

I planned to say, "My father had twenty of the best milk-producing cows in Jalapa." In Turkish, I said something as close to that as three months of language courses could possibly allow, and the liqueur helped by padding the poor pronunciation. *"Babamın çiftliğinde yirmi tane sütlü ibne vardı,"* I said.

Serpil—a radio and television producer and polished program host accustomed to interviewing people—leaned forward, smiling slightly, and asked me to repeat the sentence. Her face was tinged with red; perhaps she had had too much cherry liqueur.

I felt a little self-conscious repeating my beginner's Turkish to this woman, who during her long career as a host with the state-owned Turkish Radio and Television (TRT) was known to speak a pristine form of Turkish. But I was thrilled that I remembered the word for "farm" and even the names of animals that were my father's pride and joy. So I clearly repeated the sentence. Her smile broadened. She untucked her legs and leaned into me. She seemed pleased.

"Gerçekten, yirmi tane ibne mi vardı?" she asked, confirming what I had said.

"Evet!" I replied. Yes.

Serpil began to laugh uncontrollably, placing her empty liqueur glass back on the table and standing up to call Can into the living room. She spurted out the details of our conversation, and Can turned to me and said, "You've just told my mother that you had twenty milk-producing homosexuals on the farm!"

I couldn't believe my mistake. I must have made a pretty embarrassed face, because both Serpil and Can were keeled over howling, holding their stomachs tight. I could feel myself burning up from mortification.

"And it was slang! *'İbne'* is 'faggot,'" explained Can. "Just don't use that out on the street or there could be trouble!"

When I was eighteen I had come to İstanbul on a year-long exchange program at a high school in the center of downtown on İstiklal Caddesi—the undisputed center of urban İstanbul. Could I have heard this expression back then, something one of my schoolmates had said? Or perhaps to my untrained ear, *"inek"* (cow) simply sounded the same.

It didn't matter where I got *"ibne."* In an unexpected way, the ice was broken between Serpil and me. Far from being offended, she repeated the story to her friends, each time softly whispering *"ibne,"* not from embarrassment—she and her cohorts were fairly liberal—but because she would never use such a term for a simple laugh. The mistake seemed to make me—the woman who could potentially return to the United States with her son—more human, likeable, funny. Accepted. The story, repeated over and over again, began my own grieving process. I hadn't understood that I was afraid to miss him and accept his death—the farm story would inevitably leave me rummaging through my own memories.

My father's farm in Guatemala was Serpil's way of knowing me, just as America was my way of knowing Can. We had met in İstanbul through mutual friends in 1990 during my student exchange. He was studying at the nearby German high school and had recently returned from an exchange program in Pittsburgh, Pennsylvania. One of the many things that drew us together was our history of being "outsiders"—it was reassuring to hear someone else's experience of the United States.

Mine was an immigrant's America. When my family moved there from Guatemala, I was seven. The civil war in Guatemala was slowly making its deadly path through the countryside, and my parents were anxious to leave. They became waiters in a Mexican restaurant in Los Angeles and took English classes at night. Busy making ends meet, they were unable to help my brother and sister and me navigate our new world. My father wanted nothing more than to return to his farm and tried to persuade my mother that we would be better off there, but she was determined that her children grow up in America—it had been her dream. Their fighting seemed endless. My mother's quiet weeping behind closed doors made me question the only world I knew. I developed a shyness, and with the public library around the corner from our house, I became a bona fide bookworm.

Can could relate. His parents had both married and divorced each other twice—around when he was thirteen and again at sixteen—making his quest for stability and understanding as deep as my own. He was my first love and the only boy I knew who was reading Jung at seventeen. As we walked through İstanbul's narrow streets, he shared geographical and topographical details about the oddest things—the temperature of the Bosphorus Straits, the date a Byzantine wall was rebuilt, the height of a Roman aqueduct—or added romantic Ottoman intrigue to any spot in the city. I took in Can's information as easily as I sipped *şalgam suyu*, the pungent and salty pickled beet juice that he swore would heat us up as the snow entered our boots.

Together we explored İstanbul; his ability to navigate the city with a sense of ownership was the complete inverse of my life in the United States. We spent many hours outside of school together, or with his family. He felt disconnected from his friends after his year abroad, and meeting me afforded him the room to assert himself while reinventing the Turkey of his youth. Though I was unconscious of the process, Can was helping me reinvent myself too: Each story about his family allowed me the space to think about my connections with my own family.

Once I came to live with them four years later, Serpil captivated me even more by being open about her feelings and perceptions. When I moved in, Can and I were busy reconnecting after years of letter writing and sporadic visits through college. I failed to grasp Serpil's generosity, or the potential pitfalls of suddenly living with my future mother-in-law as we all began a new chapter in our lives. But in those first few months, what impressed me most was her frankness. I missed my family desperately—I had left so quickly after my father's death. With each of her own family stories, I felt my alienation thaw.

Her family was scattered throughout Turkey and Europe. I learned that she was disappointed with her older sisters' conservatism; their views around love and marriage easily categorized her as a harlot—or worse, single. Serpil characterized her mother as quiet and deferential, traditional in her acceptance of the role of subservient wife. Rather than judging them unfavorably if their choices did not match her own, Serpil seemed to understand other people's lives in context. Her compassionate attitude was a far cry from the way I observed my extended family, who carry family secrets and worries to a priest, or to the coffin. I didn't know such openness could exist in a family.

My father never explained why he was so vehement in his warnings and his worries about what fate might befall his daughters in this new America. He kept my hair cropped close to my head; I wasn't allowed to wear short skirts, lipstick, or perfume. If my mother disagreed with him, she was too busy to intervene. By thirteen I was a reluctant tomboy—secretly longing for pretty skirts and dresses even into my twenties.

Serpil, on the other hand, fully embraced her feminine self and seemed to me an unusual model of a mother and a woman. I was enamored by her morning routines, by the care she took to put on makeup. I noticed the way men would look at her and fall so easily under her influence. Her voice was direct and reassuring. She was adept at making me feel that a request was more of an understood likelihood than something she was asking me to do. "Carolina, you are going to water the plants on the balcony, right dear?" The only answer was "Yes." The technique served her at work too. Poor Ali, her gruff producer. None of his balking and screaming could hide his defenselessness against Serpil's soft but stern manner. Women saw power in her. She was someone they wanted to be, someone with an autonomous and creative life, with many close friends and a boyfriend. When Can announced I would be moving to Turkey, she seemed to think that courtship while living together was a practical solution to our young love—and perhaps even an insurance policy for a happy future. My mother-in-law would be a welcome bridge between the healing I needed and the growing up I had to do.

Can learned his directness from his mother, and used it on her. One night he told Serpil that she should stay out of his sister's marital problems unless asked to intervene.

"How can you ask me to stay out of my daughter's life?" she retorted, and he calmly answered that his sister needed to solve her own problems.

"It's not like you know any better," he said.

I thought Can had been rude, so I was trying to think of something to say in Serpil's defense when he followed with, "Mom, you've been divorced twice, and you're dating someone incapable of a commitment." I tensed for what I thought was coming. Serpil would surely break down or blow up at that comment.

But instead, she chortled and said, "You're right; if she wants to get a divorce, who am I to stop her?" And so dinner went on—no emotional crisis, no tragedy.

As Can and his mother continued to talk and joke, they seemed to be so many of the things I could not be—independent, emotional, free to express, free to make mistakes. A sensitive topic was broached and survived, even laughed about. That evening, for the first time, I decided to add my thoughts to the conversation without regard for my mistakes in Turkish. In doing so, I added myself to the complex relationship between this Turkish mother and her child, where opinions were welcomed and respected.

Soon I was expressing myself more easily with Serpil, unafraid of what would happen. When she complained that my Cypriot friend at work was adversely influencing my use of Turkish, I countered that at least someone bothered to speak Turkish with me in a town where English seemed the lingua franca in educated circles. She nodded in agreement, and said, "You're right, *canım* [my dear], and you've made a friend." And then she playfully whispered, "Just make sure you make other friends too." She began asking me for my opinion on *her* wardrobe, television shows, family matters, and even her boyfriend.

Actually having fun with the Turkish language, the way Serpil did, was a challenging adjustment for me. My memories of learning English were ingrained with the serious economic and social consequences it had on my family. But Serpil was a consummate educator, actor, performer, and broadcaster —professions that demanded her language be playful and lyrical—and she coaxed me to have fun with it. I befriended people who considered themselves outsiders in Turkey—Kurds, French/Turks, Cypriot/Turks—from whom I learned comic words or mannerisms that infused my Turkish. My growing use of *"iğrenç"* (gross) made my mother-in-law crack up.

Serpil and I played other games with language. We would try to identify Turkey's many regional accents on the streets of İstanbul. As we walked through the bustling alleys in Tahtakale, a neighborhood next to the famous mosques and bazaars of historic Eminönü, she would point out where each craftsman came from, explaining just how his speech betrayed him. A carpenter changed each 'g' at the beginning of a word to a 'j' sound: "A typical northern affectation," she'd said. Then it would be my turn to identify a home region. Once, I was alone on a bus from Taksim to Şişli—two major transportation centers on the European side of town—and I overheard two well-coiffed older *hatun* (the vernacular for "urban lady") discussing an upcoming wedding in Ladino, a medieval language made up of Spanish, French, and Turkish. I couldn't wait to get home to tell Serpil about the rare incident: İstanbul women speaking the language of the Jews expelled from Spain.

People told me that I was lucky to have learned Turkish from Serpil, who many considered to be one of the best TV speakers at the time. But now I was less concerned with my accent and grammar and more excited about the level of intimacy that the language now afforded me with my Turkish family. It was exhilarating to share my impressions of Turkey with Can and his family—such a contrast to my experience with learning English as a child. In America, even though the whole family was trying to learn English, my parents communicated with me in Spanish, and as I progressed in English and felt the world around me grow, I didn't share it with them. Instead, English seemed like just one more barrier between my parents' world and mine.

Once language was no longer a barrier, I began to experience Serpil on many new levels: sometimes as a concerned mother; other times as a coy, sweet woman wrapped around the phone, talking to her boyfriend; sometimes as a level-headed business woman; and many times as a friend. One day I came home early from class and found her on the phone crying to her boyfriend. She took a glass of wine and a cigarette out onto the balcony. I followed, gave her a hug, and sat next to her, lighting a cigarette in solidarity. I was upset too. That day, Can and I had had an argument about why he wouldn't speak in Turkish with me. I wanted to practice with him, but he always insisted on speaking in English with me. And sitting on that balcony, feeling her vulnerability next to me made me realize the changes between Can and me. At that moment I felt closer to Serpil than to my husband.

Serpil had been nudging me toward accepting myself as a woman. She was particularly opposed to the plain-Jane tomboy look I had always thought would protect me from a man's gaze. When I found a job with a Dutch computer company, she and I shopped for a new wardrobe. She laughed that I could not be convinced to wear skirts as she had religiously done for all of her professional life, and she gamely found a compromise between my dependable, worn backpack and a more sophisticated black briefcase. In the mornings, she would examine my face and offer to tint my lips with a dab of lipstick or to powder my face.

By example she showed me how a woman could own and balance the many warring sides of herself. Until then, I always felt like a handful of totally different people: a Guatemalan, an American immigrant, the shy bookworm, a young wife, a funny loud friend, the watchful child of an alcoholic, the uncertain foreigner in Turkey. Serpil was a typical Turkish woman, as well as a completely radical version of a Turkish woman. Like many Turkish women, she dominated in the private spaces of the home: She ran the kitchen, supervised her children's education, and through a simple gaze, she could tip the balance of power in the family. As a mother, it was her clear determination to provide a safe and welcome hearth for her family. But she also grew up in the powerful cultural and political upheaval of the 1960s: She harnessed her intellectual imagination through law school and eventually in her full-time job. She fiercely relished her work as a radio producer in the 1970s, when Turkey was coming out of its shell.

It became a long-standing joke among Can, Serpil, and me that we were in fact establishing a new trend in Turkey. An unmarried couple living with a twice-divorced celebrity mother sounded more like a French novel than an actual family in socially and culturally conservative Turkey—however proud it might be of its European leanings.

Can and I eventually moved into our own apartment and enjoyed discovering the sweetness of living together, just the two of us. We would still occasionally pick Serpil up from her show and share a late dinner together, but I also missed our quiet evenings reading in her living room, and her company when Can was out of the country. I missed her.

I never stopped thinking about my own family or about returning to California. Once Can and I had settled into daily routines and I had made some close friends, my urge to visit my family grew stronger. After six years, they knew little about my life in Turkey, and I knew little about theirs. I needed a bridge back to the people I had fled. The loss of my father traumatized everyone, but when I left, I took my hurt with me, leaving no opportunity to share. I didn't want to run away from my family anymore.

Can began traveling for work, each time leaving for longer periods of time. I felt like I was living a life separate from him; a sense of abandonment was trickling into our phone conversations. Slowly I distanced myself emotionally from him. I decided to end my marriage to Can and return to the United States. Serpil helped me make the decision.

It was a summer evening, and Serpil and I were smoking together on the balcony. She was not surprised when, with tears in my eyes, I said, "I don't think I can stay in Turkey any longer, Serpil." I lit another cigarette and could feel myself traveling up the mountain into my father's hometown of Jalapa—the jarring sensation of not knowing what to expect around the next curve, my hopes and dreams and fears tucked tightly into my backpack. Serpil looked into my eyes and said slowly, firmly, in that voice of hers, "Carolina, trust yourself and your feelings."

The words seemed so simple, but I had no idea what they meant. To trust my young, confused self scared me. But I trusted Serpil's experience and her guidance. A deep sadness spread through my body, like the warm breeze from the Bosphorus settling into the trees. I would leave Can and Turkey; yet the world Serpil had introduced would live on around me, in the lilt of a radio announcer's perfectly turned phrase, in the harmony of families who talk, and in my own rising voice.

The Food Factory

BY CATHERINE YIĞIT

"*W*hat should I do first?" *Anne*, my Turkish mother-in-law, asks rhetorically as I wash the breakfast dishes. The morning meal is barely finished, but she's already preparing for this afternoon's event.

As I work at the sink, my mind is back in my own kitchen in Çanakkale, in northwestern Turkey, watching the tankers moving up and down the Dardanelles. My husband, Özcan, and I moved there for his university job after meeting in the United States during our postgraduate studies. Far from both our families, we live a quiet life, with frequent trips to Ankara, Ireland, and here, the Black Sea region. In Çanakkale, I cook in Turkish style for the most part, learned by observing others and by trial and error in the safety of my own kitchen. I am a homemaker for the first time in my life. Staying home has given me time to adjust to the culture and lifestyle of Turkey and has offered a vital break after the pressure of my academic research in geology. And now that I am five and a half months pregnant—and amazed by the strengthening kicks and movements of my baby—I'm looking forward to watching our child grow and learn, feeling fortunate not to have to work outside the home.

"I will make *köfte* and *dible* and *dolma*, and Saniye will bring pastries," *Anne* says, listing the traditional meat and vegetable dishes we will prepare and the dessert that the second of her two daughters will contribute for today's special visitors.

Almost two years ago, in 2001, when I moved to Turkey to marry Özcan—the third son in his family—my mother-in-law had welcomed me into the family as their daughter and told me to call her *Anne*, the Turkish word for "mother." In Ireland it is unusual to call in-laws by the familiar terms used for one's own parents, so it sounded a little strange, but I grew accustomed to it. Calling her Kebire, her given name, would not be polite, and Mrs. Yiğit was too formal.

The whole family is gathering to meet Burcu, the potential *gelin* (bride) of Özcan's youngest brother, Hüseyin. Burcu and her family are coming from nearby Karademir village to Tirebolu—a reciprocation of the visit that *Anne;* my father-in-law, *Baba* (father); and Hüseyin had made to them last week. In much of Turkey, custom dictates such a visit to indicate parental approval, which allows courtship to officially begin. With an exchange of *söz yüzüğü* (matching narrow-banded gold promise rings), the couple enters a period of *söz.* After getting to know one another a little better, the couple decides whether to get engaged.

Burcu's village—nestled in the hazelnut gardens of the rising mountains, with a view of the Black Sea coast—is also the location of the Yiğit family farm and previous headquarters. The rough edges of the steep slopes, softened by brambles and ferns clambering over every surface, remind me of Ireland, though home never seemed so lush or so wild.

We had been visiting Özcan's parents for three weeks, long enough for the novelty of our visit to have worn off: We are incorporated in the family routine. I help with the housework while Özcan works in the family-owned market on the ground level of their five-story apartment building. *Anne*'s kitchen is on the fourth floor.

I am still not used to the crowd, I think, as I maneuver the vacuum around the furniture-cluttered living room and anticipate the gathering of more than two dozen people. My quiet Dublin childhood, with only a sister and brother, was no preparation for dealing with the dynamics of a family of six siblings, plus their respective spouses and children.

My claustrophobia is heightened by the sense of unease I feel—aware of expectations, but uncertain whether they are mine or those of my husband's family. Having spent nearly two years in Turkey, I should be more comfortable; I am no longer a stranger in the family or the culture. But language plays its part. My understanding is good, but my spoken Turkish is not. Painfully aware of this shortcoming, I cannot be myself. Distorted by the broken lens of language, the image I present to my Turkish family must be fractured and discordant.

Anne is sitting on the rug in the kitchen, her usual position when preparing food, chopping and mixing above a large circular tray. She dices an onion while it's cupped in her palm, then tosses it into a bowl containing ground beef and breadcrumbs for *köfte* (meatballs) as her head scarf falls down her back. I would lose a finger, at least, if I tried to cut anything this way, but she deftly manages the knife with an ease only experience can bring.

"I remember when I got married," she tells me in her Black Sea Turkish, rapid and accented with an adenoidal rush of air, "I left my village and thought I would never come back. In those days my village was as far away as Ireland is from here." She looks up and smiles at me, sympathetically.

I return her smile, uncertain how to reply; the distance she crossed was in space alone, not culture or language. I wrinkle my forehead. I'm being ungrateful; she's trying to relate to me, and I shouldn't reject that.

"*Baba* was immediately sent to do his military service, sailing to England for three years. He came back but went to İstanbul to work, and after that to Germany. Nineteen years he was gone, only returning for the hazelnut harvest each year." By the time *Baba* returned permanently from Germany, the family had opened the market and moved to Tirebolu, using the village land only for farming vegetables and hazelnuts.

Anne rises to get the olive oil and asks me to bring an egg from the fridge. Crouching beside the bowl, she mixes with her hand, squeezing the meaty pulp through her fingers. Dealing with an expanding family and looking after her husband's aging parents could not have been easy, but only in the last few years has any gray appeared in the sixty-one-year-old woman's dark hair.

"Mothers always worry about their children far away. At least you and Özcan are in Turkey now. Hüseyin will get married and run our market downstairs; that will be good." She smiles, happy that her youngest is about to marry and she will have another *gelin* to talk to. I hand her a plate for the *köfte* as she shapes each meatball into a thin oval the size of her palm.

Sadiye, a no-nonsense woman with a quick wit, arrives looking like a taller, thinner version of her mother. She hugs me and, smiling, pats my growing belly. Gülşah follows her in; she is the nineteen-year-old daughter of Sadık, the eldest son in the family and a teacher. Gülşah is a serious medical student, full of important questions and deep thoughts. Sadiye kisses her mother on each cheek, hugs her, and replies to *Anne's* welcome. Gülşah does likewise and sits at the table beside me, hand on my bump, hoping to feel the baby kick.

"Were you able to clear the undergrowth in the hazelnut gardens yesterday?" Sadiye asks *Anne* about their uninhabited farm in Karademir. Gathering an onion, some ground beef, and rice, Sadiye begins preparing *yaprak sarma,* also called *dolma* (stuffed vine leaves).

"We cleared it with Özcan's help. Is everyone ready for the harvest?" *Anne* asks about Sadiye's in-laws, also Karademir villagers, who have their own crop maturing in the following month.

"I don't know; I'm not going to go up for the harvest this year." Sadiye chops the onion, detailing her plans to spend August in Giresun with her two teenage daughters instead of in the village with her husband.

"Don't you get bored at home?" Gülşah asks me, suddenly coming out of her adolescent reverie.

"No," I hesitate a little in replying. "The house keeps me busy, and I've been very tired lately." My lack of a job is easier to explain since the pregnancy; the excuse of needing time to adjust to the culture and learn the language was beginning to sound a little weak after two years, even if it was true.

I bring the vine leaves to the table, following *Anne's* orders willingly but not confident of my understanding. I repeat the instructions; my fear of doing something wrong is slightly irrational. Perhaps I am the only one who expects I should know exactly what to do; working in anyone else's kitchen means following orders. Stuffing the grape leaves with Sadiye and Gülşah is a slow job for a beginner. I copy them inexpertly, placing the leaf across my palm, removing the stalk, adding the rice filling and rolling the *sarma.* I roll too loose or too tight, too long or too short, and everyone laughs at the worst ones. I laugh too as Sadiye rerolls one of my failed attempts. The slimy leaves are gossamer thin, and they tear easily. Slowly I begin to get the knack, feeling a sense of achievement as I speed up a little.

Another daughter-in-law, Arzu, arrives with three-year-old Doğukan, who clutches toy cars to his chest. Only on my second visit to the Black Sea did I memorize people's names. The unusual sounds and rhyming names are difficult to learn: Sadık, Sadiye and Saniye, Osman and Özcan, Hüseyin. In common Turkish style, they start with similar letters, with each change of letter indicating an age gap of more than two years between the siblings.

"Will you not let me hug you, *yavrum*," *Anne* says, calling Doğukan by the affectionate term for "young one." She is upset as he hides from her behind his mother's legs, pulling on her trousers. He is wary of contact with anyone, but especially of the overaffectionate hugs of his grandmother.

Arzu washes her hands and sits, having warmly greeted everyone in turn. She is married to Osman, the second son in the family, and rolls the *sarma* with practiced ease. As teachers on their holidays, Osman and Arzu spend their time shuttling between their families, helping out wherever necessary. Arzu is comfortable with her in-laws and is well able to speak her mind. I am slightly envious of her. I merely follow instructions; I don't feel confident to do things my own way, knowing my limited knowledge of the language won't allow me to explain what I'm doing and why.

"There's a baby in her stomach," Doğukan shouts and points.

"So how many babies do you want?" Gülşah asks me.

"Em . . . two, three would be good," I reply honestly.

Anne hugs me where I sit, showing her approval.

"Not six, like *Anne?*" laughs Sadiye, a mother of two. "Or four, like Saniye?"

Arzu is quiet. Doğukan is an only child; a rough pregnancy dampened her enthusiasm for more. Some people feel a brother or sister would be good for Doğukan, but Arzu is resolved, so it isn't mentioned.

Saniye arrives with a kilo of *baklava*, a tray of wrinkled pastries called *burma boreği* from her own oven, and a bag of soft drinks bouncing against her ankle-length leopard-print skirt. She takes off her jacket and breathlessly kisses everyone's cheeks before standing in front of the mirror to tighten her head scarf above the cap worn to cover her hair. She and Sadiye, like *Anne,* both wear head scarves, though Sadiye's is only worn in public, loosely tied for respect-ability, as my Irish grandmother might wear one. *Anne,* sitting once again in the sunlight on the floor, chops the wrinkled-leaf *karalahana* (black cabbage) and asks after Saniye's in-laws. Saniye answers quickly, more interested in the preparations for the afternoon and finding out what still needs to be done.

I put the pot of *sarma* on the stove and go sit on the couch under the window, the July heat stifling. Sinking a little under the crowd, allowing the conversation to flow over my head, I watch the family work. They work indi-vidually but seem to form a cohesive team; Sadiye chops onions as Arzu cleans the table and Saniye puts a pot of water on the stove. The comfortable *gelin,* Arzu is weaving a dance between the two sisters and *Anne,* respectfully allow-ing them to take the lead yet knowing exactly what to do herself. Discovering the sugar is low, Arzu phones the market, and Gülşah dangles a woven shop-ping bag on a string out the window.

Leaning out the window to cool down in the sea breeze, wondering whether I will ever settle into my place in the hierarchy, I glimpse the Genoese castle on its promontory. St. Jean Castle is now a teahouse, standing sentinel above the little harbor, where water glistens in the summer sunshine. It is one of the three castles in the area that give Tirebolu its name, derived from "Tripolis." St. Jean's squat defensiveness is a contrast to Irish castles, which are mostly stately homes in disguise, without a real defensive purpose. Behind the house, the hill climbs steeply—a verdant background to the quiet town. My husband, Özcan, waves to me from the street before rejoining his elder brothers, who are sitting in the shade at the corner outside the market. Sadiye fills a pot with the cabbage, rice, and onion, adding a chopped tomato and salt to the water. The steam-cooked *dible* is a traditional dish in the Black Sea region, sometimes prepared with finely chopped green beans instead of cabbage.

"So when will the wedding be?" Saniye asks *Anne* as she stirs the sugar syrup bubbling on the stove. The syrup will be poured over the dry *burma boreği*, fine layers of nuts and wafer-thin pastry rolled around an *oklava*, a narrow roll-ing pin. The pastry is then pushed together and eased off the *oklava* to form a wrinkled, hollow roll and then is chopped into finger-length segments.

"We have to meet the girl first!" her elder sister Sadiye laughs, though every-one knows that the conclusion is foregone—the engagement will be soon.

"I think they should have it after the harvest but before the schools start." Saniye makes the plan, surprising me with its haste; the hazelnut harvest will be over by the end of August. In Ireland, planning a wedding usually takes a year at least.

Anne looks up from checking the pots, filling the room with the steam and the smell of cooking *sarma*. "We have to move downstairs first, and before that, the floors need to be sanded and polished."

Hüseyin will take the apartment in which we are working and *Anne* and *Baba* will move downstairs. The newlywed's house is generally provided by the groom's family while the bride brings furniture for several rooms—Turkish traditions not always followed these days. The bride also brings her *sandık*, or chest, full of her *çeyiz* or trousseau: towels, tablecloths, sheets, and pillow-cases, all hand-decorated with delicate crochet work by the bride herself or her mother. Saniye continues thinking aloud of shopping trips and about the new couple's future. With four children, the oldest in university, the youngest ten years old, she is a natural counselor. Bringing the saucepan from the stove she pours the warm syrup over the wrinkled *burma böreği*, taking care that each piece should soak its share.

Sitting at the table again, I peel cucumbers, fresh from the farm, for the salad; Arzu chops tomatoes and onions. On my first visit, I had been the guest, waited on and treated with astonishing generosity. Now I am one of the family, included without special treatment. I try some nearly cooked *sarma*, soft and juicy; the leaves melt in my mouth with an explosion of taste. *Anne* tries to get Doğukan to eat some, but he refuses, running for cover again.

"That child doesn't eat; he is so thin." *Anne* looks concerned. "Mine were all big children, like this . . ." She puffs out her cheeks in a comic imitation of her children's chubby cheeks.

Doğukan giggles and points at his grandmother, who repeats the perfor-mance for him, edging closer to gather him in her arms. Everyone laughs as he wriggles out of her reach, looking to me like a perfectly normal, active child.

The worry fleets through my head: *My baby will probably be like Doğukan; dealing with these sorts of comments won't be easy.* I still try to explain that skinniness is a family trait whenever someone comments on my weight, or rather lack of. Arzu chops, heedless of the comment about her son; perhaps she has learned that the best way to handle it is to ignore it.

Sadiye has cut potatoes to be fried, and *Anne* begins to fry the *köfte* as my husband Özcan and his older brother Osman arrive to rearrange the furniture in the living room. Osman, full of energy, swings Doğukan to shrieks of delight as Özcan catches my eye across the kitchen, silently enquiring how I am coping with the crowd. I smile in answer, and our exchange is caught by Saniye, who says "Don't worry, my brother, we're taking good care of her."

Salad made, I survey the food: stuffed vine leaves, steamed cabbage and rice, Turkish meatballs, fried potatoes, and *Anne*'s homemade *yoğurt*, with pastries, *baklava*, and *burma boreği* for dessert. *Anne*'s butter and *yoğurt* are always homemade from fresh milk. The smell of the food is rich and warm, soothing. Saniye, standing beside me, claps her hands as she makes a sudden realization.

"There's no soup! *Anne*, what were you going to make?"

Anne suggests a packet of instant soup from the market, lamenting the lack of time and all the things she still needs to do before the guests arrive.

"Never!" Saniye replies, not wanting to serve instant soup to such special visitors. "We'll make *şehriye* soup," she suggests, referring to the orzo pasta cooked in a watery broth of tomatoes, onions, and parsley. But *Anne* fusses, unwilling to leave us to finish the cooking while she changes her clothes before the company arrives.

"Anne," I raise my voice to be heard, taken aback by its loudness, thinking of the quiet kitchen in Dublin and a little surprised to find myself addressing everyone. "You are the manager of the food factory. You go and leave the workers to cook."

Anne laughs, echoing me as she leaves the room, "Manager of the food factory; exactly, exactly." I smile, pleased that she has understood and taken my advice.

Laughing at my comment too, the sisters start to make the late soup. I relax on the couch again, realizing that without knowing how *şehriye* soup is made, I cannot help, only interfere. For the moment I only observe. I am learning more Turkish cooking in my few weeks in Tirebolu than in a year at home. The food is finally ready; only the tea needs to be made.

Soon everyone has arrived, a total of twenty-seven people. Children run up and down the stairs between the apartment and the market, escaping from the elders, who chat together. Burcu sits alone on a couch in the living room, an island in the midst of the sea of people around her, her tight head scarf adding severity to her rounded face. Her mouth is set and her eyes are downcast; an air of sullenness barely disguises her nervousness. Hüseyin, the groom-to-be, walks in and moves through the people, kissing the hands of his elders, bending to touch his forehead to their hands as a mark of respect. On the couch it is as if a light has come on, the smile in Burcu's eyes never reaching her lips. Hüseyin sits on a chair beside the couch and leans to talk to her. Aware of all eyes on them, he is polite and formal. She smiles, and the nervousness of her youth disappears as Hüseyin suddenly wrestles with her younger brother, who has sidled up. Across the room, their mothers nod, it will be a good match.

Burcu scans the room, watching the family, especially her future mother-in-law, probably wondering how she will fit in.

At that moment, I realize that though the new *gelin* is from this culture, her worries and concerns are exactly the same as mine. Moving into a new family will always involve compromise and change. Though we have the benefit and disadvantage of living far from the family, Burcu will live in close quarters, immediately within reach of family support and family doubts. She will be the traditional *gelin*, working at home to support her husband.

I start in shock; I see myself as in a mirror. For all my foreignness, I am closer to the traditional *gelin* than I want to admit—content to stay at home and look after the baby, unlike Arzu, a teacher, or Sadık's wife, who works in an office.

I rise to help Arzu bring in plates of food, almost gleeful at the revelation. I should feel more comfortable here; I fit the role of *gelin* far better than I thought. As I return from the kitchen with plates, Sadiye catches me around the waist, hands the plates to her daughter, and sends me to sit down again in the living room.

"You are not to tire yourself or the baby," she says sternly, but with a twinkle of laughter in her eye.

Saniye joins me on the couch and slips her arm through mine. Nodding toward this person and that, she tries to explain who everyone is, but I lose track. I feel as though a weight has been lifted from my shoulders. In this crowded, boisterous room, I have gained a family who accept me as their own, without judgment. This family manages to accommodate the unconventional with the traditional—a feat in any culture. And finally I have accepted my place within the family too. Across from us on the couch Burcu is alone now, and once more looks bereft.

I nudge Saniye, who squeezes my arm in agreement, and we join young Burcu on her couch, sitting down on either side of her. She brightens at the attention, and we welcome her to our family.

Cherry Pie

BY MAHIRA AFRIDI-PERESE

On a Sunday evening in June 2004, a gentle *poyraz* wind blew its cool northeasterly draft from the Black Sea across the shores of İstanbul. It was an unusually quiet weekend in the city, with the NATO summit taking place and most of the roads closed for security purposes. Alan, my Turkish American husband, and I stepped out of our apartment building in İstanbul's fashionable Teşvikiye quarter and headed past the local landmark, an aging baroque mosque, toward the popular café-dotted main boulevard. We were going to have dinner with Sıtkı *Bey* (Mr. Sıtkı), Alan's ninety-three-year-old maternal grandfather, at his home in Maçka, a brisk ten-minute walk away.

In my husband's hands, protectively wrapped in aluminum foil, was a freshly baked cherry pie. It was a surprise for his grandfather. For months we had been dining almost daily at Sıtkı *Bey's* home, but my husband was looking forward to this particular evening. An avid baker in his spare time, he had not had time until today to make a dessert for his grandfather since our relocation to İstanbul the previous summer.

Business and food are Sıtkı *Bey's* two great passions. A veritable gourmand, he appreciates good, simple food. Nothing makes his cerulean blue eyes twinkle more with pleasure than the smooth, buttery taste of fresh *kaymak* (the clotted cream of buffalo milk) or the delivery of fresh produce organically grown at his summer house in Yeniköy, an ancient fishing village that is now one of İstanbul's graceful suburbs along the Bosphorus. A keen tennis player in his youth—and once, even the İstanbul tennis champion—athletic Sıtkı *Bey* nevertheless gained weight over the decades. He jokes, "The family name is Koçman, not Kocaman!" (The latter means "extremely large" in Turkish.)

A mining engineer, Sıtkı *Bey* once managed the chromium mines of the Muğla region in southwestern Turkey, and he became an accomplished industrialist in the young Turkish republic. After buying the mines, he started a shipping company to deliver ore to Europe and North America. Other investments and partnerships followed and were later handled by my husband's uncle.

When that uncle passed away a few years ago, it became clear that Sıtkı *Bey* would be unable to continue managing the family investments on his own for much longer. In the summer of 2003, my husband completed his MBA in New York, and the family called him to help run the family business. Having grown up in the United States, my husband had little opportunity to get to know his relatives in Turkey. He was eager to move to İstanbul and spend more time with them. I too was happy to trade Manhattan's high-rises for the low-hugging skyline of this ancient metropolis.

I had already visited İstanbul several times. A child of big cities, I found its enormity and chaos familiar and comforting. I loved the place for its untamed energy; its vibrant, gritty street life; the colorful *pazarlar* (open-air markets) selling just about anything; the makeshift fruit stalls on unexpected street corners; the familiar voice of the *muezzin* singing the call to prayer from minarets above the city's hullabaloo. It reminded me of my native Karachi, Pakistan's port city of eleven million people, where I had spent my first nine years before my father took a job in Abu Dhabi and we relocated to the United Arab Emirates. To me, moving to İstanbul was like returning home.

Crossing our neighborhood's main boulevard, my husband and I walked down Bronz Sokağı, a tree-lined lane presumably named for the bronze smiths of the old city. Now the street hosts a Gloria Jeans café, selling expensive coffee, and a trendy hair salon, frequented by İstanbul's fashionistas. We made a left on to Sıtkı *Bey's* street, Maçka's main avenue, edging the neighborhood park. On this day, the avenue had been taken over by young police officers idly cracking pumpkin seeds in their teeth as they manned traffic barricades for the NATO summit.

The elevator at Sıtkı *Bey's* building immediately filled with the aroma of freshly baked fruit emanating from the baking dish Alan was gripping. He was apprehensive that the dessert would not be to his grandfather's liking. The previous day he had paged through numerous recipe books, eventually arriving at a cherry pie. The *kiraz*, Turkey's sweet Napoleon cherry, was in full season now, its deep purple hues punctuating artful displays in fruit stalls across the city.

On our kitchen table this morning sat a bowl of these gleaming, plump cherries, worthy of a still life by Ayetullah Sümer, a favorite Turkish artist of Sıtkı *Bey's* whose works grace the walls of his dining room. Art became science as the cherries were transformed into this evening's dessert. When my husband bakes, our kitchen becomes a scientist's well-organized laboratory, as he meticulously lays out his measuring instruments and monitors the temperature of the oven. This morning he rose with the early rays of the sun to painstakingly create the dough for the crust as I, the novice cook, sleepily looked on. Depositing the dough in the refrigerator, he tidied up before beginning production on the cherry filling. The secret to my husband's success in baking seems to lie in his background in pure and applied mathematics, bringing a very precise approach to gastronomy.

Even though he inherited his love of cooking from his mother, I notice that Alan's kitchen technique could not be more contrary. When his mother cooks, instinct plays a greater role than precision. Her kitchen transforms into a factory of bubbling pots, vegetables soaking in the sink, and diced tomatoes piled on the cutting board as she bustles about, throwing pinches of spices into sauté pans.

My mother-in-law is a master of Turkish cuisine, following in the footsteps of her mother, grandmothers, and great-grandmothers—all culinary legends within the family. Taking great pride in her culinary abilities, it seems she forms an almost sacred unity with the food she prepares. She can skillfully prepare a feast without showing the exertion of turning out all those dishes. On a typical weeknight, the family dinner table in New Jersey was graced with an assortment of quintessential Turkish dishes, such as *çerkez tavuğu* (Circassian chicken, a dish of shredded chicken and walnuts), *kapuska* (a delicious cabbage stew with ground lamb), *biber dolması* (peppers stuffed with rice and pine nuts), and of course *pilav*, the staple rice dish. As we tucked into our meal with smacks of appreciation, my mother-in-law looked on with quiet indulgence.

Food preparation may have always been center stage in Alan's Turkish family, but in my Pakistani family it was a marginal matter. I never learned how to cook for the simple reason that, in my family, the tradition of preparing one's own food does not exist. My parents employed a cook. By no means an unusual thing in Pakistan or in the United Arab Emirates, having meals prepared is an affordable convenience. Growing up, my older sister occasionally enjoyed doing some experimental cooking, but I never felt the motivation. Ever since migrating to Canada, where having a full-time cook is an exorbitant luxury, my parents still have not taken it upon themselves to learn how to cook. Instead their favorite Pakistani restaurant in Toronto, from which they order home deliveries, has become their surrogate cook—much to the chagrin of my teenage brother, who craves a homemade meal every now and then.

Thanks to Alan's patient cooking lessons, I have begun to face my fear of the unknown: the kitchen. The first meal he ever made for me was a feast. When I arrived at his Manhattan apartment five years ago, clutching a bottle of wine—my sole contribution to the dinner—his kitchen table was groaning under the weight of Turkish dishes he had made single-handedly. There was *cacık* (cold *yoğurt* and cucumber soup), *musakka* (stewed vegetables with minced lamb), *köfte* (meatballs covered in a tomato sauce), and cold *meze* appetizers like *patlıcan salatası* (smoked eggplant purée) and *humus* (a purée of chickpeas and sesame paste). If this wasn't enough, for dessert he had made a sponge cake in syrup. I was beyond impressed—I was overwhelmed. I had never known anyone, family member or outsider, who went through such great lengths to prepare food and actually enjoyed doing so! He had put so much time and effort into preparing this magnificent meal purely for me, and then he took great pains to explain the various dishes.

"Where did you learn to do all this?" I asked him.

"My mother," he replied simply, belying the fact that he had spent a good part of the day consulting with her over the telephone to ensure that everything came out perfectly. Had I known better then, I would have understood that this marathon Turkish meal was a harbinger of things to come.

Since that dinner, I have learned some simple dishes and now realize that the preparation of food can be more than a survival skill or chore. Rather, it can be a means of sharing and of giving oneself to others, the way Alan's feast for me was an expression of his deep belief in companionship.

When the elevator doors opened at Sıtkı *Bey's* apartment, I was assuring Alan that his grandfather would love the pie, not only because its flaky butter crust and piquant cherry juices would be a delicious finale, but also because it had been made with such love. We were greeted at the door by the motherly warmth of Sadiye *Hanım*, a plump, rosy-cheeked Bulgarian Turk who is Sıtkı *Bey's* house-help. We handed her the pie, explaining that it was a surprise, and went to greet the elderly patriarch.

We spied him in the living room, with its pretty but now yellowed magnolia-patterned wallpaper; past the baby grand piano used by Alan's mother and uncle in their childhood, covered with family photographs; past the vast panoramic windows in their chipped wooden frames overlooking the sweep of Maçka Park and in the distance, the turquoise waters of the Bosphorus.

Sıtkı *Bey* was in his wheelchair by the window, dressed in pajamas, his silver hair combed in a neat part. He smiled as he saw us, his cries of *"Hoş geldiniz!"* (Welcome!) breaking the silence. Alan's grandmother had eaten earlier and was resting in her room, he said of the woman who was usually at his side. We each kissed Sıtkı *Bey* on both cheeks, giving the traditional reply of *"Hoş bulduk!"* that expressed our happiness to be there. We settled in for before-dinner conversation, talking about the NATO summit and how unusual it was to see the city brought to a virtual halt. The conference was close by, and from Sıtkı *Bey's* windows, we could discern the outline of police sharpshooters on the rooftops of surrounding hotels.

Suddenly Sıtkı *Bey* peered closely at his watch and exclaimed, *"Yemek, yemek!"* (Food, food!) It was eight o'clock, time for dinner. Melodious chimes began ringing through the apartment. With Sıtkı *Bey's* particular fondness for horologes, a lifetime's collection of timepieces dot the walls and tables of his home. The kitchen door opened, and Sadiye *Hanım* announced that dinner was served. The elderly patriarch led the way to the dining room with Lale, his nurse, following closely behind. After pinning Sıtkı *Bey's* white linen napkin over his chest, Lale retreated to the sitting room. He still eats without assistance. Even when his hands feel weak and his coordination is unsteady, Sıtkı *Bey* stoically cuts his own food.

A meal at Sıtkı *Bey's* is not only a culinary marathon, it's an elegant affair. Tonight the dining table was set with a crisp white linen tablecloth, the table laid with delicate black- and gold-patterned china. A bottle of chilled white wine waited to be poured. Sıtkı *Bey* asked Sadiye *Hanım* to recite the evening's menu: a salad made of his organic vegetables, *yayla çorbası* (a *yoğurt* and rice soup), *arnavut ciğeri* (fried liver and onions), followed by *zeytinyağlı taze fasulye* (the traditional chilled dish of green beans cooked in olive oil). Dessert was a fruit plate, said Sadiye *Hanım*, not mentioning the pie.

When it finally came time for dessert, the kitchen door swung open, and a perspiring Sadiye *Hanım* brought in the cherry pie, perched on a tray. The cook, who had come out of his usual habitat to witness his boss's reaction to the pie, was close behind. Lale too came over to see what was happening. Sadiye *Hanım* set the pie in the center of the dining table, its glazed and delicately sugared surface glistening under the bright lights of the chandelier. There were clucks of admiration. Sıtkı *Bey* leaned over to take a closer look, his bright blue eyes squinting in concentration. "It's made from local cherries that Mahira and I selected," Alan announced as Sıtkı *Bey* inhaled the sumptuous aroma.

"*Öyle mi?*" (Really?), responded the silver-haired gourmand, his voice an excited lilt.

Cutting a generous slice, Alan placed it on Sıtkı *Bey's* plate. "Did you make it?" the nurse asked me, caught up in the moment. Not wanting to steal my husband's thunder, I shook my head and pointed to Alan, who sat modestly receiving credit for his efforts. The three household attendants made appreciative comments about the pie.

But Sıtkı *Bey*, about to take his first bite, dropped his spoon noisily on the plate. "*Bu pasta istemiyorum*" (I don't want this pie), he declared. His voice quivering with displeasure, he asked his grandson, "Why are you wasting your time in the kitchen? You should be working. Don't you have more important things to do?"

The attendants kept silent, knowing that it was the wisest thing to do when their boss had one of his cantankerous outbursts. Wanting to rush to my husband's defense, I had to bite my lip to keep myself from saying something that would heighten the tension.

Taken aback, my husband tried to respond. *"Dede,"* he started earnestly. *"Ben bu pasta sizin için yaptım."* (Grandfather, I made this pie for you.)

Unappeased, Sıtkı *Bey* began to storm. "When I was your age, I was always working!" He leaned forward in his wheelchair, the fingers of his right hand tapping on the wheelchair's arm and his energy flagging. He lowered his voice and declared that a man's primary responsibility was to work and bring home money for the family, while it was the woman's responsibility to feed the family.

I smarted at this comment. The old walrus painted an image that was alien to me. I had always seen my mother work, and even my maternal grandmother, who holds a master's degree in English literature, continues to teach today at the age of eighty-two. The idea of expecting a woman to be in the kitchen is foreign to me; it's an idea rejected by at least two generations of women before me. Although I married into a Turkish family of serious women chefs, I had never faced any pressure from my husband or in-laws to don an apron and start whipping up a meal. Until now.

The lights seemed to dim with the room's dark mood as an awkward silence washed over us all. Sadiye *Hanım* and the cook retreated to the kitchen, not wanting to get involved in the fray. The nurse stayed on, anxious to soothe her elderly boss, her hand resting reassuringly on his shoulder. I could tell from Alan's downcast eyes, his crestfallen expression, that he was truly disappointed by his grandfather's response. Finished with his tirade, the belligerent doyen looked down at his plate, his stubborn lower lip jutting out. His slice of cherry pie lay there, cold and bereft of the appeal it had possessed.

I reached over and touched my husband's arm. As uncomfortable as I was, Sıtkı *Bey's* outburst did not come as a complete shock. For here was a ninety-three-year-old man, born when the Ottoman Empire still existed; someone who still identified with traditional, Old World values. We could not expect him to see the world through the eyes of his thirty-three-year-old, American-raised grandson.

Nevertheless, in an effort to defend my husband, I tried to express in my elementary Turkish that in today's world, it is not unusual for men to spend time in the kitchen. "Some of the best chefs in the world are men," I pointed out.

Lale, the nurse, jumped in, perhaps feeling responsible for the incident. "It's true. My son helps his wife in the kitchen," she said. Alan stayed quiet.

Then Sıtkı *Bey* picked up his spoon and began to eat the pie. He ate slowly, focusing on scooping up every morsel of crust, every chunk of cherry. It was almost as if the pugnacious patriarch had forgotten what he had just said. The storm had passed. My husband and I exchanged a glance of relief.

Finally, Sıtkı *Bey* looked up from his plate and, addressing his grandson, declared in a most warm and gentlemanly fashion, *"Eline sağlık,* Alan. *Çok güzel bir pasta yapmışsın."* He used the Turkish saying, "Health to your hands," an expression of appreciation to the person who has made the food. "You've made an excellent pie," he told his grandson.

With a big smile, my husband thanked his grandfather. Never one to deny his gourmandise, the nonagenarian spoke again, his blue eyes lit. "Next time, make a peach pie."

At these words, my husband and I laughed. The lights in the chandelier began to twinkle. Once again, the loving preparation of food in a Turkish home was the ultimate social salve.

Water Under the Bridge

BY CATHERINE SALTER BAYAR

$\mathcal{A}$ rapid, insistent, high-pitched chirping invades my sleep. Not only are live birds greeting the dawn outside with warbling, but a mechanical bird is sounding from our entry hall. The majority of Turkish doorbells seem to be frenetic birdsong instead of the chimes to which I was accustomed back in California. I suppose that birds can be more pleasant than bells, but any persistent alarm waking my husband, Abit, and me well before we need to get up is difficult to embrace.

Mechanized birds mark the start of most days. My Kurdish husband's family lives in the flat downstairs; each sunrise brings reasons for them to come up. They ask for something, give us food, or impart some information that cannot wait until a more civil hour. Since 1999, when I moved to the Western Turkish town of Selçuk—home to the magnificent Greek ruins of Ephesus, the house of the Virgin Mary, and the Cave of the Seven Sleepers—life in our combined household of fifteen family members has been spirited, to say the least.

When I first met Abit's family, I was a visitor from abroad on two week-long trips to Selçuk: one during which Abit and I met, and another, a month later, when he invited me back for New Year's. I had little time to grasp the daily commotion that reigns in this particular household. Later, as the outsider willingly joining their clan, I assumed it was my responsibility to adapt to their close-knit, homespun rhythms, as different as they were from my independent urban ones. However, several months into my first year, my tolerance came to an end. By then, I'd had enough lessons in cultural adaptation to realize that my receptiveness to change had eroded all my boundaries, and now, lack of control was turning me hostile.

One morning while I was still eating breakfast, my mother-in-law, whom we all call *Yade* (the Kurdish word for mother), came to the door, again

197

offering to help with the housecleaning, although I'd previously declined her help. When I told her it was not necessary, she replied in a tone of exasperation, "But it's my job!"

I knew from researching Turkish culture prior to my wedded life that it was traditionally the "job" of the eldest son's wife (me) to look after the mother-in-law, not the other way around. But feeling guilty for previously rebuffing her desire to help, and more importantly, annoyed at the probability of her sneaking up to clean while I was away, I relented.

Pleased at my consent, she disappeared, only to return with the garden hose. In the months I'd lived in the household, I'd stumbled over women family members moving furniture and carpets out into the stairwell or even into the street, and I surmised they were far more diligent about housework than I was to do such frequent meticulous cleaning. Our home is a typical three-story concrete and stucco building in the neighborhood's sea of anonymous modern boxes painted in clashing pastel colors and draped in grapevines, which hide the peeling plaster of shoddy construction. Our block ends in mandarin orange groves, lush nature in stark contrast to dusty concrete. The flat rooftop, instead of being the garden I'd prefer, is used for baking bread and storing wood, old broken furniture, hot-water solar panels, and water tanks. Otherwise opulent marble is inexpensive here, further cheapened inside our building. The white marble of our communal hallways and staircase is rendered functional rather than decorative by the cluttered tubs of homemade tomato paste, curing olives, twenty-five-kilo bags of flour, and every pair of shoes the family owns on the landings outside each of the three flats' front doors.

But a garden hose was a new concept in indoor cleaning for me. Perhaps she would start by watering the potted plants on our terraces, I thought as I watched her attach one end of the hose to the bathroom faucet. She then went into the front room and started folding the nomad-woven wool *kilim* rugs on the terrazzo floor, taking them out to hang on the terrace rail. When the floor was bare, she brought in the hose and asked me to turn on the water.

"Efendim?" I said, the polite way of requesting someone repeat herself. However, there was no need. I had heard right; she was actually intending to

hose down our front room! While our home does have practical floor drains in the kitchen, in the bathrooms, and on the terraces, there are none in the front room or bedrooms. These are dry rooms, filled with favorite vintage textiles Abit and I collected from all over Turkey to start our carpet business, and from my years of world travel as a clothing and textile designer. Though only a few pieces were truly valuable, they possessed a great sentimental value, helping me feel at home and representing my former life—a life over which I had control.

"What about the furniture?" I asked in rather frantic Turkish. Granted, our sofas are not upholstered; instead, they are painted iron daybeds draped in colorful embroidered Uzbek *suzani* cloths, and the tables are wooden, but the idea of any of my things getting splashed or water-soaked made me fume.

Textiles are important to me. Textiles brought me to Turkey. I first came to İstanbul in the early 1990s for my clothing design work. These trips spurred my desire to return, then stay, especially when I met Abit, a man who shared my zeal for textiles and for life. Nevertheless, as I adjust to small-town life in Western Turkey, illogical encounters with my rural-minded mother-in-law are jarring after years of having lived alone in huge impersonal Californian cities. As an independent American woman, moving in with a large, interdependent agrarian family has been daunting. Previously I had lived however I liked, with few people to comment on what time I got up, what I ate, or how my home looked. But I felt that being set in my ways by my late thirties was no reason to give up the chance to live here on the Aegean coast, with its natural beauty, hospitable people, and the ancient Greek city of Ephesus—a former Roman capital of Asia Minor (circa 1500 BC)—a short stroll away. I just didn't realize that adjusting to life in a house of fifteen would be a one-way street.

The largest shock was the discovery that for me, being a foreigner in my own home was disconcertingly akin to being a newborn, knowing nothing about how to do anything. The things I *did* know how to do were certainly not the way my new family would do them, so by default, mine was the method that had to go. The family and I initially shared no common language that created good-natured silences; real communication still remains limited, except through Abit. I do my best to learn Turkish, but the family mainly speaks Kurdish, which wouldn't help me much in the rest of Turkey or in my business. I figured one new language to learn at a time is enough! When I first moved into our household, I spent time with the other women, thinking it would make my adjustment easier by living as they did. Learning to cook Turkish and Kurdish food was fascinating. Having freshly baked bread from our own clay oven every other day was heaven, though I never learned to slap dough with bare hands on the blisteringly hot inside walls of the *tandır*—traditionally a skill that all Kurdish girls must master before they can marry.

Hours spent sitting in each other's company—drinking tea and watching chat shows while minding the youngest children (ages one and three) of Abit's brother and his wife, who lived on the 1st floor—were tedious. I realized how little besides my husband we have in common. The women love to gossip about the neighbors and relatives, to grumble about their husbands, and to worry about what tomorrow may bring. It was normal chatter for small-town life probably anywhere in the world, but enervating for me.

My early enthusiasm was dampened further when my attempts to reciprocate with multicultural Californian foods—like enchiladas, curried chicken, or even pistachio chocolate-chip cookies—were greeted with little curiosity, less appetite, and an obvious undercurrent of pity that my poor husband would have to eat such fare. *Yade* frequently sent her cooking up so Abit would not have to suffer, or at least that's how I felt when the dishes arrived minutes after we came home from work. The entire family seldom ate together, since our schedules conflicted. Though I expressed frustration, Abit saw no problem in having varied cuisine; so what if the family didn't want to try it? But as I saw it, it was the first lesson: Thanks, but keep your foreign culture to yourself.

Almost daily, I found myself explaining my way of doing things, usually only to have it fall on deaf ears. Abit had little time or patience to act as constant mediator, translating cultures for me and the other women. Abit wants no part in living the family's traditional ways but prefers not to be in the middle, and having him convey why I was upset made me feel like a child. Direct confrontations or displays of anger had only made situations worse, I recalled, as *Yade* again asked me to turn on the water.

This time I decided to try a more diplomatic way to dissuade *Yade* from soaking our belongings. To buy time, I slowly gathered breakfast dishes from the low table surrounded by cushions while asking if she still had some of my favorite homemade peach jam left downstairs. "What's the rush?" I asked. "Let me finish my breakfast; then we'll clean." I was surprised how well Turkish came to me that particular morning—perhaps adrenaline increases language retention. And my blood was rising to the fight ahead.

I am accustomed to being a woman working in a man's world. Starting our tourism-oriented textile business in downtown Selçuk was tough, but far more daunting for me is that within Abit's family's culture, a woman's role is still expected to be in the home. Sure, I know how to cook, clean, and do laundry, but housekeeping has always been something to be done rapidly on weekends, not for hours a day, every day of the week. I find little pride in these tasks, unlike *Yade*. We have so little common ground.

She wears long-sleeved peasant dresses of dark rayon challis fabric over baggy *şalvar* trousers year-round, layering one similar garment over another, depending on the weather. A long white cotton head scarf is always firmly secured around her head, covering black henna'd hair held in one long braid down her back. Her upper front teeth are entirely capped in gold, a sign of the family's former wealth and, I must admit, startling to me still.

Her days are punctuated by the chores of rural life, undertaken with many females working together. The family clings to its conventional village ways. They had been land-owning farmers, and they live as though they'd never left that timeless agrarian existence. No matter how much money she has, *Yade* would never consider buying food from a modern grocery or bakery. That Abit and I occasionally choose to eat in restaurants makes her shake her head at my laziness. Lazy is the last thing I am—overwhelmed by beginning a business and a marriage with Abit, learning a new language and culture, and trying to keep house to her standards. Housework is to be done the way she learned it in the village, whether baking bread in the *tandır* on the rooftop, chopping vegetables by hand instead of using a small appliance, brewing huge vats of tomato paste over an open fire in the yard, stringing scores of eggplants and peppers to dry in preparation for winter, or scrubbing carpets in the street on hands and knees and dragging them up to the terraces to dry. My second lesson: Do it our way to do it right.

Yade clucked her tongue and raised her eyebrows, the Turkish sign for "no," then shook her head at the idea that I could linger so long over a meal. *"Sonra, sonra"* (Later, later), she responded. Then she called down the stairs for one of my five sisters-in-law to bring a mop. *"Yade,"* I countered. "We must remove everything from the room first." I started folding sofa covers and stacking pillows. Our walls are covered in travel souvenirs and are lined with packed bookshelves; *what to do about keeping those dry,* I wondered? *Yade* stopped my careful work, only to take everything I'd gathered—plus small tables and folding chairs—and dump them in a huge pile on the unswept terrace outside. Great, now we'd have wet and dirty fabrics! For someone who so valued cleanliness, I couldn't understand her hierarchy of dirt!

Beyond housework, there were also general lessons about living within our Kurdish abode. My third lesson: Privacy in this small town of twenty-five thousand is a family concern, not a personal one. In every Selçuk neighborhood, all windows have curtains, rarely left open. When I removed the sheer tulle curtains from windows to let in more light, I came home to find them replaced. Abit explained that not having curtains in the windows gave the impression that we were too poor to have them, that we were shamelessly trying to show off what we did have, or worst of all, to expose what we were doing. That passersby could look into our house is unacceptable in my in-laws' village-oriented view, especially since my foreignness provokes increased curiosity. So curtains are kept closed, despite my preference.

Half our neighborhood is inhabited by Abit's extended family from the rural east; the rest are farming Turks who park their tractors outside, instead of cars. Turkish and Kurdish pop or folk music floats from nearly every nearby window. The sound of spoons tinkling against tulip-shaped tea glasses marks the end of meals eaten while seated around a tablecloth on the floor—the traditional Anatolian style of dining. Early in the mornings, a rumbling truck arrives to take my sisters-in-law to work in the surrounding fields, picking oranges, cotton, grapes, or olives. Weekdays, the youngest children clamor to get ready for school. I tell time by the sounds of running, yelling kids heading home to eat at noon, and again at three, when classes are finished. Though my mother-in-law and her elder daughters never attended, my husband is determined that the youngest siblings be well educated, even if the family thinks it's a luxury. They get along fine without it, though they acknowledge that it's necessary for those who live in the wider world. To them, my college education in art history only seems useful here for such things as speaking to visitors interested in ancient history.

No amount of studying Greco–Roman civilization could prepare me for living in modern-day Selçuk. The ancient Ephesians had hot and cold running water in their homes two thousand years ago, though we seldom do. I'd bet they even used hot water to clean house.

Another diversion for *Yade* and her garden hose came to mind. (I had discovered through our carpet business that stalling was a respected passive–aggressive tactic in the time-honored art of bargaining here.) "*Yade*, let me see if we have any hot water; we can't clean properly without that!" Our house rarely had hot water this early in the morning, since the solar panels had had too few hours of sun. I ran the tap and held my hand under it.

"Hot water is too expensive to use for cleaning floors." Or washing dishes, or taking showers daily, I added silently to myself. She refused to believe that the solar-heated water cost the same as the cold. "*Haydi.*" (Hurry up.) "Turn on the water!" *Yade* was out of patience.

I studied this woman standing in front of me, strong-arming me into doing what she thought best. In my own home I had no control and I had no way to close the door on her maternal coercion. The lesson about privacy has an important corollary. Asserting a need for personal privacy has become my most stressful challenge in communal living. There is little time alone within our house. My habit of keeping our front door closed to curtail free movement by family members into our flat at any time was initially greeted with protests that

I was being rude. Abit has explained my need for privacy for solitary activities of reading, painting, and writing. I occasionally stay home to pursue my latest project while Abit minds our business. But when they see him leave, someone in the family downstairs comes up to "keep me company." That I would be lonely being by myself is obvious to them. Not wanting to be inhospitable, I invite them in for tea or to show them what I'm doing. It is unimaginable to them that I may actually desire solitude.

Individuality is an unusual concept within our family. Asserting my own form of independence without causing offense is an ongoing endeavor. I work in town, preferring to walk the two kilometers by myself. The family considers this bold behavior, since the other women in our extended Kurdish family only venture to town in groups on market days.

The independence I was accustomed to in California is challenged in a more crucial way, however. Though I have a close relationship with my family in California, Turkish commitment to family is far more demanding, at least in our case. My husband, the oldest of ten children, is traditionally responsible to provide for parents and siblings, a burden that I think is rather excessive. Being in love initially muted the harsh realities of my new life, married to the family provider. Though I found his devotion to family appealing, I had not really understood what that commitment meant, nor the limitations it would place on us as a couple. We live in Selçuk to look after the family, not because it is the best location for our business. Our obligation to provide for them curtails our ability to live independently from them, or to spend money on things that do not benefit the entire family. Abit jokes about being the "bridge" that spans cultures, but it is a serious stretch to have one foot in traditional Kurdish culture and the other in the modern world of competitive tourism.

Abit knows how to live independently, but he also realizes his filial responsibility forbids it. He lived in the southeastern Turkish town of Derik until age thirteen, when he came alone to Selçuk (several years before the family followed in 1985) to work many jobs before mastering the art of carpet selling. Our Aegean town is a jumble of modern buildings, astounding antiquities, abundant agriculture, and the influences of roughly one million foreign visitors per year. Time spent with tourists taught Abit English. Though he lived alone for a decade in İstanbul and Brugge, Belgium, the bulk of his earnings were always forwarded to his family. He had purchased a home for his parents and siblings a few years before we met. We never intended to live in the building, with its three separate flats, though when I arrived, we found ourselves staying in the uppermost floor for financial reasons while starting our business in 1999. The slowing of international economies and tourism worldwide, coupled with our interdependent relationship with the family, leaves us coping with the inevitable conflicts such close proximity will bring.

Suddenly an uproar from downstairs. My father-in-law, a proud, authoritative man, always quite properly dressed in a suit, or at least a waistcoat in warmer weather, complained loudly for fresh hot tea. Maybe his distraction would be my way out? A man of few words, he speaks only when he thinks something is being done incorrectly, at which point his advice can go on for days. But at this point, I was willing to endure a lecture if it would keep our belongings from being ruined. "Cleaning can wait. Let's get his tea." No, *Yade* said, one of the girls can do that. It had been months since she'd last forced a housecleaning on me, and she was determined to finish the job immediately.

I do admire *Yade* for being a very warm, hardworking woman. She accepted me as part of the family from the day we met, though I knew the family had reservations about Abit marrying a foreigner. I was grateful for her approval of me when I arrived, though it soon became obvious we did not agree on how daily life should be lived. These conflicts are troubling to me, since I generally feel affection toward her because of the good-hearted man she raised. But I want to live the independent life I've envisioned with Abit, and she knows of no other way to live than her own.

Yade was heading for the bathroom faucet to turn on the hose. I had to stop her, but putting my foot down and just saying "no" would cause endless grief. I had learned that losing my temper would cause much drama and gossip, unsettling the entire tribe for days as they complained to Abit. But I'd finally had enough of our territory being invaded. Obviously, subtlety and distraction was not going to work. "Let me get the mop," I said, heading out the front door.

Too late; one of her daughters was already coming up the stairs with a mop and a long-handled squeegee. Though I have similar tools in plain sight leaning against our bathroom door, every housekeeper has her instruments of choice, I suppose. I tried to take the mop, but my sister-in-law just smiled and moved toward the bathroom while asking her mother if she was ready for the water.

My sister-in-law entered the bathroom to turn on the tap. Taking a deep breath, I knew I had two paths: either allow them to clean the rooms their way and seethe about the ruined furnishings, or break my habit of giving in, without causing another cultural collision. I had learned the ways of my new culture, but my new family had yet to learn about mine. Blending our lives together couldn't be based upon my abject conformity; the family would have to acknowledge that I was not the same as them—*and* we were still family.

Saying, "Wait," as calmly as I could, I ran to the hall outside to collect two large plastic buckets, newly purchased for rising bread dough. "In my country, we use these to hold the water. This is my flat, so let's do things my way here, okay?" I put the end of the hose in a bucket. *Yade* started to say, "No, that's for bread," but she caught the look of determination in my eye, then shrugged and grinned, as if to say, "Why not?" Perhaps she could also see it was time for us to start building the bridge between my urban West and her rural East, instead of expecting Abit to do it for us.

Five years later, with many more bumps along the way, Abit and I bought a lovely old two-story stone house with a large garden, just under Selçuk's sixth-century castle, the Citadel of Ayasoluk, in the fall of 2004. Just for the two of us, at last. . . . Well, now only five other family members inhabit a separate floor. As for blending our cultures in one household, dynamics are changing, but ever so slowly. We are still the same people, after all. At present, *Yade*'s goat lives in the part of the garden where I'm planning to put in a swimming pool someday. We'll cross *that* bridge when we come to it.

SEVEN

Peddler in the Bazaar

*With the historic Silk Road coursing
through Turkey and ending in İstanbul's
Grand Bazaar, vending is in the Turkish
blood. The brisk market scene is a way of life.*

The Business of the Bazaar

BY DENA SUKAYA

*T*wenty years ago, I was a serious young career woman in Northern California, climbing onto the first rung of a retail sales executive ladder. Liking my single life, I wasn't planning to marry or have children, and I could clearly see the road ahead. I was transferred to a different city every year, and I planned to end up in the company boardroom in New York. One day, one of my store managers suggested I meet her "Turkish brother." Her family had hosted a Turkish university student, and after graduation, he took a position with an engineering company in San Francisco. Although often assigned overseas, he was now in town. Curious, I agreed to meet him and fell in love. One year later, we married, and I veered off my career path to travel the world with him. Soon we started a family.

I set out to conquer my new life the same way I'd eyed the boardroom in New York. First on the agenda was acquiring my husband's language. Apparently a slow learner, I continue to struggle. Moving to İstanbul in 1998 helped, and I can finally carry on a conversation. Delighted by my efforts, Turkish friends and family never corrected my mistakes; they simply kept talking to me. For many years, I ordered "tomato socks" for lunch, confusing the *çorap* we use to keep our feet warm with the *çorba* we slurp from a bowl. I was confused for fifteen years about the verb "to work." When I wanted to defer a buying decision to my husband, I confidently announced that he would join me at the store when he was finished urinating. Shopkeepers grinned when my husband finally arrived but hesitated to offer a traditional cup of tea.

I made other rookie mistakes in my new environment. There were times I felt alienated and incompetent when language and cultural barriers loomed large. Frequently unable to handle the smallest transaction, each time I left the house it seemed I was climbing on stage. I needed to be primed for the performance. Often it felt easier to just stay home.

But the fascinating city of İstanbul fueled my curiosity, driving me out of the house and into unexpected adventures. Exploring, I got lost as I practiced using public transportation and began to enjoy chance meetings with interesting people.

I discovered it is the Turkish people who make living in İstanbul so worthwhile. Whenever I was lost, or had the wrong change, or couldn't figure out which bus to get on, someone stepped up to offer the help I needed. Strangers have given me bus tickets when I misplaced mine. Regularly tripping on cobblestones as I gawked at architecture and street scenes, others have picked me up, brushed me off, sat me down, and served me a refreshing tea. Unknown shopkeepers have closed their businesses to lead me to sites I just couldn't seem to locate; and once, a taxi driver returned to my front door to deliver a sweater I had left in his cab earlier in the day. This level of personal interaction seemed inordinate for a metropolis of over twelve million people, and I loved it.

Yet of all the places I explored, the one that kept drawing me back was overwhelming: the legendary Grand Bazaar, or Kapalı Çarşı. Originally founded in 1453 at the command of the Ottoman Sultan Mehmet the Conqueror, the immense covered market has over four thousand shops, restaurants, workshops, banks, and mosques. It also has its own administration, an army of maintenance people, and its own police force. The final stop on the Silk Road trade route between the Far East and Europe, the Grand Bazaar was the birth mother of modern shopping malls. For a woman like me, with retail in the blood, the Grand Bazaar represented the source of all inspiration.

My first visit was mind-numbing, as it is for almost everyone. I went with fellow American Linda Caldwell, who had lived in Turkey on and off over thirty years until she and her husband retired and made İstanbul their home. With a strong love for the Bazaar, she knew it well. Beside the baroque Nuruosmaniye Mosque, we joined the crowds of people who thronged the main gate: a huge wooden double door banded with iron and crowned with the gold-trimmed seal of the Ottoman Empire. Passing into the Bazaar, I was struck by the vision of glittering gold and jewels in the windows lining a broad boulevard paved in travertine tiles. Overhead, the soaring ceiling was a combination of arches and painted domes pierced with small windows letting natural light in. There seemed to be no walls—only shop windows, open doorways, or arches leading down other streets. Anything that might have been a wall was covered with Oriental treasures, hanging and stacked. Two or three salesmen stood by the entrance to each shop, and as we walked by, they called to us in English. When we didn't answer, they switched to French, German, and even Spanish, trying to guess our nationality.

"Where are you from?"

"Let me spend your money for you," said one, who obviously banked on the appeal of humor.

"Do you want a carpet?"

"It is my turn, now," said one as he stepped into my path.

"Come to my store for your leather jacket."

I began to keep my eyes lowered so as not to meet their gazes. Too many people wanted my attention. Linda ignored them all and plunged down a small side street and up a staircase, around a fountain, and through a narrow corridor. Following her, I was hopelessly lost, a mouse in a maze. I was on sensory overload, surrounded by colorful merchandise, overpowering salesmen, the din of voices, and the glare of lights. Suddenly Linda ducked into a tiny shop filled with samovars and wonderful old metal objects stacked floor to ceiling. Commotion was left outside, and peace reigned in the small space. This was L'Orient, one of Linda's favorite shops. The smiling owner, Murat Bilir, her friend for many years, stepped from behind a miniscule showcase to greet her. Holding out both his hands to shake, Murat *Bey* motioned us to the small, carpet-covered benches tucked amongst his merchandise, then called for tea. Together we shared a glass and conversation. As Linda and Murat conversed, I caught a glimpse of what the Bazaar really was, and I was hooked.

I learned that day that, much like İstanbul itself, the appeal of the Bazaar was its people. In the Bazaar, one generation of shopkeepers pass down the knowledge of their culture's history and craftsmanship to the next generation. Interested visitors are graciously included in the process, and long-term friendships are forged. I realized that the business of the Bazaar is most importantly about preserving Turkish traditions; connecting and building friendships based on an appreciation of fine craftsmanship, love of learning, and curiosity about different cultures. For the Turks cradled in this tradition, a good day was not simply making quick sales to strangers never to be seen again. Being vast enough to accommodate all kinds of people, the Bazaar also includes the obnoxious and aggressive barkers, but I noticed they did not have a place in any of the shops Linda took me to.

As I continued to visit regularly to get my fix of history and retailing, I wanted to share the Bazaar I was enjoying with other people, especially newcomers and foreigners like me. Whenever I heard people relating their negative experiences, it saddened me, as I knew there was something very different to be found. The shopkeepers I knew didn't deserve to be lumped together with the harassing, loud salesmen many people saw before fleeing the market, exhausted and empty-handed. So I began introducing newcomers to the Bazaar through tours and programs I organized within various international women's social groups. Later my head began to fill with the idea of creating a shopping service through which I could show people the best the Grand Bazaar had to offer.

I began searching for vendors with a history and good reputation in the Bazaar, vendors who were lovingly immersed in the knowledge and lore of their product, who were able to educate in addition to producing and selling. I looked for honest people well respected by their peers, ones who could beautifully present the Turkish traditions of hospitality to my guests. Linda helped by introducing me to her many friends in the Bazaar, as well as to some of the local artists who sometimes sold their art at Linda's gift shop in the Bosphorus village of Arnavutköy. Later Linda opened a second branch of Deli Kızın Yeri (The Crazy Lady's Place) in the Bazaar, possibly the first American woman ever to do so.

Within three years of landing in İstanbul, I combined my city orientation programs and knowledge of the Grand Bazaar and opened my own business: Know İstanbul . . . Shop İstanbul. The service was designed to guide expatriates and foreign visitors around the city and to my special vendors, where they could consider the best merchandise Turkey had to offer without the usual stress and struggle. For shopping, I covered the Grand Bazaar and other historical areas, such as Sultanahmet—which was the governing center of the Ottoman Empire—and the Mısır Çarşısı, the 17th-century Egyptian Spice Bazaar. Sixty shopkeepers in the Bazaar formed the foundation of my Shop İstanbul family; they were Turks who had become close friends and were always willing to try the new programs and projects I dreamed up. Together we put on art shows, workshops, and educational programs for the foreign community. We arranged a program for an international child-welfare organization's summit, and when NATO convened in İstanbul in 2004 and found the Grand Bazaar too much of a security challenge for VIPs, we created an in-hotel Bazaar for the American First Lady and White House staff.

The basis of my shopping service was that a client should not feel disoriented and defensive in the Bazaar (the main reason visitors cited for not enjoying the experience). Instead, I was determined to make a foreigner in İstanbul feel part of a wider network of trusted people who were there to support her, in true Turkish interdependent fashion. Grounded, she would have a home base and an extended family of shopkeepers ready to help with whatever she wanted, whether it was to locate the nearest restroom, get a watch repaired, or find a gift that an elderly Turkish friend might like—or even more difficult, the perfect present for a teenage nephew back home.

Home base in the Bazaar was the fine jewelry shop, Milano, owned by one of my staunchest supporters, İlhan Güzeliş. Easy to locate just inside the main Nuruosmaniye Gate, the shop was used as a meeting place for first-time guests using my service. I could always count on İlhan and his staff to create an oasis of hospitality for visitors and to help to orient them to the Bazaar.

Further into the maze of the Bazaar, in its very center, my other foundation vendors had shops in the İç Bedestan, or Old Bazaar. The grid of main streets radiates from this ancient stronghold. With its great, locking doors, the İç Bedestan was originally a secure area for the most valuable of merchandise, and the same can be said today. Here are precious old textiles, artwork and calligraphy, jewelry, meerschaum, and antiques of every description.

In my Bazaar programs, this was one of my first stops. After taking tea with Murat Bilir, I would turn the corner to visit Nick Merdenyan. Nick's shop consisted of just a display counter, behind which Nick himself was perched, working on his laptop or arranging beautiful calligraphies on dieffenbachia leaves. These hand-painted designs and calligraphy, applied directly to the delicate leaves, represented prayers, sayings, or emblems of Islam, Judaism, and Christianity, and were always a solid cornerstone in my art shows.

Then I would head to Halıcılar Sokak, Street of the Carpet Makers, to visit my favorite carpet shop, Adnan and Hasan. Historically, similar businesses were housed together on streets with descriptive names such as Terlikçiler Sokağı (Street of Slipper Makers), Kalpakçılar Caddesi (Avenue of Fur Hat Makers), and Yağlıkçılar Caddesi (Avenue of Oil Lamp Makers). Only remnants of that tradition are still to be seen, as merchants modernize or try new products in their centuries-old shops.

Linda opened her shop on Halıcılar, and just up the street was Mehmet Özyurt, in a tiny space simply called Gift Shop. Mehmet was known as "the Box Man," as his shop contained a wonderful selection of Anatolian carved and inlaid boxes.

Next door was the Galeri Apollo, a leather store. Although the coats were enticing, I remember best the plush sheepskin throws in sumptuous colors and the tiny sheepskin baby booties. On an afternoon, I would bundle up in a sheepskin throw and enjoy a cup of Turkish coffee with shopkeeper Sancho, running ideas by him for a new program for one of the İstanbul ladies' groups.

Turning on to the Street of the Head Scarf Sellers, a row lined with textile shops, I would seek out Tarkan, the owner of Dalida Ceramics. Tarkan stocked modern-day productions from the towns of İznik and Kütahya, both centers of Turkey's strong and refined ceramic tradition that has been practiced for centuries. All of the dramatic floral- or geometric-design faience tiles on the walls of the Grand Bazaar, in landmarks like the Blue Mosque and Topkapı Palace, were created in İznik. Bowls, water pitchers, platters, and tableware— also beautifully hand painted with floral or geometric patterns—came from workshops in Kütahya, a central Anatolian town.

Whether I was guiding others or not, I liked to arrive at the Bazaar early in the morning. Observing the market begin a new day was like watching a great beast shake itself from slumber and come to life. Every morning at eight-thirty, the enormous Bazaar gates were pushed opened, and twenty thousand workers flowed through the main streets, making their way to work in the multitude of tiny shops. As it was not a time to try to travel against the tide, I would step back just inside the gate and people-watch. In just a few minutes the rush would slow, the streets almost empty. *Where did they all go?* I would marvel, as the Bazaar absorbed thousands.

Then, after an initial settling in, activity would begin again in a rush. Shop gates and grills were opened or rolled up with a clatter, carpets shaken, shelves dusted, merchandise arranged. *It is the same in malls all over the world,* I would think, ever the retailer.

Suddenly though, there would be a great rushing around of the youngest or newest shop workers. They would pop out of their shops with a bucket and head to nearby fountains, which are located with frequency throughout the Bazaar. A huge marble one with gold-leaf inscriptions stood by the main jewelry street, and one made of blue İznik tiles was set into a corner of the İç Bedestan. Others stood in the intersections of major streets, and all provided potable water for the entire Bazaar. The bucket brigades would return to their shops with full, sloshing buckets and mop their store, as well as the portion of the main street in front of the shop—apparently an age-old collaborative custom that makes the Bazaar as sparkly as old stones and tile can get, each and every day.

When the mopping and hustle of setup was done, the tea shops and tea boys got busy. Tucked throughout the Bazaar were tiny tea kitchens, strategically placed to serve a distinct neighborhood in the market. The tea boys, who ranged in age from fifteen to seventy-five, emerged from their appointed kitchens and rushed to and fro, swinging suspended circular trays loaded with little tulip-shaped glasses of steaming tea as they made their first big delivery of the day.

A lull would fall over the Bazaar as shopkeepers sat, relaxed, sipped tea, read the paper, and conversed with the neighbors. It was one of the quiet times in the Bazaar, daily savored, before the rush and crush of business began. This is when I would join my friends for a cup of tea and a discussion about our upcoming projects, or just sit back with them and get ready to watch the world flow by.

Just as in malls in the United States, I noted that the atmosphere and pace of the Bazaar varied with the seasons and with the arrival of holidays. Ramazan, the Islamic month of fasting, was one of my favorite holidays in the Grand Bazaar; its rhythms were unique. During Ramazan the daytime pace was slower, the streets quieter. Then, as the sunset hour for breaking the fast drew near, activity and noise would increase. Energy surged through the streets; I could feel it building. On some streets, big planks were set up into long makeshift tables; the copper seller might set out a big copper tray and short squatty chairs. Some shopkeepers simply cleared off a counter or table inside their shop. Everyone—shopkeepers, salesmen, and helpers—would wait to sit for the *iftar* (the breaking-of-the-fast meal). Most customers would leave to share *iftar* at home, but in many shops, the Turkish tradition of hospitality would be extended to any customers remaining. Other shoppers would prepare to take their meal at one of the numerous Bazaar restaurants. The restaurants, kitchens, and tea shops hummed with activity. Anticipation ran through the streets. People had worked hard all day and were ready for their meal.

When the appointed time arrived, signaled by a cannon blast from a local mosque, the *muezzin* sang the *ezan* (call to prayer), audible all over the Bazaar via loudspeaker, and the streets would suddenly fill with noise. An army of boys and men, laden with heavy trays of food, made their swift way through the narrow streets. Breads and soups, cooked vegetables, *pilav,* bean dishes, *şiş kebap,* and meatballs known as *köfte* were delivered. Almost as one, chairs and benches were pushed back, and all sat to eat. Silence ruled until the food was gone; then conversation began to hum. Time for tea and the first cigarette of the day, as even cigarettes are forbidden during fasting.

I considered this the best time to shop for those who preferred a hands-off approach. Satisfied, happy, and perhaps just a bit sleepy, shopkeepers would be happy to let a customer browse unattended.

As for the seasons of the Bazaar, wintertime was my favorite. During winter the Grand Bazaar became a cozy haven against the rain and cold. Each little shop radiated heat, the mass of humanity warmed the corridors, and bright treasures dispelled the short day's gloom. When the workday wound down and most of the customers headed home, the lighting in the old structure began to change. Lights seemed to soften, shadows lengthened, and a kind of foggy mist worked its way through the streets. The Bazaar slowly hushed, ready to sleep.

A friend would offer me a chair at such a time, and over quiet conversation, we would sip a cup of *salep*, an orchid-root drink that reminded me of sweet eggnog. As we breathed in the heat of that wonderful cinnamon-doused drink, sitting comfortably outside of a shop, it was easy to sense the centuries of history in the Bazaar, and to feel, for the moment, that all was well with the world. No boardroom could beat that.

Unpacking *the* Pazar Arabası

BY VALERIE TAŞIRAN

*W*hen I arrived in İstanbul with my Turkish husband, I was an American determined to immerse myself wholeheartedly in the business of really living here. Although I would not be working during my first few months in the country, neither did I plan to become a resident tourist, nor to inch myself slowly into life in the "mysterious East." I assured Serdar, my husband, that I would handle all of our household administration: opening and monitoring bank accounts, getting my *nüfüs cüzdanı* (national identification card), and registering our residence with the local *muhtar* (city clerk). I vowed to run the house with an efficiency equaled only by that of Serdar's mother, an exemplary homemaker. No matter that we were in a new country; since he was beginning work immediately upon our arrival, I assured him I'd take care of everything else, from government paperwork to grocery shopping.

Before starting a graduate degree in history at the University of California, Berkeley, I'd never thought much about Turkey. But living at the International House, a dormitory filled with students from all over the world, I had met a group of friendly Turkish and Turkish American students. My best friend among them, a computer science PhD student, became my husband at the end of 2001, four years later. By then I had gained an appreciable knowledge of the Turkish language and culture from Serdar, his friends, and my Turkish teacher, who taught me a great deal about the culture as well as the language.

When Serdar accepted an engineering position at an İstanbul university in 2002, I was already a dual citizen through marriage, proficient in Turkish, and determined to do everything in a proper Turkish way. I had already received a stamp of approval from my mother-in-law, Gülen, who had praised my performance as a *gelin* (a Turkish bride and daughter-in-law) during her previous visits to the United States. Even before Serdar and I started dating, Gülen appreciated the fact that I had stocked her bachelor son's apartment with all the necessities of civilized life—towels, decent sheets, comfy blankets, and so on—in advance of one of her visits to California. On her first visit to our house after we were married, I was thrilled when Gülen pronounced everything *tertipli* (extremely neat and clean) and commended me on the crisply ironed sheets in the guest room. I'd visited enough immaculate Turkish homes, in Turkey and in the U.S., to realize that a home's orderliness was considered the best indicator of how well a woman cared for her family, whether or not she did the actual housekeeping herself.

Although the degree of familiarity I had gained with Turkish culture should have made me feel prepared when I moved to İstanbul, instead it made me more nervous. I realized that, in fact, I knew just enough about Turkish culture to be dangerous; not only did I know when I was making a mistake, but too many people realized how much I knew to allow me to feign ignorance! My mother-in-law's approval, which had meant so much to me during her visits to America, set an impossibly high precedent once I actually lived in Turkey. Preparing for a mother-in-law's visit is one thing, always keeping the house *tertipli* is another. In the U.S. even my smallest attempt at playing the good *gelin* had been met with enthusiastic approval, while any missteps had been politely overlooked. I worried that when I lived in Turkey, I might be held to a higher standard.

Some aspects of Turkish culture are easy to embrace—the delicious food, the warm society, even the language. However, once we moved to Turkey, I felt that my eagerness to please and my need to be accepted as an exemplary *gelin* had opened the floodgates of, well, Turkishness. It seemed that acting in a proper Turkish way was no longer a choice, but an obligation; I was afraid that everything—my cooking, hospitality, conversations with relatives, even the furnishings and cleanliness of my home—would be subject to what I perceived as the fixed and ritualized dictates of Turkish morals and manners. No one forced me to assume this pressure: I took it on willingly, and my inner perfectionist proved to be my harshest critic.

Through her example, Gülen had confirmed for me the importance of having a beautifully kept and well-appointed home, with a kitchen that was always fully stocked. We'd visited enough of Serdar's extended family to give me the notion that a proper Turkish home—the kind inhabited by respectable grownups—had to have several key items.

The most important item, a *çaydanlık,* the double-boiler teapot used to brew tea in many Turkish homes, was among the first things I bought in Turkey. It is essential to have such a teapot, or two, in order to serve guests the freshly infused loose tea that is brewed in the upper teapot, then diluted to each person's taste with hot water from the lower teapot. Turks drink tea with breakfast and throughout the day, so it is a practical item in nearly constant use in many Turkish households, including ours. My years of socializing with Turkish expatriates in America, as well as visits to Serdar's relatives in Ankara, had left me with the impression that freshly brewed tea was an important part of life in Turkey. In fact, I had even tracked down a *çaydanlık* in America to give to one of my students, a young Turkish woman, as a wedding present.

While tea is an important daily staple, visits to Turkey and Turkish friends had also impressed upon me the importance of being able to make a good cup of Turkish coffee. I grew up in Fresno, California, a town with a significant Armenian population, and therefore was familiar with the strong, thick coffee long before I met my husband. However, my friendships with Turks in America had given me a new perspective on its importance. My friend Aslı was anxious to teach me how to make it; my male Turkish friends all teased me about the standard bride's trick of making a bad cup of coffee to test her husband's character. When a Turkish man and his family come to ask for a woman's hand in marriage, my male friends had explained, it is the woman's duty to make impressively smooth and foamy-topped Turkish coffee for everyone. Traditionally, the bride-to-be substitutes salt for sugar in her fiancé's cup, then he confirms his love for and loyalty to her by proclaiming it delicious nevertheless. To top things off, I even heard of an American friend offending her Turkish mother-in-law by eating dessert while drinking a cup of Turkish coffee; when made properly, the coffee is so good, it must be enjoyed on its own!

Clearly, it seemed, since we were living in Turkey, I needed to buy a *cezve,* the small, long-handled pot used to brew Turkish coffee slowly over the lowest flame possible. My friends did a lovely job of teaching me how to brew a perfect Turkish coffee, but to my surprise I have had little occasion to do so. In the past two years, I've rarely used my *cezve*. I don't particularly like Turkish coffee, and Serdar prefers espresso. The only visitors I have ever managed to impress with my ability to make a foamy cup worthy of a traditional Turkish bride were Serdar's cousin and uncle, who were not given the option to decline. Because Turkish etiquette requires a guest to ritualistically decline proffered food and drinks, I simply cornered them and forced the already prepared coffee into their hands.

The *cezve* was just one of many poorly conceived purchases I made during my first few months in İstanbul as I tried, literally, to equip myself for life in Turkey. Another was my *pazar arabası*, a small cart to transport the fruits and vegetables purchased from the weekly neighborhood open-air market, or *pazar*.

I had decided to do all our grocery shopping at the *pazar*. As impressed as I'd been with the sprawling city's huge, modern grocery chains like Migros and Carrefour, they seemed sterile and inauthentic with their piped-in music, stadium-sized floor plans and fluorescent lighting. I hadn't come halfway around the world to shop in a European version of the stores I was used to in America. The *pazar*—with its rutted muddy paths, vendors hawking their wares in catchy singsong chants, and mounds of artistically arranged grape leaves or fresh hazelnuts—seemed so much more ethnic and authentic. In preparation for my life as a *pazar* shopper, I bought a bright purple *pazar arabası* that looked more like an oversized backpack on wheels than the typical rectangular plaid cart pulled by urban-dwelling grandmothers in the United States. When I called my husband and proudly announced my big purchase, his reaction was, "You bought a what? Why?"

I was puzzled that he wasn't as excited as I was. After all, a *pazar arabası* was so Turkish. His American wife's plan to shop at the *pazar* should have made him proud! He had certainly loved it when I did "Turkish" things back in California. I'm not sure he's ever recovered from the day he came home from work to find me in the kitchen of our San Francisco Bay Area home, rolling out dough for *baklava*. Not only that, but since we had both lived for many years in Berkeley—a progressive, politically correct town on the San Francisco Bay—he should have been pleased that I was choosing to support local farmers and merchants, and that I was protecting Turkish culture and customs by avoiding Westernizing megamarts. I wasn't acting the scared foreigner in a new land, sticking to familiar patterns. Embracing my new environment, I was practicing my Turkish and resisting the Americanization of Turkey. He should have been glad. Overjoyed, even.

When I put down the phone, deflated, I realized my husband and I had very different ideas of authentic Turkish life. I needed to rethink mine.

I never considered myself among those people who subscribe to an Orientalist concept of Turkish life. I dread trips to the touristy Covered Bazaar and don't consider Turkey any more exotic or mysterious than, say, France. But because my introduction to the culture came mostly through friendships with longtime expatriates living in the United States, much of my initial sense of what constituted real Turkishness was a reflection of their outdated ideas. Most had left their homeland in the late '80s or early '90s, bringing with them memories and artifacts of a Turkey just beginning to be changed by the open-market and globalizing reforms of Prime Minister Turgut Özal. They created in their homes, hearts, and minds a Turkey with ideals and aesthetics that many of their contemporaries back home were abandoning. Becoming familiar with the manners, objects, and tastes of my friends' imagined homeland, I believed that I was prepared to live in Turkey.

My picture of Turkey was not exactly quaint or Oriental, but it was certainly far from the modern, globalized İstanbul in which I found myself. I remember, just before moving to Turkey, rationalizing my "investment" in some relatively expensive designer sweatpants to my mother. "It is not like America, Mom," I explained. "I can't just wear any old thing around the house—people might drop by unexpectedly. I have to be presentable."

"It's true," Serdar confirmed at the time. "In fact, it can actually be considered rude to call before going to someone's house, because if you give too much advance warning, it will seem like you expect them to prepare something special." This is how Serdar remembers things from his childhood, but we have not had one unannounced visitor since we've lived in İstanbul. Although the practice of not calling ahead is perhaps still common in some circles, we both soon found out that it is certainly not the norm among our thirty-something professional crowd.

Not only was some of my knowledge of Turkish culture out of date, but as an outsider, I had failed to grasp the symbolism attached to particular activities, like shopping at the *pazar*. I thought the *pazar* was Turkish, my husband thought it was backward. For those who, like Serdar, had left Turkey just as global consumer goods were becoming widely available, making the conscious choice to shop at the *pazar* seemed a mark of lower socioeconomic status. While many segments of middle- and upper-class İstanbul also share this idea, it is much more widespread among those who left Turkey just as the country was opening its economy. My husband, for instance, remembers the relative scarcity of Western goods under the import-substitution economy of the '60s and '70s, which made them seem more desirable and even inherently superior to their Turkish counterparts. Combined with the traditional Turkish equation of Westernization with modernization, it is no surprise that shopping at Migros rather than *pazar* should have seemed to Serdar an indication of status and modern thinking.

Turkey was unfamiliar territory for both of us when we arrived in İstanbul in early January 2003. We knew it would be a foreign country for me, but we hadn't realized Serdar might find it foreign as well. In the twelve years since he moved to the United States, Turkey had undergone massive political, economic, and physical changes. Among other things, he was amazed by the proliferation of relatively wide roads, Western-style strip malls, and general changes in attitudes about customer service. "Be careful," Serdar used to warn whenever I would buy something, "you can't return it!" Only now is he beginning to adjust to the fact that exchanges, even refunds, are allowed in most stores. Most of these modern changes are not particularly in evidence at the *pazar,* where the customer, though generally treated well, is certainly not always right.

Our views of the *pazar* epitomized the difference between our reactions to living in Turkey. Serdar's stance on the neighborhood market was rooted in childhood memory: all the Sunday mornings of his youth spent loaded down with a week's supply of food, trudging through open-air markets that were, depending on the season, dusty or muddy. For him, stores like Migros represented a much more appealing vision of the country, as well as our life in it. I saw the *pazar* as a quaint, but fun, outpost of authentic Turkey and a source of hormone-free, organic produce; a larger, less expensive version of a farmer's market . . . that also sold underwear. My husband had always enjoyed going to such markets with me in the U.S., but now he didn't want to. Shopping at *pazar* was a way for me to resist the Carrefour-ization of Turkey; for my husband, patronizing the *pazar* reinforced backward, inefficient obstacles to modernization.

Nevertheless, he bit his tongue and for the first few months I shopped at our local *pazar* every Wednesday, pushing my way through the crowded streets, my little purple cart bumping along behind me. Soon enough it became a duty and stopped being so much fun, and I eventually began to see my husband's point. Perhaps it was desirable to support the big grocery stores; they *were* better, more efficient and modern. As the novelty wore off, I began to feel that a few unscrupulous *pazar* vendors were overcharging me because I was a foreigner, taking advantage of my linguistic and cultural difficulties. The *pazar* operates on a cash-only, no-receipt basis; prices can be flexible, and confident customers bargain them down ferociously. Such an informal economy makes it necessary to ask the price of everything, which can be daunting in a country where, until 2005, nearly everything was priced in the millions.

Approaching a vendor with fresh-looking beans, I might ask, "How much are these beans per kilo?"

"One million, two hundred thousand *lira*," the vendor would reply.

"And these," I'd ask, pointing at another pile.

"Seven hundred and fifty thousand."

Okay, so, three kilos is . . . er . . . about three million lira, *right? Wait . . . is three kilos too much? How much* is *a kilo?*

"If I buy two kilos?"

"One million *lira* total."

Well, that is a big discount. . . .

"What about the *Ayşe Kadın* beans?" I'd ask, gesturing to another of many tasty varieties of fresh beans available in Turkey during the summer.

"One million seven hundred fifty thousand for two kilos."

"Okay, two kilos of *Ayşe Kadın* beans, two bunches of parsley, and a kilo of organic tomatoes, please." *Wait, how much did he say a kilo of tomatoes was again?*

"Ten million *lira.*"

The total would sound a bit off, or my change would not seem right, but with all the zeroes in the currency, I found myself unable to remember and calculate what vegetable had been how much for how many kilos.

Compounding my difficulty, some of the vegetables, such as fresh garlic shoots, were unfamiliar to me, and others, like melons or squash, came in more varieties than I'd ever imagined. I was unable to tell what a particular item was, let alone how to pick a good one or how much a kilo should cost. Among my most dreaded moments at *pazar* was when I would ask for a kilo of something and the vendor would hand me a small plastic tub and ask me to pick my own. This is supposed to be a good thing, being allowed to choose the best produce myself. For a metric-impaired American though, it caused stress and uncertainty. I have no feel for how many tangerines, or anything else, amount to a kilogram. I suspected that I'd actually put in five hundred grams and was nonetheless being charged for a whole kilo, or maybe that I'd put in one kilo and was told semiapologetically that it measured one and a half kilos. Since the scale is generally obscured behind heaps of produce, it was hard to be sure. I have no real cause to believe I was ever cheated, but I sensed the potential lurking in nearly every encounter.

When I started teaching at two İstanbul universities, it was no longer time efficient to shop at the *pazar*. Stopping at one of the large supermarket chains, with their large, free parking lots, on the way home was much more convenient. Although in the U.S. I had always tried to support local stores against the influx of chains, I find that hard to do in Turkey. Here, with a bit of guilt, I patronize the big multinational chains for the values they represent: convenience, standardization, efficiency, reliability, and variety.

Before coming here, this would have been unimaginable. One of the reasons my husband and I chose to live in Turkey was to get away from chain stores and strip malls and their impersonal implications. We used to dream about living a more authentic life; we wanted to interact with the guy selling us our tomatoes. But my work in Turkey leaves me with even less time to chat up the tomato man than I'd had to talk with the produce manager of our local Safeway in California. Eventually my little purple cart began collecting dust on the kitchen patio. What had seemed to be an essential part of authentic Turkish life had gradually become, as it has for many Turks, a marginal part of my life here. Concerns about what was authentic faded in light of the practical demands of really living in Turkey. My mixed feelings about shopping in Turkey summed up a complexity that I could not have prepared myself for: the issue of how to live in Turkey as both a Turk, since I am a naturalized citizen, and a foreigner.

It seems this process is paralleled in the experience of many urban Turks, as the blind preference for Western or imported goods has begun to recede as the popularity of *otantik,* traditional Turkish or Ottoman style, resurfaces. Whether because of local pride in the face of globalization, an increasingly sophisticated consumer society, a desire to capitalize on a world focused on the East, or just plain nostalgia, classical Turkish things seem to have come into fashion again. Home-decoration magazines feature photo spreads of the elegant homes of the Turkish rich and famous, most of which prominently display at least one piece of Oriental Turkish art: *hat,* Ottoman calligraphy; caftans; *ebru,* marbled paper; *ferman,* handwritten decrees from sultans; and other artifacts from the region's Ottoman past. A recent explosion of cafés promises to re-create the five-hundred-year-old tradition of *nargile keyfi.* Now coed groups of young Turks gather to do something their parents' generation might have looked down upon as backward—smoking tobacco through a water pipe.

As a nonsmoker I've never tried a *nargile,* but over my husband's initial objections, I've hung a piece of calligraphy and even some antique textiles on our living room walls. However, by hanging these alongside prints and artifacts from other aesthetic traditions, I hope to at least somewhat alleviate any potential Orientalism in our decor. Our *cezve* sits on top of our espresso machine, now more ornament than instrument.

During the summer breaks from my teaching positions, I shop at the *pazar* occasionally when I have the time and the inclination. I could not bring myself to use the *pazar arabası*, though. Not only do I no longer need it, since I only pick up a few bits of whatever produce is fresh rather than a whole week's worth of shopping, I also have the feeling it would mark me as a regular *pazar* shopper, which I am not. In fact, in Turkey, just as in the U.S., I am not any one thing. Having first embraced as authentic—and then rejected as Orientalist—traditional Turkish ideas, symbols, and places, I am now working them slowly back into my life, on my own terms and with significant reinterpretation: I no longer refuse on principle to go to the touristy Sultanahmet district, or avoid shopping at the *pazar*. I see such things more clearly now that they have been demystified and stripped of exotic trappings. Shopping at the *pazar*, like so much else about Turkey, has become just one of the dizzying array of choices from which I can construct my own Turkish life, my own Turkish identity.

EIGHT

Charms and Soothsayers

*Believers in talismans, Turks have clung
to their shamanistic roots for centuries.
Does the witchy wisdom of old wives' tales
and the insight of fortunetellers apply
to everyone on Turkish soil, even expats?*

Ankara's Fertile Ground

BY NANCY LUNSFORD

I had been in Ankara about a year when I became pregnant. Every Turk I knew—friends and coworkers, schoolteachers and housekeepers—had the same reaction. Smiling, they would shrug and say, "It's a fertile country." Then the teasing would begin. Perhaps it was the water I drank from the fountain in ancient Ephesus, the one tour guides tout as bringing luck in love or procreation. Or maybe it was some fertility talisman I had unknowingly stroked in an antique shop. As an Appalachian fiddle player's daughter, I was no stranger to superstition. I had witnessed my father slipping a rattlesnake's rattle into the hollow of his fiddle to "keep the devil out." So I went along with the soothsaying. After all, in Ankara it seemed I was surrounded by mystics. I could hardly drink a cup of coffee without someone offering to read my future in the grounds.

Even my business associates had soothsaying in the blood. Nuran, the gimlet-eyed sophisticate who ran the gallery where I showed my artwork, was most poetic about it. Holding my tiny Turkish coffee cup like a delicate ornament, she would peer inside and whisper about birds and bears and dancing figures. From an old family in İstanbul, Nuran was well educated and seemed to know everyone. She hosted lively parties in Ankara, introducing me to many of the country's most respected artists. And soothsaying was in her bloodline, since one of her ancestors had been a sultan's fortuneteller. That link to the otherworld shone in her eyes, lit by some inner, magical source. Kohl-rimmed and all-seeing, they reminded me of the effigy goddesses at the Museum of Anatolian Civilizations in Ankara.

Nuran had power—like a priestess in some ancient belief system. She had the power to make things happen on slow gallery days when we sat sipping tea, passing time. Her eyes would widen, and in a conspiratorial voice she would say, "Let's make popcorn!" It was more of a spell than a snack: Every time she made popcorn, someone would walk into the gallery and buy a painting, or the postman would deliver a letter from a dear friend. As a logical person, I accepted her popcorn hocus-pocus with a grain of salt, but its mystery appealed to my artistic sensibilities.

When I became pregnant in Ankara in 1987, I was pleased. I already had a three-year-old son; he had been weaned in the East Indies, where my husband's work as an attorney for international joint ventures had taken us. Despite the initial cultural displacement and language barriers in Indonesia, I adapted quickly and enjoyed rearing my child abroad. He thrived on a local diet of rice and tropical produce. Turkey was very different from Indonesia; compared to the Far East, it was much closer to my own culture. I felt good about having my second child in Ankara. I was healthy, had a reputable Turkish doctor, and my first pregnancy had been uncomplicated. But perhaps most of all I was looking forward to having a baby in a country where motherhood is honored and where breastfeeding has always been encouraged.

Turkey is, after all, the land of Cybele, the ancient multibreasted mother goddess worshipped in Anatolia by the Phrygians in the 8th century BC. Although breastfeeding might be common now in the States, at the time of my first child's birth, visits to Tennessee to see my family were filled with furtive feedings in closed rooms so as not to offend certain relatives. This time, my newborn would sleep in a cot beside me in my Ankara hospital room, unlike my first child, who was born in a hospital in Brooklyn, New York, where infants were kept in a communal nursery and only brought in for nursing.

Nonetheless, paying homage to the shamans of modern medicine and appeasing the gods of extended family, I traveled to New York for a sonogram, which showed in my second or third month that everything seemed normal. Being thirty-six, I discussed with my American doctor the risks of pregnancy at my age and whether or not an amniocentesis—the extraction of fluid from the placenta to test for genetic disorders—was necessary. Such procedures, routinely done in the States, were at that time not so common in Ankara. I decided to forgo the amniocentesis, ignoring the suggestion of a worried relative to remain in the States to have the baby. *Bearing a child is a natural, universal experience,* I thought. *My own mother successfully delivered all thirteen of her children without the benefit of a sonogram or amniocentesis.* I was trusting fate.

And I was trusting the many people around me in Ankara who took such good care of me. Among these were the *kapıcı* and his family. Although it literally means "doorman," a *kapıcı* is more of a concierge or superintendent in charge of building maintenance, a person who performs daily grocery shopping for each tenant. And our *kapıcı*'s wife helped out with housekeeping duties. I found this Turkish custom a great arrangement, especially for a foreigner just settling in.

His youngest daughter, Zübeyde, a wide-eyed and energetic fifteen-year-old, delivered the newspaper and ran errands for us. She was quick in deciphering my hieroglyphic grocery lists and learning the English words for bread, eggs, fruits, and vegetables. One evening—with sign language, drawings, and primitive Turkish—I hired her to baby-sit our son. It was a trial run; I knew I would need a regular sitter when I began furnishing our apartment and looking for a painting and sculpture studio for myself. I was taking a risk with Zübeyde since she seemed so young and unexposed to the world. Her family had moved to Ankara from the village years ago, but like many of the rural immigrants in the sprawling capital city of Turkey, they brought the village with them. Her very old-fashioned father had taken her out of school when she turned twelve, declaring that all a girl needed to know was how to read the street sign where she'd get off the bus.

Zübeyde and my three-year-old had already established a warm and funny nonverbal rapport of broad gestures and exaggerated facial expressions. I left her emergency telephone numbers, kissed my son goodbye, and left knowing I would be sick with worry until we returned home. The next day my son reported they had a good time. When pressed for more detail, he said they had both jumped on the bed and thrown books at each other, like children without adult supervision. But Zübeyde had also fed him, bathed him, and put him to bed, caring for him as young girls from her village had been tending their own babies for generations.

Zübeyde was a window into another way of life, a Turkish cultural land-scape quite different from the heady, sophisticated, high-art environment I enjoyed with Nuran at the art gallery. Besides studying portraiture and illustration in college, I had earned a degree in art history, focusing on non-Western traditions, like the arts of Asia, the Pacific, and Africa. Now I was immersing myself in the study of Turkey's illustrious art history and chal-lenging my development as an artist. But I was also drawn to the parallel culture of the Anatolian village and its earthy simplicity. I wanted to paint rural scenes and soon was invited to Zübeyde's village, about an hour's drive outside Ankara.

But when we arrived, the car's trunk packed with art supplies, I quickly forgot the landscape and was riveted to scenes of village women making *yoğurt* in clay amphorae, stirring pots over an open hearth, kneading dough on a broad hand-carved board that was smooth from years of pressing flour and water together. Female village life fascinated me. Hardy women performed back-breaking farm work and housework—hoeing the fields, hauling water from the well, endlessly cleaning and preparing food. Then, as the sky grew dark, their hands would move in the rhythmic, concentrated flutter of crocheting or tat-ting, looping and knotting thread and beads into graceful lace trims for linens and head scarves.

I was Zübeyde's patroness in town, but here the hospitality extended to me by her family and their neighbors seemed genuine and natural rather than obsequious. I was plied with tea and *ayran*, a salty mixture of *yoğurt* and water with a taste similar to buttermilk, and *meze*, local appetizers like stuffed grape leaves, homemade cheese, and freshly baked bread.

I felt welcomed into their midst. I sketched them and photographed them and ate with them and spoke broken Turkish. They laughed at me and put up with "Madame's" curiosity about the most mundane things, like a discarded head scarf in the garden. The fabric was so worn it seemed that the dirt alone held it together, edges still trimmed in a delicately crocheted scallop. In front of an amused audience, I fished it out of the muck and later used it in an abstract series of painted collages.

The village light helped me to understand Zübeyde and the traditions from which she descended. I saw her mother as if for the first time. In Ankara she seemed an anachronism in her veils and voluminous skirts and pantaloons, head bowed and silent, but here among her sisters, she was a wizened crone with rosy cheeks, mischievous eyes, and a sense of humor. She was not as old as I had suspected, misreading her weatherworn skin, untended teeth, and grandmother status. She was probably in her midfifties, younger than my own mother.

The only discomfort I ever felt in Zübeyde's village was with the women's high level of physical familiarity. The hard kissing and hugging I quickly got used to, but when asked whether I still nursed my son, for example, the language barrier was quickly broached with a pat to my breast and a point to my son.

When I had just begun to show my pregnancy around the fourth month, I ran into Zübeyde, her mother, and one of her aunts in the apartment hallway. They smiled, tested my breasts and belly, and conferred amongst themselves, laughing and shaking their heads. When I asked Zübeyde to translate, she held up two fingers and said, "*İkiz! İkiz gelecek!*" (Twins! Twins will come!)

Twins? No way. My New York doctor hadn't mentioned twins. I tried to explain, in broken Turkish, how I knew they were mistaken. As I pantomimed what a sonogram was and how medical doctors can see what the baby looks like before it is born, the women listened to me politely and then dismissed the results as they said goodbye.

"*İnşallah, ikiz gelecek, inşallah*" (Twins are coming if God wills it), they said.

The meeting sparked a stormy afternoon of confusion. I was suddenly fed up with these charming villagers. Just before I saw them in the hallway, I had been on the phone trying to convince my worried, overprotective older sister that I was going to be all right, that Ankara was a modern city with perfectly adequate hospitals, good doctors, and medical facilities. Perhaps I was trying to convince myself too. And then any illusions I might have had about where I was evaporated. These toothless women—wearing village *şalvar* (loosely gathered slacks) under mismatched printed skirts, and donning the beaded veils that so enchanted me just a few months ago—now worried me with nonsense. *Who were they to give me a prognosis,* I pouted. Feeling me up, predicting twins with their *"inṣallah"* and *"maṣallah."* (God willing, God protect me).

A few months later, I missed my prenatal appointment. Since my belly was so huge, I had lost my balance, fallen, and broken my ankle. When I finally went to my local hospital for a sonogram, I was in my eighth month. The Turkish technician was explaining the sonogram process to an assistant, and I understood her to say, "Here's one head . . . and here's the other head."

Fearing I might be bearing a monster, I asked her if the baby had two heads. She looked at me very seriously and said, "Twins. You don't know? You're having twins." Apparently the sonogram in the States was too early to pick up identical fetuses, in the same placenta, one hiding behind the other. *So those toothless women in the veils were right,* I thought, lying on the examining table. They told me months ago that I was carrying twins, and in a moment of blind faith in Western medicine, I refused to believe them. They may have known nothing about sonograms, but they knew quite a bit about pregnancy and childbirth.

When I got home and told Zübeyde, she said there were many twins in her village and that her mother and aunts had personally assisted in their births. Their diagnosis was right, but she didn't want to believe it. Zübeyde had already worked for two other women who had twins after they hired her, and she knew how much work would be involved. In the end, my younger sister came to live with me to help out, and so, with a lightened load, Zübeyde stayed with us until we left Turkey. But I told her she could make a good living hiring herself out as a fertility talisman. (Of course, her patroness would have to visit Zübeyde's village and drink the *ayran* and eat the stuffed grape leaves and succumb to the occasional clutching of a breast.)

Bearing twins forced a hiatus from my artwork. But when I finally returned to the studio, my creative energy and ideas seemed to have doubled, inspired by my Turkish surroundings and the land's fecundity. I found an old wire cradle in a flea market, and I draped it with strips of cloth, tying them to the frame the way wishing trees in Turkey are tied with rags by those hoping for a dream come true. I produced so much work that Nuran offered me a solo exhibition, a very personal show—and she made popcorn while we sent out invitations. As we saw it, this collection of new sculptural work represented my coming of age in a natural world inspired by the earthy sensibilities of the Anatolian village. At the entrance to the gallery, I incorporated fresh heather into a sculpture that greeted the visitor with the smell of the fields—a link to my own country childhood in Tennessee.

Then, on the day of the opening, disaster struck. There had been mounting tension for weeks about the possibility of war in Kuwait and neighboring Iraq. The morning news reported that American bombers had already left Turkish air bases and the first Gulf War had begun. Ankara, the seat of parliament and the capital of Turkey, was within range of Saddam Hussein's missiles. The mood grew darkly somber and nearly all social events were canceled. A grim populace, preparing for the worst, hurried to stock up on flour, bottled water, and batteries in the event of a greater crisis. Nuran and I were distraught. I was an American guest in a country threatened by a war now escalated by American intervention. I couldn't see myself having a reception on such an ominous day. People began to call the gallery to ask if we would be open later that evening. As we regarded the quiet walls filled with images imbued with the everlasting promise of cycle and rebirth, we decided to make a stand for peace and art and life in the face of war and opened the doors at the scheduled time. Soon Nuran's establishment was thronged with diplomats, businessmen, and socialites displaced by canceled dinner parties and other events; it was a subdued but much larger crowd than we were expecting. Although the talk was of war and politics and an uncertain future, many people were seeking respite from the events of the day, looking for a hopeful new perspective.

A Mother's Charms

BY Maria Yarbrough Orhon

"**W**here's your belly button?" my Turkish boyfriend İbrahim asked me one night in the 1970s as I sipped white wine at a fish restaurant beside the Bosphorus.

"Pardon me?" I sputtered, hoping I hadn't dribbled on my silk blouse.

"Your belly button. Where is it?"

"Oh, İbo, for goodness sake, it's here, of course," I snapped back, pointing vaguely toward my middle, annoyed that he was being so silly.

"No, no, I mean the part that falls off later," he went on.

"Oh. You mean the umbilical cord," I mumbled, glancing around to see if anyone was overhearing this oddly intimate exchange. "I don't know. They probably threw it out at the hospital or something." As I spoke, I realized I had no idea what Americans did with a newborn's dried umbilical stem.

I rearranged my napkin daintily in my lap, wondering where this strange conversation was going. "So where's yours, anyway?" I said, deciding to put the ball back in his court.

"My mother has it, safely tucked away. You're supposed to keep it as a kind of amulet to ward off harmful things. Too bad about yours," he said, cutting into his salmon.

I sat there staring at my sautéed shrimp, feeling slightly squeamish. I'd known İbo for four years and I had always thought of him as being very modern and European. Certainly in Turkey, his native land and my home on and off for nearly a decade, there were superstitions, particularly the fear of something called the "evil eye." With a father who was a Middle East specialist, I grew up in Beirut, Tehran, Ankara, and Athens and went to high school and later taught in Turkey—all experiences that had exposed me to many different customs and superstitions. But I'd never heard my pragmatic, American-educated mate confess to believing in any of them. That was the first time.

Four years later, we'd married, and our daughter Alara was born in İstanbul. On her tenth day, while I was changing a diaper, the shriveled stump of her umbilical cord slid gently onto the changing table. I picked it up gingerly, hesitating, remembering that conversation. I put it carefully into a small plastic bag, wrapped it with tape, and placed it in a tiny wooden box, along with her identification bracelet from the hospital. For some reason or other, I felt relieved, knowing that even though I didn't believe in that stuff, at least I knew where it was, just in case.

In the ensuing weeks, relatives and friends came to visit, bringing traditional gifts of gold coins for the baby. She was also given tiny blue glass beads resembling eyes, strung on gold chains or mounted on pins. They were supposed to shield the child from harm. Turkish mothers made sure that their children always wore these *nazar boncuğu,* or evil eye charms, especially when in public or on journeys. Such talismans were thought to protect the wearer from the evil eye—bad luck or bad intentions of others.

I didn't drape or pin any charms on Alara; instead, I stored them in a miniature jewelry box, like the finery and valuable gold that they were, until she was older. It amused me sometimes when people would stop me in the park, remarking on her beauty and then in the next breath admonishing me because I failed to display a blue evil eye prominently on her clothes.

When Alara was a month old, there was a big family birthday party for one of the cousins at a restaurant along the Bosphorus, and everyone admired her. My mother-in-law, Renan, came back to our house for supper that night.

"Excuse me, Maria. Where's the salt?"

"In the shaker in the dining room," I answered, puzzled. She had been in our house frequently over the years and of course knew where it was.

"Oh, no, I mean lots of salt, from the kitchen."

"How much?" I asked, trying unsuccessfully to keep a suspicious tone out of my voice. *What was she going to do with a lot of salt?*

"About a handful, I guess. Maybe half a handful would do," she replied, looking down at her open palms and weighing the imaginary salt.

I led her to the kitchen and rummaged for the salt. Alara was fussy after the day's excitement, and I wanted to settle her down, so all this salt business was a bit of a bother. Without explanation, Renan took the canister from me and tipped a large white mound of it into the palm of her beautifully manicured hand.

Spellbound, I followed her into the baby's room, where she proceeded to carefully wave her hand about, palm filled with salt, making circles above her granddaughter's head, taking pains not to spill the grains. She whispered something over and over. I strained to hear, fascinated.

"God protect this child from bad things, from evil eyes," she was saying. Then she returned swiftly to the kitchen, where she lit a burner, turning the flame to high. She poured a white stream of salt onto the fire, which sparkled and spat. Transfixed, I watched my modern mother-in-law in her tidy suit and silk blouse as she leaned over the stove, performing some kind of ancient rite.

"Maria, come see," she said with warmth, taking my hand. "The eyes there. See the eyes of those who loved Alara too much today? Loving too much invites envy, the evil eye."

I studied the glowing white and gray pile on the stove's burner. On the surface, a few small craters had formed. Mesmerized, I stared at the tiny, eye-like dents.

"Well, now. Everything will be all right," she assured me, satisfied. She lit a cigarette with her gold lighter, exhaled with a sigh, and went back to the living room. I remained, watching the flames. *There must be a chemical explanation for what had happened to the salt,* I thought.

From time to time in the next few months, Renan would again perform the salt-burning ritual. My skepticism made it difficult for me to accept, though I pretended for my mother-in-law's sake. Each time, I felt torn between intense guilt at witnessing this primal ritual in which I had no faith, and my secret irrational wish that it would indeed work, that my daughter would be magically protected from everything.

One night, when Alara was about a year old, Renan called.

"You must burn some salt," she announced. "Far too many people admired her today when we were at the New Year's party."

I cringed.

"Me? I can't. I can't say those things. I don't know how to do it. It will be all wrong." I struggled with my conflicting feelings. The salt ritual was not me. But I also felt a strong mother's instinct to guard my child in any way I could.

"Well, I can't do it from three kilometers away, you know. İbo can help you. You'll do fine." She hung up.

For a long time I just stood, wondering what to do, wondering if such an act could actually do any good. I was also gripped with an overwhelming sense of wanting to do everything I could to protect my daughter. I finally decided it couldn't hurt to try it. I went to the kitchen, opened the cupboard, and clutched the salt canister. I poured a tiny bit into my hand. *This is ridiculous*, I thought. I went to Alara's room. Summoning my composure, I straightened my shoulders and began making the circling motions, trying to approximate the right words.

I heard a noise behind me; I swung, startled. My husband was leaning against the door frame with a funny expression on his face.

"Don't sprinkle it on her head," he quipped, intending affection rather than flippancy. Embarrassed to be caught trying this superstitious ritual, I turned back and finished the circles with determination. It wasn't my custom, but I would do it just in case, for Alara. When I turned around, İbo's face had gone soft. As I passed him, he reached out and pulled me to him in a tender embrace, an embrace of thanks. I leaned in to his warmth, still gripping my handful of salt, and we lingered there in the silent hall, listening to Alara's breathing, feeling like a family.

Then, enveloped in a kind of calm quiet, together İbo and I went back to the kitchen. He turned on the flame as I poured the salt onto the burner. It glittered in the semidarkened room. We watched in silence, each pointing to the little pits on the surface of the white dune.

When Alara was two, we went to the United States to see my parents. My mother, a true South Carolina belle, delighted in her granddaughter's company that summer, taking her to the beach, cooking special dishes, spoiling her, and generally making up for all the time they couldn't normally spend together.

"Renan's so lucky, seeing her granddaughter every day," mused Mom one afternoon as we watched Alara paddling in her little baby pool. "She takes good care of Alara, and gives her lots of love."

The day we were to return to Turkey, bags packed, standing by the door, suddenly I remembered the blue charm. "Where's Alara's evil eye? Renan will expect to see it when she meets us at the airport. Oh, now we're going to be late," I said to my mother, dropping my purse and starting to rummage through the trinkets on the coffee table. Alara had a gold and blue *nazar boncuğu* she wore on a chain on long journeys, when Renan would remind me to put it on her. I'd taken it off on our arrival in June, forgetting about it entirely.

Besides hearing all my stories of superstitions and rituals in İbo's family, my mother had also spent a few years in Turkey with a young family, so she understood why an evil eye talisman would keep Alara's other grandmother happy. But my Southern belle mother surprised me that day, saying, "Turks have such willingness to believe that there's a solution or potion or remedy for everything. Few places in the world inspire such hope. Maria, we've got to find that charm!"

I opened the suitcases while she looked in cupboards, coin jars, and under the furniture. We searched for half an hour in every room in the house, patiently, and with a vigor that shocked us both. "Found it!" Mom called triumphantly, pulling it from an old silver mug on the mahogany sideboard in the dining room. She placed it around Alara's neck, trying hard to blink back the tears as she kissed her granddaughter again. "Is there anything else I have to do, dear?" she asked, sounding concerned.

"For what?" I said, rummaging in my purse for one last check of tickets and passports.

"I don't know, to make sure you have a safe trip. Do I need to—burn salt or something?" she asked solemnly in her soft, Southern drawl, gently wringing her hands.

"No, Mama," I said, drawing her to me one last time, encircling her in a hug. "We'll be just fine." I held her, imagining this diminutive Episcopalian lady, hand moving in rounds, pouring salt grains onto her built-in electric range like a Turk. Every mother everywhere wants in some way or another to draw invisible circles of love around her children, keeping them safe.

It was many years later when I returned, in a moment of despair, to the ritual of burning salt. It was one of those weeks when everything seemed to go wrong. Things were crazy at the private school where I taught, with everyone preparing for holiday festivities, classes being canceled without notice, kids leaving early, the office demanding reports and papers. Both Alara, then nine, and my son Altan, who was four, were sick in bed with the flu, and I had been up three nights in a row with them. İbo had just called to say that his business trip had been extended for five more days.

Going into the kitchen to make a cup of coffee, I pushed the button on the electric kettle and then began to load the dishwasher. I turned on the tap. It just hissed. The water had been cut off—a typical yet unpredictable İstanbul occurrence in the 1990s. Looking at the pile in the sink, I burst into tears, feeling tired, frustrated, and defeated.

I can't remember just how long I remained there. I do remember slowly going to the cupboard and taking down the salt, holding the jar to me, the tears slow but constant. First I measured out a small amount, and then more, just to be sure. Twisting the knob as far as it would go, I lit the burner. Around I spun in the kitchen, arm outstretched, reaching in my mind's eye to all the corners of the house.

"Mommy, what are you doing?"

I stopped, frozen in my pajama-clad daughter's gaze. *Caught again!* Just like the last time I was interrupted in the act, I remained determined to continue my adopted custom.

"Alara, sweetie, come here," I said. She watched as I put the salt on the fire, a frightened look clouding her face. Then Alara moved closer, touching me for reassurance.

"I want to tell you a story," I said, draping my arm across her shoulder and wiping the tears from my cheeks. Then I began to explain to her about the salt, and how her grandmother had believed that it would help protect us from harmful things.

It was time to show her the contents of the tiny box in my room, the remnant of the essential physical bond that connected us.

Together we went to my bedroom, where I found the brass-studded box in the back of my scarf drawer. Perched on the quilt that my Southern mother had sewn for me as a girl, my daughter held her breath, eyes wide, as I opened the box.

Looking in, she groaned with all the disgust a nine-year-old can muster.

"Ew, yuck! You really kept that? How gross, Mom."

Then she was quiet. Cautiously holding the corners of the plastic bag, Alara studied her umbilical cord, holding it up to the light and turning it over. Then she put it back in the box, closing the clasp with a short, snapping sound.

"I suppose you can keep it," she conceded. Suddenly, she leapt up. "The salt!" She raced to the kitchen, where I had left the salt in the flame on the back burner of the stove. I found her there, on tiptoe, looking at the twinkling flames and the pitted pile of salt, all those evil eyes being banished, all our troubles burned away.

"Mom, look! It works!"

I leaned over to watch the salt glow and crater. A little hand crept along my waist until her arm stretched around me in a soft, protective embrace.

"Everything will be all right, now," Alara said, surrounding me with her hopes, just as I had encircled her with mine.

Evil Eye Exorcism

BY ANNIE PRIOR ÖZSARAÇ

A few years ago, my Turkish husband, Koray, and I moved into a new flat in Arnavutköy. A quaint waterfront fishing village north of İstanbul's city center, Arnavutköy is now part of the city. The apartment was quite small but had a cozy bedroom loft, a spacious kitchen, and large windows that let in a beautiful Bosphorus view.

After eyeing the neighborhood for quite some time, we were thrilled at the prospect of spending our days in such a pretty place. When the real estate agent called and announced an available rental, we thanked our lucky stars. Quickly we made arrangements to move out of our furnished, ground-floor flat in the high-density, hilltop of nearby Etiler, to trade a dismal view of the neighborhood mosque for the natural vista of sky and water. As a young couple on the limited budget of English teachers, we didn't have much furniture of our own yet, and I hadn't shipped any when I moved over from my home in Washington State. But we couldn't pass up what was obviously a fantastic opportunity. We ordered a dining set, a couch, and new appliances, and we moved in to the bare space, content with life. However, it wasn't long before things began to go awry.

It started with the brand-new refrigerator. Without warning or reason, we would either come home or wake up to a warm fridge, its contents well on their way to being spoiled. Five times it went belly up on us, two times just an hour before a dinner party. Once we were able to save the evening by shifting all the food to an icy window ledge. Every time the appliance company's repairman came, he would try something else, replacing a different part or jiggling a new connection, intent on exhausting all possible causes rather than giving us a new fridge.

The electrical lights in the apartment came and went, turning on at times that didn't suit us, like in the middle of the night. The delivery of our dining and living room furniture was delayed repeatedly, leaving us with only our bed to sit and dine on. The apartment's old combination space heater/water heater broke down several times, usually during morning showers. To my surprise, the landlady announced it was our responsibility to have it repaired, and Koray agreed this is the way it works in Turkey.

We had just forked out a billion *lira*, or one thousand U.S. dollars, for car maintenance when the muffler sprang a loud and obnoxious hole. Then another car hit it as it was parked on the winding, narrow street just in front of our building, shattering the rear brake lights and crushing the fender. A local street gang swiftly relieved us of the car stereo. Needless to say, Koray and I had stopped thanking our lucky stars. Instead, we were reduced to battling each other, fed up with everything, especially our quaint little honeymooner flat.

As things spun out of control, we requested assistance from Koray's gracious parents, who helped any way they could. But all the while, they insisted the *nazar*, or evil eye, had its sights on us. In Turkish culture, it is thought that when things are going well in your life, others will look with envy upon you, inciting the evil eye, which brings bad luck.

It was true, things had been going well for us: We were lucky in love, health, friendship, and family, and we had a lovely new flat with a breathtaking view of the Bosphorus. Koray's parents insisted we allow *Babaanne*, Koray's paternal grandmother, to perform *kurşun döktürmesi*, the lead-pouring ceremony—an evil eye exorcism. The plan was to remove the evil that was tormenting us and invite good luck back into our lives. It was a novel idea, and I welcomed the cultural experience, even though I didn't subscribe to such supernatural concepts. However, I was intrigued. Two years of teaching in Guatemala near the worship of Maximón piqued my interest in black magic. Maximón is said to be the god of death and fertility, a mixture of Mayan and Christian principles. I once paid an eight-year-old to take me to see the top hat–wearing effigy that sat in his village shrine, surrounded by offerings of alcohol, cigarettes, and food.

The lead ceremony was a shamanistic practice, one increasingly rejected by younger generations of Turks, who don't embrace the mystical folklore of bad luck that surrounds the evil eye.

"It's just superstition," Koray explained to me. "It doesn't really work." But he didn't add that he had undergone the *kurşun döktürmesi* when he was eight years old, having come home for the third time with a broken arm—and that he hasn't broken a bone since. Even so, like a man grown from a reckless boy, he chose not to see any relation between the exorcism and his sturdy bones.

Then swords of ice fell from the sky.

We woke up to what sounded like bombs being dropped over our heads, explosions all over the neighborhood. When the sounds slowed, we realized that they were large shards of ice plummeting from the sky, crushing the terracotta roof tiles just above our living room, allowing the melting snow to seep through and stain our ceiling and walls. The icicle swords did not come directly from the gods; truth be told, they fell from the power lines that were suspended high above the building and that crossed to the other side of the Bosphorus. Disregarding these power lines was perhaps not the best choice we had made in selecting this new home. According to our landlady, it had been twenty-eight years since this phenomenon had occurred.

Koray and I began to mop the living room floor and wipe down the walls. We started to giggle at the ridiculous chain of events as we relived the indignities of the past few months. Soon we were roaring with laughter, our eyes welling with tears, knowing there was nothing we could do about any of it. We chose this place: a neighborhood preyed on by car stereo thieves, a building with faulty wiring, a home directly beneath power lines that sent massive icicles through our roof. When we finally sobered, we found ourselves wondering whether maybe it wasn't time for the witchdoctor antics of *Babaanne*. Maybe she could do something about our predicament.

Babaanne is a ninety-year-old woman from a small town outside of Rize, on the Black Sea coast of Turkey. Short—and even shorter because she walks hunched over—she joined her children in İstanbul twenty years ago but seems locked in another time and in a more rural place. She is known in the family as a headstrong woman, and according to my own Turkish mother-in-law, *Babaanne* fits the stereotype of a domineering Turkish mother-in-law: sharp of tongue and opinionated. Koray's parents say her heart seems like it will beat forever. But when Koray and I ask her how she is, she gives the stock answer, "I am wrestling with old age, Allah save me."

As the matriarch of the family, it is her privilege to perform the ceremony, and so we made an appointment with her when she was visiting Koray's parents for the weekend. When we arrived, *Babaanne*—her wrinkled face framed by a white head scarf, wearing her usual uniform of a flower-print cotton house-coat—was perched on the sofa in the salon with her early evening glass of tea. Koray and I greeted her in turn, using the traditional show of respect to elders by kissing her hand and lifting it to touch our forehead. In the kitchen, Koray's mom was bustling around, preparing dinner, and Koray's father was rifling through what I call his "Aladdin's cave of tools"—an immense box that holds enough tools for three households. Eventually from its depths he produced two chunks of solid lead much like the ones fishermen use to weigh down their nets. He called to his mother; the lead was ready.

Babaanne creaked into the kitchen, beckoning us to follow her. Nobody had told me in detail what was going to happen, so I figured I might as well put all of my faith into it and not disturb the process by asking lots of questions. I took my cues from Koray, who was perfectly at ease as *Babaanne*, taking no safety precautions, arranged the chunks of lead onto an ordinary household spoon before setting it over the open flame on the stove. The spoon blackened with soot, and the lead slowly turned molten as *Babaanne*'s shaky grip barely kept it from spilling all over my mother-in-law's freshly scrubbed stovetop. I looked around for my mother-in-law in order to catch her reaction, but she was busy unfolding a sheet on the kitchen table. My father-in-law was arranging chunks of bread, Turkish *lira* notes, and an onion in a large mixing bowl. Then he placed a smaller bowl, brimming with water, inside the mixing bowl. When he saw me watching him, he quietly explained that the onion was to add extra help to ward off the evil eye. I figured it worked similar to the way garlic is used to ward off vampires. The bread and money were symbolic of giving alms to the less fortunate, my father-in-law continued, fingering them in the bowl, since humility is the ultimate way to ward off the evil eye.

Babaanne signaled to my mother-in-law, who approached with a bed sheet, gently pushed me to a seated position on the floor, and draped the sheet over my head and body.

In a whisper, *Babaanne* began to recite prayers in Arabic, and then I heard loud popping. It was the molten lead being poured by a shaky hand into the cool bowl of water directly above my head. I only had a sheet between my head and the skin-searing substance, so I sat completely motionless out of fear that fiery hot metal would drop on me. Then Koray pulled the sheet off and helped me up. They all crowded around the bowl that my father-in-law held, watching the lead cool. *Babaanne* fished the solid lead out of the water with knobby fingers and inspected it, explaining that the more jagged shards there were, the better, as apparently those are evidence that the sharp, hurtful intentions of the evil eye have been taken away and sealed into the lead for all eternity. My lead had quite a few jagged shards. This seemed to please *Babaanne*, who said that there was no doubt our bad luck was an act of the evil eye. Then she asked me to bow down, said a long prayer over me, and spat into the air three times. She performed the same ceremony on Koray.

After dinner Koray and I each went home with small cloth charms filled with the lead, bread, money, and onion, and we slept with them under our pillows for three days. At night in our little Arnavutköy loft, we would grin at each other before we lay our heads down on lumpy pillows, doing this exorcism together—not sure exactly why, but willing to believe for now. Our moods improved. We got up early on the third day to avoid the rambling crowds of fishermen, old men, and exercisers, and we marched down to the icy shores of the Bosphorus, our bundles like hot potatoes in our pockets. Together we tossed them into the swift-moving waters and watched our bad luck sink to the bottom, never to bother us again.

To our own amazement, the fridge began to work like a charm, the car hasn't needed further maintenance, the lights turn on when we flip the switch, and our lives have been nothing but marital bliss ever since.

Knock on wood.

NINE

Homespun Hospitality

Misafir perverlik, *traditional Turkish hospitality, is both legendary and inescapable, especially for expatriates who seek to challenge it.*

Rescued by Village Intelligence

BY CLAIRE UHR

I try desperately to fall asleep. My throat is raw, and every swallow brings a cry to my lips. I pray to God and then curse him for causing my pain. I attempt an "Our Father" prayer but get stuck on the seventh line. Having been lazy in my Catholicism since seventh grade at Saint Agatha's Primary back in Brisbane, I can't remember what comes after "as it is in Heaven." So I recite the abbreviated verse like a scratched CD, then give up, apologize to God for my waywardness, and plead for someone more earthly to rescue me instead.

Mentally flicking through my list of acquaintances in Turkey, I realize most of my help-in-a-crisis friends are on the coast, between Çanakkale and Antalya, where I worked as a tour guide until two months ago. But they are thousands of kilometers and another world away. In my new central Anatolian town of Göreme, whom do I know? Superficially, it seems like everyone in Cappadocia. But in a crisis? Making friends is a serious challenge in touristy Göreme's off-season, when I can count the number of people on the street on two hands. In between sips of tea at Mercan Restaurant, one of the few cafés still open on the main street during the off-season, the teenage waiters would teach me grammarless *Tarzanca* Turkish ("Me Tarzan. You Claire."). But I couldn't compromise their values by asking them to come to a single girl's house anyway. The teachers at my school—well, we try to socialize in between classes, but certainly not enough to have asked for phone numbers. And even if I did have a phone number to call, I don't have a phone. Some homes in Göreme have homing pigeons, but not mine.

A brief but vibrant image flashes before my eyes: my decayed twenty-seven-year-old body being found several weeks from now by my landlord when he comes to investigate why I haven't paid the rent. Shuddering, I return to my mental list of possible saviors. My newly ditched Turkish boyfriend? No, I

253

ditched him because of his unreliability and general lack of concern for me. He wouldn't be of any help. *Think, think, think!* I shriek internally. But I can't think of a single person who might search me out. Despite the bitingly cold weather and the thickening pile of snow outside my door, I am sweating. Burning up, I have no energy, and I know I am dying. Alone.

Moving to this town of three thousand at the beginning of winter, the plan was to experience Turkey at its most traditional. After the brash commercialism of the Aegean coast, I wanted to try living among a community less consumed by tourism, less prone to call after me "Aussie, Aussie, Aussie" based on my looks alone.

This cement box I call home, set amidst the moonlike, fairy-chimney landscape of Cappadocia, is the best I could do on a miniscule budget. Its triangular living room is the size of a windsurfing sail. A kitchen bench runs along one wall, and I have overlapped five threadbare Turkish rugs on the concrete floor to cut the cold underfoot. My now excommunicated boyfriend donated the grubby foldout sofa I'm lying on helplessly, as well as the coffee table, now filled with dirty plates. With the fridge against the wall, the tiny room is positively cluttered. But it has become my only living space, as winter has made the bedroom leading off it too cold to inhabit. That door is sealed, awaiting spring, which shows no promise of ever beginning.

The only other piece of furniture in the room is an old blackened coal stove with a tin pipe leading up out of it, precariously held by wire, running parallel to the wall and then right-angling up into the ceiling. Every night, I load dirty black lumps of coal and kindling into a bucket and dump it into the stove to burn. But I haven't mastered the art of lighting it, so I spend frustrating hours trying to keep the fire burning long enough for the coal to catch alight. I have discovered, by mistake, that spraying copious wafts of men's cologne into the bucket sometimes does the trick, although I haven't admitted that to the shopkeeper as I stock up on bottles of the stuff at the corner shop. I don't want anyone to know that the new foreigner in town is struggling with everyday life, although what he must think instead is probably far worse than the truth.

But for the last three days and nights, I haven't had the energy to stand up, let alone battle the stove. I'm too dizzy to shuffle around making tea or toast. And my medicine supplies haven't even dented the agony in my throat. In the room that has become my prison, I wish desperately for my illness to pass. The Lonely Planet guidebook and several assorted English course books lay discarded at arm's length—as my only choices of light reading, they fail dismally. I don't have a television, and my transistor radio has slowly died under the strain of the past twenty-four hours.

Today is the third day of surviving in my pajamas, damp with sweat, putrid and braless. I need a shower, but unless the weather is dead still, with no breeze and no rain, my gas hot-water system, plugged to the wall, won't light either. It seems most people in Göreme aren't concerned by several days without water to bathe anyway; they only get wet once a week in winter, according to the waiters at the café, who explained that for the rest of the week, villagers strip down to the last few layers of clothing at bedtime, and in the morning replace the same top layers.

This may be acceptable to them, but I am utterly miserable. I cry in bursts but become quickly exhausted, the exertion hurting my throat more. My bones ache, my eyes hurt, my thoughts have turned desolate. I am too ill to go in search of help, although my rented box is only two hundred meters from the town center, with its carpet dealerships and now boarded up cafés. The box is surrounded by a large expanse of uneven yard, but the worst of the weeds have long ago been hidden under snow. A long sinister black stain runs from my door, testament to the coal dust that I empty from my stove each morning. I know I should be more environmentally responsible and deposit the sinister dust in the rusting council barrels down the lane as I have seen the other villagers do, but I lost interest when faced with trudging further into the bitter cold. Around the yard is a high stone fence that's collapsing in places; a solid iron gate with a stiff catch serves as entry. I have twice been unable to open it, so it is now askew, and snow has piled up on both sides, so it can no longer be swung. But I forgive the house its grot because rising above it on all sides are magical fairy chimneys—giant anthills of creamy volcanic tufa, with peepholes and arched entrances gouged out by generations of cave dwellers, the Hittites, and then a few centuries of Christians fleeing marauding Arabs.

Now my windows are snowed over, the view forgotten. I fall into a depressed reverie, thinking longingly of my mother in Australia and the shiny packets of paracetamol fever-reducers she would line up on my bedside table. *Mum and Dad must be sleeping soundly in the sultry heat of their inner-city Brisbane terrace house right now,* I sniff. Then, as a shadow darkens the frosted glass of my door, I let out a scream. Was that a knock? It isn't my feverish imagination. Someone is outside.

I stand up, stabilize my dizzy head, and wrench open the door. A mustachioed man with almond brown eyes looks back at me. He wears no coat but dons coarse woolen trousers and a yellowing shirt. I glance down to confirm socks and sandals, the uniform of the traditional Turkish man in small towns. The man speaks slowly, but I still catch only a few words.

"Merhaba . . . komşunuzum" (Hello, I am your neighbor), he says with small measured gesticulations, pointing to a house up the road. *"Bir kaç günden beri sizi göremedik. İyimisin?"* He has noticed that I haven't come or gone from my home in several days. He wonders whether I am okay. Choking with emotion and embarrassment, I croak that I am fine and close the door in his face. I don't want him to see me burst into a flood of tears. Falling onto the sofa, I cry anew but try to check my tears when another knock sounds.

I gingerly unhitch the latch. The door is firmly pushed open and in marches the mustachioed man. Behind him in a train are four more people: a young woman in head scarf; a primary school–aged girl with lively, curious eyes; an older village woman; and a gray-haired, round-girthed man dressed like the first. They don't bother to introduce themselves; instead, they push me down on the sofa and lay out an array of food on my table. Lentil soup, an oily meat stew, fresh bread, and *yoğurt. "Ye,"* they order, urging me to eat. Stunned, I do as I am told. While I swallow the scratchy bread and slurp the hot liquids—both painful and relieving—the women begin washing days of dirty crockery in my sink, and the men busy themselves with my stove. The young girl just stands at my side, staring and occasionally stroking my arm. I feel self-conscious in my days-old pajamas, but they either don't notice or don't care. When I begin to cry silently in relief, they pretend not to notice that either.

After I have eaten all I can, they introduce themselves. They speak no English. The mustachioed man is Fatih; his young wife, wearing a mismatched floral blouse and baggy trousers, is Hanife; and the girl smiles widely as they present her as their daughter. The older couple are also apparently my neighbors; they live in the dilapidated farmhouse up the road. One family lives downstairs and the other upstairs. I struggle to recognize them. Apparently I have said hello to them in passing several times. But then I say hello to everyone I cross, and even the street dogs recognize my voice after eight weeks in town.

Kindness envelops me. They ask me questions, although they already seem to know so much. For instance, they know I am an English teacher working in a nearby village two days a week. They have seen me lugging bags of coal up the road. They know I have a Turkish boyfriend; they don't know I am not speaking to him any longer. Or maybe they do and are too polite to say. Either way, I prefer not to appear fickle with affection, so I don't correct them when they mistake the ring on my left hand as his instead of the family heirloom it actually is. They even know I have yet to make any real friends.

The older couple gently clothe me and help me out of my cement prison and up the road to their house, where they prepare a special medicinal tea and put me to bed. They sit with me on the bed watching an incomprehensible local soap opera on television, the only modern technology they appear to have in their one-room winter living quarters. Then they bring photos of a young man in military uniform, standing tall with his gun held proudly, and I share my stories of family with them as well. The story is well rehearsed on my part, having memorized the Turkish vocabulary after six months of living amidst curious Turks.

They gasp as I reveal my age and then mock me kindly, shaking their head and saying, *"Evde kaldın, evde kaldın."* I'm a girl left at home. They think I've been left on the marital shelf. Most local girls in town are married at eighteen. Then I explain that I am the youngest of four and that my other siblings are married with children. They are normal, if I am not. The fact that I have a big family seems to reassure them. With such little Turkish knowledge, nothing I say or understand is certain. But I watch their faces and weigh the emotion in their eyes. We all nod, cementing our kinship.

I recover. It was only a terrible flu. But I am now in the habit of visiting my neighbors every couple of nights; some nights sitting upstairs with Fatih and his family as he works his trade of mending and stitching carpets, his daughter playing with the markers and little whiteboard I have brought. Other nights I watch TV downstairs with the older couple in serene silence, drinking my specially brewed medicinal tea.

When the snow finally melts, I gather with the women in the garden and sort drying sultanas that are handpicked from the family garden up in the hills. We speak little, but grin largely. The sun grows stronger and the air warms. Then the locals begin to come out of hibernation, and the town buzzes again with the promise of a long and clear summer.

The Headman's Pajamas

BY JESSICA LUTZ

"*I*t's late," said Sheyhmus, looking up into a dark, star-punctured summer sky. "Time to get inside." The hour was barely seven, but here in Görümlü, a hamlet in the far reaches of southeastern Turkey, a machine-gun enforced curfew started shortly after sundown. This desolate spot, deep in the mountainous Kurdish borderlands with Iraq, was a world apart from my penthouse on the Asian shore of İstanbul, with its dreamy view of the Sea of Marmara and the green peninsula of Topkapı Palace. Instead of the continuous upbeat roar of the metropolis, here, silence made my ears ring. For now.

As we went inside, Sheyhmus seemed concerned, his grooved face furrowing deeper. A red-and-white checkered scarf was loosely wrapped around his head and was topped by a dark flat cap, the typical dress of Turkey's Kurds. "Where do you want to sleep?" he blurted out, clearly uncomfortable with the question. "You might feel better with the women, but then . . ." He paused, embarrassed. "I mean, you're different. You can stay here with us too."

The faces of Sheyhmus's six sons lit up expectantly. They had made themselves comfortable on flat cushions, which were spread out on the dark red, factory-made carpets that covered the floor. At their backs, a set of stiff pillows lined the bumpy mud-brick wall of the spacious living room.

Obviously, their father was a rich man by the standards of this Godforsaken mountainside near the town of Silopi. He had three wives and could afford to keep them under lock and key—not that any of the doors of the house actually needed to be bolted. The chains of tradition and the treachery of living in a war zone were enough to keep the women within their proscribed boundaries. I had spent hours on the veranda of his house, chatting with the menfolk of the village, without seeing wives or daughters—only a pair of female hands extending tray after tray of sweetened tea through a crack in a half-opened door to a young man who served it. Such segregation would be most unusual in the western part of Turkey, where village women work the fields and joke with the men, but here, some people still indulged in illegal polygamy and employed the most restrictive traditions of the harem. These men, even if monogamous, would have considered it an offense to drink tea with each other's wives, but due to the circumstances, I—a foreigner and a reporter—clearly defied categorization.

The year was 1993. The first half of the 1990s was a bad time for Turkey, and worse for the Turkish Kurds. Many of them had been seduced by the dream of an independent country. Naturally, the Turkish state defended itself against regional secession, but the rebels were tough. As a freelance journalist for Dutch- and English-language radio and newspapers, I traveled regularly to the region to cover this bitter war. On this particular trip, I had met Sheyhmus in Silopi, and he had brought me to his village. Now he was asking me where I wanted to sleep.

"Where are your wives?" I countered his question with my own.

"Ah yes, you're a woman," Sheyhmus replied pensively, as if he suddenly remembered that under normal conditions he would never sit in his living room, the men's domain, with a woman. "Why don't you go visit them?" he continued with an encouraging smile. So his eldest son, a slender boy of seventeen, took me to the women's quarters, which were forbidden to males other than those of the family.

I had to bow my head to get through the door, and I took a few steps down into a small room, in which the main feature was a huge, shiny, light blue refrigerator. Crouched at its base sat three women, dressed in bulky *şalvar* (trousers) of dark, flowered fabric. The stocky, round figures reminded me of pumpkins. While trying to keep rebellious strands of henna-red hair under their black head scarves, they pushed away the four or five children around them and spread thick gray blankets on the concrete floor.

"They're preparing their beds," the son explained to me. "They have to get up early to bake the bread and feed the animals."

I had always imagined the innermost part of a Muslim house to be luxurious, a place where a man could while away his leisure time with his wives. In the face of this poverty-ridden harem, I understood I had certainly read too many books romanticizing the East while studying Turkish literature and history at a university in my home country, Holland. There was nothing enchanting about this place.

As much a shock as it was to find their quarters to be so different from the Orientalist painting in my mind, my appearance must have been equally disconcerting. To these women, I must have looked like a space alien, with my field jacket full of pockets, bulging with the tools of my trade: microphone wires, pens, notebooks, and camera lenses.

A girl came in with a huge tray. She could barely lift it as she placed it in the corner of the room, on top of a television that I only now noticed. It was on, but the sound was switched off.

"Why's the sound off?" I asked. "Too busy to watch, I'll bet?"

The son laughed and said something in Kurdish to the women. It made them laugh too. "They'd love to understand what's going on in the soap," he translated. "They watch it every day, but it's in Turkish. So they make up the story themselves."

Like many others, these Kurdish women didn't speak Turkish because they were never sent to school. In university, I had mastered Turkish, which allowed me to communicate with their men, but all we women could do was smile hesitantly at each other, recognizing we had nothing in common—language being the least of it.

Still, I wasn't quite able to believe what the son was telling me. "So they sleep here, on the floor?" I asked, to be sure.

"Yes," the son nodded. "It's close to the courtyard where they do the cooking."

Indeed, a rough wooden door was all that divided them from the thick summer heat that hung between the courtyard walls, which had the pale color of bone-dry earth.

At dawn the next morning, I was to see the women out there—one of them was sweating above a small wood fire, over which a thin domed sheet of metal was placed. On it she slapped rounds of unleavened bread to cook.

In the shade of the corrugated roof that covered part of the courtyard and provided some coolness in the early hours, the two other wives helped each other lift heavy plastic drums of water off their shoulders onto the stamped earth. Each morning they filled the containers at the stream that ran through the village.

At first glance, it seemed life here had been the same for centuries. My arrival at their village, however, was a sign of the tremendous upheaval the whole region was experiencing.

A few days earlier, the atmosphere in the town of Silopi had been so tense that it had set the hair on my back tingling. People scurried around nervously, pressed to finish whatever business they had in town as quickly as possible. Traveling in the dark was extremely risky, because the rebels took control of the roads. During the day, at countless military roadblocks and checkpoints, vehicles were searched from top to bottom and the identity papers of every passenger were scrutinized, making any trip nerve-wracking. When I entered a teahouse, fourteen pairs of black eyes had met me with a suspicious glare.

Of course, this was a place reserved exclusively for men. Fair-haired, tight trouser–wearing women were a rare sight in teahouses, even in normal times. More upsetting for them was that I was obviously there to ask questions, when it was best not to talk in these troubled days. On previous reporting trips, people had asked me time and again: "What if the enemy reads what I said and comes to find me?" I would then explain it was highly unlikely that anyone involved in the conflict would read a Dutch newspaper, and that the news had to get out if they wanted the world to do something.

Apparently Sheyhmus had understood this even without my explanation. As I stood indecisively in the middle of the teahouse, he and two friends invited me to sit with them. With tears in their eyes, the three men were soon telling me of the disastrous impact of the war. The fruit trees of their village had been cut down. All of their wheat harvest had been burned. Then the major of the nearby military post informed the villagers they could no longer go up the mountain to let their animals graze, because the rebels might rustle the sheep to eat them.

The men insisted that I come see their besieged village. That would be hard. Because of the fighting, the government strictly forbade reporters from traveling into the countryside. Conspiring on stools around the low teahouse table, the men constructed a plan to get me there. One of them tensely jiggled his leg up and down. None of them had shaven in a while. Their faces were half-hidden behind the red-and-white checkered scarves loosely wrapped around their heads, topped by dark, flat caps, like Sheyhmus, whom they respectfully called *muhtar*, the elected headman of the village.

Out on the street, we split up as agreed. My companions vanished like bedbugs into a mattress, and after a moment's hesitation I walked off quickly in the opposite direction, careful not to trip over the pungent refuse littering the broken pavement. In the midst of a guerrilla war, nobody cared about cleaning up the streets. In a back alley, I found the three again; they were standing by one of the rickety minibuses that served as public transport. It was full of people and clearly waiting for me.

"I can't go in that," I protested, surprised at their naiveté. "I'd be picked out immediately at the first checkpoint."

My remark caused a buzz. The male passengers started whispering in Kurdish to each other, while a middle-aged, head-scarved woman invitingly patted the empty seat next to her.

"*Gel,*" Sheyhmus said. "Come on, get in. We've sorted it out," he urged. He was sitting in the front seat next to the driver. I sat behind him, squeezed in between the friendly woman and the skinniest of my three guides, who extended a hand with a grip like a vise.

"I'm Ali," he said, smiling. "Don't worry. We're taking an alternative route. We're not allowed to take this road anymore because it's dangerous, but there won't be any checkpoint. The driver says he knows where all the landmines are."

"Mines?" I squealed. I hadn't expected a busload of people to risk their lives, and mine, to smuggle me into their village. I wasn't prepared to die, but in the face of their courage, I could hardly turn back.

Sheyhmus looked around. "We'll be all right," he grinned, reassuring himself as well, no doubt.

Over a sandy trail through fields of wheat stubble that turned a warm gold in the glow of the lowering sun, we bumped toward the middle of nowhere. My heart was in my throat. It was impossible to spot anything irregular on this road, let alone landmines. Apart from us, of course. We must have stuck out like a red flag for any soldier with binoculars. I knew there were military lookout posts on many of the mountaintops. To be on the safe side, I dug out a black scarf from one of my pockets. It was part of my gear since, on a different trip, a local religious leader I wanted to interview demanded I cover my head before he'd speak to me. On the minibus, the woman next to me nodded in approval when I knotted it under my chin.

My fellow passengers seemed without a care and chattered all the way. Just over the first mountain pass, we rattled into the hamlet.

"Keep your head down," Sheymus suddenly hissed, and I struggled to disappear under the seat. The minibus stopped. Ali opened the door and beckoned me to follow him out. We hurried to the safety of a tiny alley. "We're nearly there, but there's a checkpoint in the middle of the village," he explained in a low voice. "We'll have to walk around it."

I had landed in the Middle Ages. A trickle of stinking sewage meandered through the narrow, unpaved alleyways. Barefoot children with crowns of uncombed hair and dirt-streaked faces were playing around it. A toddler dressed only in an oversized t-shirt squatted by the mud-brick wall of a house, defecated, and jumped up to continue chasing a scruffy chicken with a stick. A small boy spotted me and let out a yowl of delight. Within seconds, I was surrounded by a troop of children who pushed and stretched to press grubby fingers onto my camera lens. Ali shooed them away and quickly steered me into a doorway.

"The searching of the minibus will take a while," he said. "The soldiers check all our shopping. We're only allowed a certain amount of food per family to make sure no extras go to the rebels. Take off your shoes."

Here at Ali's cousin's, we were going to wait until the inspection of the minibus had finished. I crouched to undo my shoelaces. In the whole Muslim world, from the Mediterranean to China, shoes lined up by the front door are a familiar sight, a habit of domestic cleanliness maintained even in wartime. I wondered whether the children had to wash their feet before they were allowed to step on the threadbare carpets inside.

I exchanged formalities with Ali's cousin, who was just as skinny as he, and we sat down. The room was small and cavelike and had pillows along the wall. I noticed a swaddled bundle in the middle of the room. Our host followed my gaze. "My youngest child," he sighed. "She's ill. I don't know what to do about it."

"Isn't there a doctor in the village?" I asked.

"I don't have enough to feed the rest of my children," the man shrugged as I kneeled down by the baby. She was pale and ice cold. Her crying only produced the faintest of sounds.

"Can't you keep her warm at least?" I asked, eager to do something, even if I didn't know what.

Her father waved his hand in powerless resignation. "Without help, she's probably going to die. You can have her if you want."

That shocked me into silence. Was he serious? But what would I do with a baby—me, Ms. Independent, who had learned very quickly after moving to İstanbul how to deftly avoid the typical impertinent Turkish inquiries about my reproductive plans and tiresome advice about fertility. Where was the baby's mother anyway?

Ali had come to my rescue. "This lady is here on another mission. Let's have some tea, cousin, and then we should go," he said. A few minutes later, his cousin appeared with the first of many glasses of tea I was to drink in the village.

"The soldiers will be back at their post now," Ali said as we continued our way through the steep alleys.

"How far are they?" I gasped, breathless from carrying my reporter's gear in the heat. The village didn't seem that big, although it was hard to get an overview from between the walls.

Ali had snorted and pointed vaguely to the left. "The checkpoint is just there, over by the brook. Their post is above the village. They won't come out anymore until tomorrow. They're really afraid of us," he boasted, even though it seemed to me to be the other way around.

Our destination was the house of Sheyhmus. When we arrived, the veranda was already filled with men. In the shade of a corrugated metal lean-to trimmed by a vine, they sat upright, cross-legged. A vibrating shriek of crickets hung in the sweltering afternoon air as the men in the circle watched me take the place next to Sheyhmus. Then, one by one, with soft voices, they started to tell their sad stories, while I scribbled frantically. Soon my head was spinning.

"We're innocent. We're not helping the rebels, honestly," they kept saying, inhaling nervously the acrid smoke of cheap tobacco. Although I was a smoker myself and we were in the open air, that afternoon I felt sick. Each man must have smoked at least three packs of cigarettes. It was only later, after they left and the poisonous cloud of tar and nicotine lifted, that I became aware of the sharp smell of a small herd of sheep, condemned by the war to live in a stable under the veranda.

At dusk a large meal of rice and mutton appeared. Hungrily we all dug in with our fingers. As the guest of honor, I got the first pick, then Sheyhmus had a go, and soon there were only a few bony pieces left on the savaged heap of rice. The tray was then sent back to be finished off by those inside, the women and children of the house. I felt sorry for them and hoped at least the children had had a chance to nibble on some of the meat before it had been devoured by the ravenous pack around me on the veranda. I figured it was not often they ate meat.

A few men belched appreciatively after the meal, as they do in the East, and lit yet more cigarettes. Enjoying the silence, I looked up at the stars. My Turkish husband back in İstanbul was probably eating out with some friends in a *meyhane* restaurant by the seaside, feasting on exquisitely prepared fish, or squid, or roasted eggplant. He had no desire to travel the east of his country and could hardly believe what I, a foreigner, told him about it. I wondered whether he could have enjoyed the crude meal I had just consumed.

That's when Sheyhmus declared it was bedtime. "Let's go inside," I heard him say. "Normally we sleep on the roof in summer, but that has become too dangerous with all the shooting."

We said goodbye to the men who had come to share their stories. Once inside, I was confronted with a confounding decision: where to sleep. Surely the proper thing to do was to join the women. I regarded the red carpets and the thin mattresses Sheyhmus's sons were laying out in the men's quarters. I considered the women's quarters, where the concrete floor by the refrigerator had just a blanket to cushion it. I was ashamed by my lack of fortitude. Had I known Kurdish, I would have gone to the women, I told myself to justify my conclusion.

"There's hardly any space in the kitchen," I said sheepishly.

"It's more comfortable here," Sheyhmus agreed. "I and my sons will go to one end of the room so you can have the other." He disappeared briefly and came back with a bunch of white bedclothes, which he shyly pushed into my hands.

Shortly after I lay back on my bed in a corner, an explosive rattle of a machine gun not far away made me bolt upright. "Lie down and keep away from the window!" Sheyhmus warned from the other end of the room. "The soldiers are supposed to shoot over our houses. It's just a measure to keep us inside and the rebels away, but sometimes the bullets stray. One of my cows got killed that way. The wall will protect you, though." As I tried to ignore the sound of the gun and the occasional thump of a bullet that hit the wall, I swallowed hard and felt grateful for not having been born in a Kurdish village.

Two years later I was in Silopi again. The war was raging with full force, making it even more difficult to travel or gather information, but I decided to try my luck. To my astonishment, I was able to drive up to Sheyhmus's hamlet without being stopped. At his house, the local army commander was sipping tea. Pretending I didn't know Sheyhmus, not wanting to implicate him, I greeted the headman. He welcomed me with a broad smile.

"I remember," he said. "You were here when we still supported the rebels." As my cheeks went red, he turned to the major and continued, "We smuggled her in, you know. She stayed the night."

The major smiled benignly. "Thank God such things are no longer necessary now that you support the state," he said.

"A state for ourselves would have been great, you know," Sheyhmus added to my amazement. "But the rebels weren't strong enough. And they started kidnapping our children to make fighters of them. That was the limit."

The Turkish State showed its presence in Görümlü with a small dispensary, built and manned by the army. A school was on its way. Food was no longer rationed, Sheyhmus updated me. Then he began to chat about me to the major as if I were an old friend.

Bewildered, I slowly realized that this apparent change of heart was an opportunistic flexibility that had also made him put aside the region's strict rules regarding women during my first visit. With my behavior of traveling alone, smoking, and freely interacting with the village men, I broke all taboos. But I was a woman with a difference—a foreign reporter—and they had needed me to get their story out.

Most of all, however, Sheyhmus made me understand that Turkish hospitality overrides all other possible concerns. No matter how odd or inconvenient— or even potentially dangerous—a visitor is a guest from God. During that frightening curfew two years before, Sheyhmus had honored this principle with his awkward offer of the white bundle: They were his own pajamas for me to sleep in.

Hijacked

BY KATHLEEN HAMILTON GÜNDOĞDU

*W*hen I set out alone on a trip across Turkey in 1981, friends and family thought I was insane. What kind of foolhardy twenty-three-year-old American woman plunges into a country in the grips of civil unrest? I decided to go in spite of all the well-meaning warnings and pleas to consider a safer place to vacation. Perhaps being a rough-and-tumble Texan who could rope cattle gave me a sense of self-reliance, though my six-foot stature was enough for people to assume I was more imposing a figure than I actually was, and they gave me a wide berth.

My first stop was Konya, in order to visit the tomb of the Sufi poet Rumi and to witness the Whirling Dervishes of Turkey. None of my friends were interested in either the 13th-century mystic poet or the turning ceremony performed by men in long robes and high hats, but I didn't mind. I enjoyed traveling on my own.

Foreigners on intercity buses in Turkey were a rarity at the time. The trip from İstanbul to Konya, in central Anatolia, took twelve hours, so during the tedious, dictionary-intensive conversations with fellow travelers to pass the time, everyone on the bus soon knew I was an American traveling alone, that I was going to Konya, and what hotel I'd be staying at. In those years, even a Turkish woman traveling by herself was an anomaly. Consequently, by custom and for the woman's comfort, only another woman or child could sit next to a lone female passenger. Therefore, I was seated directly behind the driver, with two seats to myself.

The long overnight trip obscured the landscapes speeding past in the darkness. I'd memorized my guidebook's images of towns that were now only reflective green highway signs on the night road south: rolling green mountains of Bolu, dusty pine forests of Ankara, dry, craggy steppes near Konya.

After many rest stops at bus company–owned restaurants, we finally arrived before dawn at the Konya station. While the other passengers quickly disembarked and collected their baggage from the hold, the driver refused to let me depart, insisting I stay on board. I was confused. Maybe this wasn't Konya. It was still dark outside, and I had dozed off right before we arrived. Maybe I was supposed to get off at the next stop. I had to think fast before he and the bus left the station. I fumbled deep in my purse for my dictionary as I tried to communicate with him.

"I have to get off here! Here! I must get off!" I said, pointing to the bus terminal.

He didn't understand me. I didn't know any Turkish, couldn't find my dictionary, and my frantic glances around the station told me all the other passengers had promptly claimed their bags and dispersed. I was left alone on the bus. This wasn't right. The bus driver stepped off the bus, took my bag from the luggage hold, and put it on the floor next to my seat. He then closed the bus doors, and off we drove.

"Excuse me, but I want to get off in Konya! Is this Konya? Where are you taking me?!" I had trouble controlling the tremor in my voice, trying to get the bus driver to answer in some way that I could understand. He only replied quickly in Turkish and continued driving, seemingly oblivious to my concern.

I started recalling all the stories I had ever been told about women being abducted and disappearing. Was this how it started? We turned north, back out of town. It wasn't that I had to get off at the next stop. We weren't heading toward the next stop.

As the bus wound through consecutively smaller streets, my doubts seemed to be confirmed. I quickly lost any sense of direction and knew that there was no way I could find my way back to the bus station. We were in a residential neighborhood, and since it wasn't yet seven in the morning, no one was on the streets. I sat back and tried to look relaxed in case he looked in his rearview mirror—I didn't want him to know I was on to him—but inside I was in a state of panic. I began trying to figure out how to get away from the bus driver when we stopped. Surely he was up to no good.

Though the day would be hot, it was still cold and dark, and I started shivering from the morning chill and my rising adrenaline. After about twenty minutes of driving down progressively narrower rural roads, with me carefully trying to memorize landmarks for my escape, we stopped in front of a small house. The driver motioned to me to stay on the bus while he went to the door of the house. Was that where he was going to hold me? I considered making a break for it. He began banging on the door and yelling. Not good. I crept down the stairs of the bus and peered out of the door, trying to decide which direction would offer the best escape—back where we came from, or somewhere out into the beyond? A man's head popped out of the upstairs window of the house. How far could I get carrying my purse and heavy suitcase? I couldn't leave my suitcase—it had my plane tickets in it. *Open it quickly, Kathy. Get your ticket and just start running,* I thought as my hands fumbled clumsily over the clasps of my suitcase.

I looked back at the house. The man and the driver conferred for a minute, and then a woman stuck her head out the window and looked at me poised in the door of the bus. I paused. What was a woman doing there? The man and the woman both withdrew their heads from the window, and a few moments later, at the sound of a latch being drawn, the downstairs door was opened. The man and woman motioned for me to get off the bus and quickly come into their house. I would have to; I couldn't yet get the clasp open on my suitcase. Hesitantly I made my way toward the house, hoping that with another woman in the house I would be safe. Unless, of course, she was in on whatever plan they were hatching.

Their modest house was, like the other houses we passed, a nondescript concrete block that looked mint green under the fluorescent streetlight. I was shown to the living room, where the modest furnishings included a table with plastic tablecloth, white plastic patio furniture chairs, woven carpets on the floor, and a wood-burning stove in the middle of the room.

Thankfully, the man started loading and lighting the stove. I was freezing. I told myself to memorize every detail of the room and the appearances of these people in case I would need to testify about them later. The woman motioned for me to sit down, and I chose the chair closest to the door, just in case I needed to quickly bolt. The woman went into the kitchen, and soon I could smell eggs and sausage cooking while the two men continued talking to each other and glancing at me. Minutes later, the woman brought in tea for all of us to drink. Finally after a glass of tea, the man whose house I was in began to talk in halting English.

"My name Mustafa." He pointed to the woman. "Wife Meryem." He indicated the bus driver. "My friend bringing you my house for waiting. Now eating."

That's it? What did he mean? I didn't know what we were supposed to be waiting for, but my growling stomach made the decision for me, and for the time being, I stayed put. Whatever was going to happen to me, let it happen on a full stomach. I would need my strength.

Meryem brought in a huge breakfast of fried eggs, cheese, olives, meat, and bread. My wariness must have excited my appetite, because I couldn't stop eating. It was delicious. At this rate I would be too full to run. I glanced warily over each bite but mostly kept my head down. I was still unsure why I was there, so the meal was consumed hastily, in a tense silence.

Finally, after finishing breakfast, Mustafa began again, "You foreigner. My friend bringing you my house because. You alone, and you don't know things."

I swallowed hard on my last sip of tea. I wondered what he was trying to get at. What didn't I know? That I was about to be sold? Kidnapped? Ransomed? Worse?

"Your hotel not opening this time, my friend say," explained Mustafa. "Doorman not going work this time. Too early. He bringing you my house because I speaking English and my wife feeling you safe. No sitting street waiting doorman. No good. You need eating."

My face flushed hot with shame. I clapped my hand to my mouth. How could I have such suspicions about the driver and his intentions? I shook hands with Mustafa, his wife, and the driver, thanking them profusely for their kindness, with tears of embarrassment and relief barely blinked back. God, did they know what I'd been thinking about them?

Now very relieved that I hadn't made a scene or a mad dash down a deserted street, I thought back on the trip, remembering that the driver had gone out of his way to ensure that a female passenger showed me to the ladies' room at each rest stop, and that he had seated me with a family to drink tea with before reboarding the bus. He had been looking after me all along and didn't feel that his job had ended when we'd reached the bus station. Instead, he had extended the Turkish hospitality my guidebook kept mentioning by looking after me and making sure that I wouldn't be left unprotected on the street in the brisk, predawn air, waiting for the hotel to open.

Reassured, I untensed my knotted muscles and sat back in conversation with my Good Samaritans as I began to answer their many questions about life in America and about my travels through Turkey. Three hours later, with a full stomach, a relieved mind, and some new friends, the bus driver and I boarded the bus again. I waved goodbye to my kind benefactors, Mustafa and Meryem, and the driver took me directly to my hotel.

His service didn't stop there. When we arrived, he carried my bags inside, and confirmed with the clerk that my room was ready so that I wouldn't have to sit in the lobby by myself. Confident that he had finally secured all possible comforts for me and had safely delivered me to my destination, the driver was satisfied that his duty was finished. He shook my hand and boarded his bus. With a wave, my thoughtful hijacker drove off.

Failed Missionary

BY RHONDA VANDER SLUIS

"**W**hy did you choose Turkey?"

I get asked that question a lot, after an effusive recitation of the highlights of eight years I spent living and working there, after running on about my adopted Turkish family and my recent and upcoming trips back to visit them, trips that are never more than six months apart.

I hesitate. Do they really want to know? Or, more to the point, do I really want to tell them? Should I get into the missionary stuff? I'm a little bit embarrassed to admit it, but the reason I went to Turkey in the first place was to evangelize Muslims—"unreached peoples," in missionary lingo. I had done a stint in Pakistan and was uncomfortable with the restrictions imposed by a strict Islamic state. Turkey was more modern, easier; you didn't have to wear a head covering and could move about quite freely as a single woman. But I would still be bringing the message of salvation to the group of people that, at least in the eyes of my mission superiors, needed it the most.

Because proselytizing in Turkey was illegal, I had to come up with some other convincing story for why I had left a lucrative nursing career in the States. "To learn Turkish," I insisted brightly to anyone who asked. I misinterpreted their polite silence and subsequent "Don't ask, don't tell" indulgence of me, thinking they had fallen for my ruse. As it turned out, my long denim jumpers and conservative lifestyle marked me as a religious worker anyway; the only one I was really fooling was myself.

Living with a Turkish family was encouraged by my mission organization as an excellent way to learn the culture along with the language. After securing a spot in a Turkish language school, I turned to my church colleagues for advice on finding a suitable family. Katie, a missionary veteran, was quick to oblige. "Mustafa *amca* and Gülsüm *teyze;* they're the sweetest couple," gushed Katie, using the Turkish honorifics for "aunt" and "uncle" out of respect for their age. "Their son is getting married, and they want to rent out a room for extra cash. It'd be a perfect place for you."

Katie arranged to accompany me and the mission director's wife to the family's four-story concrete walkup apartment, minutes from İstanbul's bustling city center of Taksim. We were met at the door by Gülsüm *teyze*—smooth-faced, gracious, with a head scarf tied neatly under her chin. Mustafa *amca*, right behind her, was tanned and handsome, with a striking white mustache. They ushered me to a spot behind the chunky living room table, where I sat, wedged up against the wall, with no avenue for escape. The two women I came with chatted amiably with our hosts. I understood nothing. As we were leaving, they showed us the room where I would be staying. It was no more than ten feet by ten feet, with a foldout divan shoved up against the back wall and a round metal table, with an oversized television set on it, squeezed in between the door and the bed. A cheap, fiberboard chest of drawers leaned precariously against the other wall. I disguised my dismay at the bleakness of the tiny space with an enthusiastic nod, and with that, the deal was sealed.

Two days later, while unpacking my meager belongings, I paused to pray for God's blessings on this momentous beginning to my fledgling missionary career. I asked God to protect me from the influence of the Muslim faith, which I had been programmed to believe was Satan-inspired and dangerous. I asked God to use me to draw this family closer to Him through Jesus Christ. It never occurred to me that perhaps some members of this family were closer to God than I was, or that they just might be more in tune with the spirit of Jesus's teachings than most Christians. This proselytizer was about to meet her match.

Gülsüm and Mustafa were a modest, hardworking couple with roots in a southern mountain village just north of Antalya. They had recently retired from the *yoğurt*-making business and were now reinvesting a good portion of their prodigious energy into making me feel welcome. As an American whose mother had long since ceased to interfere in her personal life, the intense nature of the attention was a bit overwhelming for me. Suddenly, I had someone who was concerned with the state of my ovaries; if I didn't keep my slippers on, I would freeze the fragile organs and forfeit my life purpose of having babies. I quickly became a member of the Impossible to Clean Your Plate Club. Until I learned to pat my tummy and insist emphatically, at least three times in succession, that I was indeed full to bursting—*Doydum!*—the portions kept on coming. And it was very difficult to get any time alone.

There is a word for privacy in the Turkish language, but in this household, it remained a vague concept, not a practical reality. People simply did not spend time alone behind closed doors unless they were sleeping or dead, or engaged in some kind of unmentionable activity. Five minutes after arriving home and collapsing on my bed, I would hear a gentle *tap, tap, tap*. *"Gel çay var"* (Come have tea). Determined not to cause offense, and lacking the language skills to defend my need for downtime, I would join Gülsüm *teyze* for five o'clock tea, or *beş çayı*, as it is affectionately known among the Turks.

Initially, our conversations were limited to my halting replies to her gentle, simply phrased queries: "What did you do today? Where did you go? Who did you see?" Before long, she had coaxed out my entire life history—my family back home, my life as a nurse, my daily routines, and the names and foibles of all my friends. She was a shrewd judge of character, with a calm authority and quiet wisdom that belied her humble village origins. I was becoming as addicted to her wry humor and insightful social commentary as I was to the hot fragrant Turkish tea.

Soon, I was bringing home friends in long denim jumpers to meet her—friends who had also, coincidentally, moved to Turkey "to learn Turkish." Aside from general references to "the church," we were careful not to volunteer any information about our real agenda, and Gülsüm *teyze* never asked. She welcomed us warmly, as individuals, with impeccable Turkish hospitality. I felt nurtured and loved in a completely unexpected and wonderful way.

The rest of the family was just as welcoming. The older son, Hasan, lived downstairs with his wife, Nazmiye, and their four-year-old daughter, Sinem; the younger son, Mehmet, and his new wife, Dilek, lived upstairs. They all absorbed me easily into the rhythm of family life, except for Sinem, who sensed a threat to her position as the house sovereign and center of attention. But it didn't take her long to discover my value as a live-in playmate, and soon my room was even less private than before. She chattered on in simple, understandable Turkish, unconsciously correcting my imprecise phraseology. It was the perfect way to learn and gave me the courage to tackle conversations with the adults.

Tentatively, I joined them for evenings in front of the television set, watching maudlin Turkish movies and raucous comedy skit shows, drinking more cups of piping hot tea. At first, I politely excused myself at ten o'clock sharp, exhausted from the mental effort of trying to pluck a few meaningful words from the swirling soup of conversation that flowed about me. But gradually, my bedtime became more flexible as I began to relax, basking in the simple warmth and lively camaraderie of a close-knit Turkish family. I was given a Turkish name—Rezzan, and a family position as *hala*, the paternal aunt. It was feeling more and more like home.

But wait, I was here to evangelize. I couldn't sit around all day drinking tea and watching television. I had to justify my existence to the eager supporters back home. We had all decided that these people were lost; it was up to me to bring them the message of salvation. Trouble was, it was more often me who needed the rescuing.

One sweltering August day, we went to a relative's home for a *mevlut*, a ceremony of thanksgiving that is held forty days after the birth of a baby. As the major attraction, upstaging even the baby, I was fawned over and passed from person to person—no doubt so everyone could share equally in the humor of my mangled Turkish. The room was filling up; every seat around the edge of the room was occupied, mostly with hefty matrons clad in the silk head scarves and long raincoats that constitute one of the more popular uniforms of conservative Muslim women in this country.

"Otur!" (Sit!), commanded one of the raincoats. She pulled me down to the springy sofa cushion between herself and her amply proportioned mother and handed me a head scarf. It was then that I realized that I was about to take part in a Muslim prayer session. I glanced around in panic, looking for my handlers. Just then, the cadence of Arabic prayers began.

The two women next to me wiped their faces with their hands and raised them to Allah, indicating that I should do the same. I panicked. I was a Christian. I couldn't pray to Allah. Or could I? I didn't want to be impolite, but I didn't want to betray Jesus either. Was I supposed to take a stand for Jesus? Confused, I covered my head awkwardly and tried to block out the incomprehensible drone of Koranic recitation. I repeated Bible verses silently to myself, praying furiously for God to forgive me for any real or potential transgressions.

After what seemed like an eternity, the prayers ended, and glass party plates with tightly wrapped stuffed grape leaves and stale breadsticks started arriving. I bolted from the sofa, desperate to escape from the heat and the humiliation of my predicament. I pressed through the crush of bodies, looking desperately for a familiar face. Where were they? Where was my family? By then I was sobbing, completely unable to articulate my angst to any of the concerned faces around me. Then, my savior Nazmiye appeared. Without a word, she whisked me off to a cool dark corner of the house, where I could rest and compose myself. She kept the curious well-wishers at bay, slipped me some grape leaves and a cola, and, in the process, taught me a gentle lesson about compassion.

Other lessons were forthcoming. All of the good Christian values that I had been led to believe were the result of Jesus's transformative power were alive and well in the lives of this typical Turkish family. They weren't acting like they were "lost."

Service. The motto of my mission organization was "We take servanthood seriously." That could've been Mustafa *amca*'s motto. He rose selflessly before anyone else to build a fire in the wood stove every morning and would run to get the bread from the bakery up the road when those younger and healthier were too tired. He insisted on being the one to stand in line to pay the electric and phone bills and would heave my oversized suitcases up three flights of stairs when I arrived back from vacations, despite my protests. In a society where male machismo behavior is common, Mustafa *amca* regularly took up the teakettle and served the rest of us.

Stewardship of God's gifts. Nothing was wasted in this household; all of our casual discards were carefully stowed away in the "flea market," the upstairs bedroom of their village home, awaiting careful allocation to people in need. Gülsüm *teyze* knew which young man needed a suit of clothes for a job interview, which construction worker's wife had just given birth to triplets, what little boy needed a toy car or a pair of socks.

God's provision. "God provides for my needs before I even ask him," Gülsüm *teyze* once marveled, unconsciously repeating a Bible verse that I thought was the exclusive province of Christianity. "Just last week I realized that I needed a rug for that space in front of the washing machine, and this week your friend Ruth gave me one that is the perfect size." I remember my surprise at hearing a Muslim pray to God for mundane things in the same way that we Christians did.

Justice. Gülsüm *teyze* told me the story of their hired hand, who, after many years of faithful service, absconded with their butter machine, forcing them to shutter the family *yoğurt* business they had run for thirty years. Their son Hasan was furious and wanted revenge. Gülsüm and Mustafa decided to leave the matter in God's hands. A familiar Bible verse came to mind: "Vengeance is mine, says the Lord. I will repay." Sure enough, years later, the man turned up on their doorstep, ruined and begging for forgiveness. "You sinned against God," they said. "Go to God for forgiveness."

Patience and kindness. Learning a language is a humiliating experience. It is also a very tedious process for the people who have to listen to you. The temptation to make fun can be irresistible. My family worked overtime to unobtrusively run interference for me in interactions with relatives, interpreting the intended meanings of my half-sentences and mispronunciations. I felt like an autistic child with a special language that only the close family members could understand. But they never laughed at me.

Eventually, my Turkish did improve, and we were able to talk about deeper, more important things. One late night, between more sips of more hot tea, Nazmiye popped the question, "Just what do you mean when you say that Jesus is the Son of God?"

There it was, my opportunity! Missionaries live for questions like that. In my head, I quickly reviewed the main points of my trusty Four Spiritual Laws booklet, the missionary shortcut guide to salvation: "God loves you; God has a plan for your life. We have all sinned...." But no, there was no textbook answer for the kinds of questions that we were discussing. We were fellow seekers, trying to understand the mysteries of the universe. I struggled to find the right words in Turkish, in any language, to explain the doctrine of the Trinity.

Nazmiye was eager to help. "God has a son whose mother is a virgin?" she prompted. "So he is half-man, half-god?" Her eyes widened, and she cocked a skeptical eyebrow at my subsequent explanation.

"All god, all man? How can that be?" She eyed me quizzically. I shrugged helplessly. Doctrines like this, it seemed, made a lot more sense in the church pews of my youth than they did in an İstanbul living room.

Nazmiye and I had other conversations. About prayer. About religious piety and rampant hypocrisy in the fundamentalist sects of our respective faith traditions. About heaven and hell.

"Christians believe that all Muslims are going to hell, and Muslims believe all Christians are going to hell," observed Nazmiye wryly. It was a turning point for both of us, as we realized that neither one of us was willing to consign the other to eternal damnation, as the tenets of our respective religions demanded. Cracks in my airtight belief system started to appear, as I found myself face-to-face with a Muslim individual who was anything but "dangerous" or "evil." We were partners on a sacred adventure, probing the reaches of our understanding, speaking honestly of what we truly believed and allowing space for mystery in those areas where we weren't quite sure.

As my worldview and my understanding of the meaning of spirituality was expanding, my life as a missionary was becoming increasingly constricting and, in a word, exhausting. Sunday was anything but a day of rest, full to the brim as it was with church services, postchurch tea-and-biscuit duty, and assorted committee meetings and social obligations. By this point, I had a job working as a nurse at the American Consulate, but my days off were not for me; they were devoted to "ministry," a euphemism for "taking care of everyone but yourself." As my experience with the language and culture increased, so did my responsibilities.

"You're doing too much," said the family. "Come home and rest."

"Can't you do one more thing?" said the church. "We can't find anyone else to organize the food at the Spring Fair."

I was also tired of living a double life. Before, I was a missionary masquerading as an ordinary citizen. Now, I felt like an ordinary citizen masquerading as a missionary. While I had a great deal of love and respect for many of my missionary compatriots, I no longer shared their zeal for conversion of the so-called heathen. The Turks that I had come to know in my new family circle had a vibrant spirituality that infused their daily lives with meaning and served as an example to me. The God that I was coming to know was too big for the boxes that fundamentalist Christianity wanted to put him in. I was no longer sure what I believed, and I was tired of feeling like a hypocrite.

The growing crisis of integrity, aggravated by an impossible workload, resulted in an emotional meltdown. It happened one morning in church. Exhausted after a late night ministering to a neighbor woman dying of cancer, I had wearily settled myself into a pew after the morning service to administer hepatitis B injections to a newly arrived missionary couple. A harried church member came running up, brochure in hand, saying "Rhonda, it's Spring Fair time!" The next thing I knew, I was stumbling out of the building in tears, fleeing to the one place that I knew I would find rest and comfort and unconditional love. I needed to be with people who loved me for who I was, not for what I could do for them. The family.

Within the week, my Turkish family had spirited me away to their mountain village home for a much-needed rest. I lazed on the sofa, sleepy from the wood-stove heat, my tummy full of Gülsüm *teyze*'s famous eggplant *kebap*. Mustafa *amca* hovered attentively, filling my teacup and ensuring that the biscuits were within my reach. I gazed out the window into the swirling snow and thought about my future. I didn't want to leave Turkey. I didn't want to leave this family. But the suffocating demands of my life in İstanbul and my growing disaffection for missionary life were taking an emotional and physical toll. I vowed to change my habits. I would delegate more of my responsibilities. I would do whatever I had to do to be able to stay.

But it was not to be. When I returned to İstanbul, I developed a severe case of bronchitis that threatened to land me in the hospital. When I got the news that my mother had been diagnosed with cancer, I knew that it was useless to fight anymore. God was emphatic; my dysfunctional Christian service in Turkey was over. Anger, confusion, sadness, relief—a storm of emotion clouded my memories of those final days in İstanbul and continued to dog me in the ensuing months as I tried to make sense of my experience.

I had joined the evangelical Christian movement when I was a junior in college, as part of a general search for belonging and meaning. Emotionally immature and accustomed to acquiescing to authority, I absorbed the doctrines and teachings of the faith without question. I progressed through the ranks to what I considered to be the pinnacle of Christian service—missionary work abroad. I had come to Turkey with the best of intentions, as an idealistic do-gooder. Pressuring people to change their religious faith was never part of my strategy; I believed in the power of personal example and the ability of God's spirit to change people for the better. I never expected that the most powerful personal examples would be those lived in front of me by Muslim friends. I never could have guessed that the person who would be changed for the better would be me.

I had failed as a missionary. But I didn't feel like a failure in the eyes of God. I had forged a bond of mutual love and respect with my Turkish family that transcended cultural and religious differences, as well as a formidable language barrier. My own understanding of spirituality had been radically transformed. Thanks to Turkey and this special Turkish family, there was one more citizen of the world celebrating the validity of the many diverse roads to God. And there was one less fundamentalist Christian, insisting on just one path.

Pronunciation Guide

a short 'a' as in 'father.' Example: *merhaba* (hello), pronounced MEHR-hah-BAH.

e as in 'send' or 'tell.' Example: *yedi* (seven), pronounced YEH-di.

i 'ee' as in 'see.' Example: *iyi* (good), pronounced ee-YEE.

ı 'uh' as in 'fuss' and 'plus.' Example: *hayır* (no), pronounced HAY-uhr.

o as in 'phone.' Example: *yok* (there isn't; no), pronounced YOHK.

ö as in 'annoy.' Example: *göbek* (center; stomach), pronounced goe-BEHK.

u 'oo', as in 'food' or 'blue.' Example: *doydum* (I'm full), pronounced doy-DOOM.

ü as in 'screw' or 'cute.' Example: *güle güle* (goodbye), pronounced gew-LEY gew-LEY.

c 'j' as in 'jet' and 'jar.' Example: *cadde* (street), pronounced JAHD-dey.

ç 'ch' as in 'church' and 'chatter.' Example: *çay* (tea), pronounced CHAI.

g always hard, as in 'go,' never soft, as in 'gentle.' Example: *garson* (waiter), pronounced gahr-SOHN.

ğ never pronounced. It serves to lengthen the preceding vowel. Example: *doğu* (east), pronounced doh-OOH.

h as in 'half' and 'high.' Never silent. Example: *hamam* (bath), pronounced ha-MAHM.

j 'zh' like the 'z' in 'azure.' Example: *jurnal* (diary), pronounced zhoor-NAHL.

s 's' as in 'stress.' Never 'zzz' as in 'tease.' Example: *saz* (lute-like instrument), pronounced SAHZ.

ş 'sh' as in 'show' and 'should.' Example: *teşekküler* (thanks), pronounced TEH-shey-KOOWR-ler.

v a soft 'v' sound, halfway to 'w.' Example: *var* (there is), pronounced VAHR.

About the Contributors

A native of Pakistan, **Mahira Afridi-Perese** grew up in Karachi and the United Arab Emirates. Her love affair with Turkey began in 1994, when she visited İstanbul on a family holiday. Five years later, she met her Turkish American husband on a blind date in New York City. In 2002, after earning a graduate degree in international affairs from the Johns Hopkins School of Advanced International Studies, in Washington, D.C., she worked in Cairo researching migration issues in the Middle East at the International Organization for Migration. In 2003, Mahira and her husband moved to İstanbul, where she now looks forward to focusing on migration issues concerning Turkey and the surrounding region.

Archaeologist **Maureen Basedow** has been working at Troy since 1990 and spent three years in Anadoluhisar, İstanbul, as a Fulbright fellow. She met and married her architect husband, Lynn, in İstanbul. Both Americans, they consider Turkey "home" and relive their romance with the country, its people, and each other every time they visit. Currently a professor of classics at Miami University in Ohio, near Cincinnati, Maureen can frequently be found preparing lectures while listening to Turkish music on her iPod.

Ever since her first international trip, at age fourteen, unaccompanied by parents, traveling the world has been a life goal of **Catherine Salter Bayar**. She developed her skills as a designer just for the opportunity to spend time observing cultures in faraway places. A childhood in Santa Barbara, California, gave her an appreciation for balmy climates and Mediterranean architecture, so she quickly felt at home in Turkey. Catherine and her husband, Abit Bayar, own a vintage textile shop and Turkish wine house in the Aegean town of Selçuk, where they now travel the world vicariously through the visitors they meet.

After having studied music for two years at an Ohio university, a chance meeting with a Turkish man changed **Katherine Belliel**'s life and prompted her to earn her degree in history from Eastern Michigan University. Katherine left her native city of Grand Rapids, Michigan, in 2003 for an exciting new life in İstanbul, where she currently resides in the seaside district of Tarabya, spending her time researching Turkish history and culture.

Diane Caldwell's primal language is dance. She has performed and choreographed throughout the United States. Diane began writing poetry at the age of fourteen and ran away from her home in Philadelphia, Pennsylvania, at sixteen, to hang out with the Beat poets of New York City. She has been writing ever since, and her works have been published in New York and in Seattle, where she lived for twenty-two years before moving to Turkey. In Seattle, Diane worked as a professional actress for twelve years, followed by a decade as a psychotherapist. She plans to spend her next ten years in İstanbul, teaching English, writing about her experiences, and dancing to Gypsy music.

Amanda Coffin grew up in coastal Maine, moving just a bit south to complete a fascinating and impractical degree in linguistics from Wellesley College. She drifted into a technology career, which amused her for twenty years. That was enough. Now she lives a footloose life overseas and revels in her uprootedness. She has paused in Southeast Asia at the moment, catching up on her reading, knitting, painting, and wandering. Studying yoga in Sri Lanka and raising llamas in Chile are still on her to-do list, unchecked.

Ana Carolina Fletes was born and raised in Guatemala until the age of seven, when her family emigrated to the United States. At seventeen, she came to Turkey as an exchange student at the French-language high school Galatasaray. She studied political science at the University of California, Berkeley. Ana married a Turk and lived in İstanbul for six years, where her Turkish mother-in-law, an erudite television and radio personality, taught her to speak Turkish with an unrivaled accent. Currently she lives in San Francisco and works for a Latino contemporary art gallery. She hopes to make films about women in the Middle East.

Wendy Fox was born and raised in Tonasket, Washington, a rural agricultural town in the north-central region of the state. After she completed her MFA and taught for a year in the Spokane Community College district, she moved to

Kayseri, where she instructed English and literature at Erciyes University. She also lived in İstanbul, working at a private university. She currently resides in Seattle.

A former public relations professional from Chicago, **Dana Gonzalez** and her American husband have lived overseas since 1996—half that time spent in Estonia, and half in Turkey. Enamored of Turkish culture, she admits to a certain amount of joy in the mysteries of the country remaining unsolved. Dana has taught English at Bilgi University in İstanbul. She currently lives in Tallinn, Estonia.

An instructor of writing at the University of Colorado at Boulder, **Sally Green**'s first visit to Turkey, as a teenager in 1978, changed her life. She studied Turkish at Bosphorus University in İstanbul, and later met Varol Tuncay, her Turkish husband of eighteen years, while teaching English there. She also taught at Bilkent University, in Ankara. Currently she is writing a novel about an American who travels to Turkey on a religious "Footsteps of Paul" tour. Her manuscript has been supported by a variety of grants and awards. Sally's in-laws spend several months of each year with her family, and she and her husband plan to reside in Turkey again when their two young children are a bit older.

A Texan turned expat, **Kathleen Hamilton Gündoğdu**'s initial view of Turkey was tanks and soldiers lining the runways of the airport when she first visited in 1981 during a military coup. In spite of that dubious welcome, she continued to return for vacations until finally succumbing to the lure of Turkey and settling permanently in 1998. Married to a Turk, she is busy raising their son, who was born in 2001. In her "spare time," she specializes in writing articles about the lesser-known historical treasures of İstanbul for a number of publications when not on the road, comanaging her Texas-based silk accessories business, Sultan's Caravan.

Susan Fleming Holm is the Dorothy Donald Professor of Modern Foreign Languages at Monmouth College, in Illinois. With her former husband, Jim McHenry, she was a Peace Corps volunteer in Erzurum, teaching English at Atatürk University from 1966 to 1968. They returned to Turkey in 1974–75, living in Ankara and Northern Cyprus. During her sojourn in Erzurum, she came to love the city, with its rich and difficult history, its wealth of folk music and dance, and its ancient streets and alleys. She remembers and misses most the openness, warmth, and hospitality of the people of Erzurum, and of all Turks. She dedicates her tale to Süheyla Tinel.

Tennessee native **Eppie Lunsford** has been living in Turkey since 1987. A graduate of Tulane University with a degree in art history, she taught in the department of interior architecture at Ankara's Bilkent University before moving to İstanbul in 1992. Interested in working with children, she taught English at Yüzyil Işıl Primary School and has conducted children's art workshops. Eppie is an active member in the International Women of İstanbul, having organized their charity works and served on their board. She lives in İstanbul with her Turkish husband, Ergun, and two children. Eppie is the sister of fellow contributor Nancy Lunsford.

Nancy Lunsford is an artist presently living in Brooklyn, New York. Born and raised in southern Appalachia, Nancy augmented her early education in mountain folklore with a degree in art history and English literature from New York University. She lived in Ankara, Turkey, from 1986 to 1991, exhibiting her work at Urart Galeri. Three years in Indonesia, six years in Turkey, and an abiding interest in non-Western art forms have all contributed to her development as an artist and as a citizen of the world.

After studying Turkish literature and history at the University of Utrecht in the Netherlands, **Jessica Lutz** moved to İstanbul fifteen years ago, where her first job was to found the cultural department of the Dutch Consulate General. She has worked as a freelance journalist in Turkey, the Middle East, and the Caucasus. When in Baghdad, four months pregnant and with war pending, she decided to slow down and settle permanently in İstanbul. The native of Holland is also a novelist and short-story writer, with works appearing in American and Dutch media. Her first book, *De gouden appel,* about Turkey, was published in the Netherlands and sold out within a year.

Maria Yarbrough Orhon has combined an English/Scottish/Irish/Virginia/ South Carolina heritage with an upbringing in Beirut, Tehran, Ankara, Athens, and İstanbul, and she celebrates the wealth that these experiences have given to her, her Turkish husband, and two children. An educator for more than two decades, she is currently Secondary School Director at Turkey's acclaimed Robert College, a premier school that has turned out many of the country's business and government leaders.

An African American with Canadian roots, **Tanala OsaYande** is a bit of a wanderer. She has taught English in Mexico, worked for a policy institute in Los Angeles, and been a budget manager for a nonprofit teacher-training organization in New York City. She lived in İstanbul for two years, teaching English to corporate clients and learning the rules of engagement on the Turkish dating scene. Her home of the moment is Mexico.

A four-year resident of İstanbul, American **Annie Prior-Özsaraç** and her Turkish husband, Koray, teach English at the Koç School, where they met and fell in love. A native of Washington State, she spent two years teaching in Guatemala, where black-magic mysticism—especially a god of death and fertility named Maximón—failed to influence her beliefs. Joining a Turkish family changed that, as she has learned to respect the power of an evil eye exorcism. She can now be heard whispering to herself, "*Maşallah*" (May God protect you) upon seeing beautiful babies and witnessing the good luck of others.

American **Dena Sukaya,** her Turkish husband, Galip, and her sons, Aclan and Ceyhan, have been visiting Turkey since the 1980s and have lived in İstanbul for six years. Dena opened a Grand Bazaar shopping service for expatriates based on the friend-of-a-friend network—a distinctly Turkish resource and recommendation method. Currently in Seattle, Dena manages her business via the Internet and is concentrating on bringing Turkish arts and crafts to the United States. She plans to retire someday to the family tangerine farm outside İzmir but will surely maintain a pied-à-terre in İstanbul, close to the Grand Bazaar.

California native **Valerie Taşıran** lives in İstanbul with her Turkish husband. She is completing her PhD in history at the University of California, Berkeley, while lecturing in American history at Bosphorus University and working as an instructor in the College of Arts and Sciences at Koç University. She has delivered academic papers on subjects ranging from Americanization, hip-hop, and regional identity in Northern Mexico to the effects of nationalist politics on Armenian intermarriage in Fresno, California. A naturalized Turkish citizen and an avid shopper, Valerie continues to construct a modern concept of "Turkishness" and admits to making a few misguided purchases along the way.

Twenty-nine-year-old Australian **Claire Uhr** was sitting in her London office one afternoon in 2002 contemplating life when she decided to change it all. Opening a map of the world on her computer screen, she closed her eyes and blindly pointed. Turkey. Two weeks later, she arrived, with one hundred dollars to her name and a desire for adventure. Now back in her native Brisbane, she was an English teacher, a carpet salesperson, a hotel travel desk clerk, a tout at the harbor, and a tour guide. She has lived in Selçuk, Kuşadası, Göreme, İstanbul, and Ankara.

Rhonda Vander Sluis was born in Primghar, Iowa. She spent ten years in New York City and conducted missionary work in Haiti and Pakistan before heading to Turkey in 1990. Coming to her senses and leaving the church in 1994, she returned to Turkey in 1997 for another four years, where she worked as a nurse educator at the American Hospital and the Koç University School of Nursing. She is the coauthor of *From the Bosphorus: A Self-Guided Tour of the Bosphorus*. Currently living in Portland, Oregon, with her partner, Cyndi, she is a pediatric nurse.

Californian **Trici Venola** is a Los Angeles visual artist with a background in digital art. After a bad case of computer burnout from creating art for a slew of video games, such as Super Mario Brothers, she fell in love with Turkey when it reawakened her talent. Drawing from life in pen and ink, she has completed an illustrated memoir of her experiences in and about Turkey over the past five years. Her tale in this book is adapted from that memoir, *Freefall in Byzantium*. She lives in İstanbul's Sultanahmet neighborhood.

Karen-Claire Voss studied at Graduate Theological Union in Berkeley and École Pratique des Hautes Études, Sorbonne. She is a past president of the American Academy of Religion, Western Region, and she taught at San Jose State University from 1985 to 1991. She is the translator of Romanian physicist Basarab Nicolescu's *Manifesto of Transdisciplinarity* and his *Poetical Theorems,* and she is the author of numerous scholarly and popular articles. She has lived in İstanbul for almost thirteen years, where she has taught at Bosphorus University and Fatih University. Now dividing her time between Turkey and Scotland, her work in progress includes two books: *Spiritual Alchemy: A Way of Being in the World* and *'Feminine' Gnosis: An Other Way of Knowing*.

Originally from the United Kingdom, travel writer **Pat Yale** became the main author of the Lonely Planet guide to Turkey after many years of backpacking around the world, working as a travel agent, and teaching other people to be travel agents. She has been living in the central Anatolian village of Göreme for six years, where she converted a cave-house into a home. She has written a book about her life in Göreme and is currently working on a handbook for people living and working in Turkey. In addition to authoring or coauthoring Lonely Planet's *Britain, London, Ireland, Dublin, Iran, Middle East, Mediterranean Europe,* and *Europe,* she has been a contributor to British newspapers, like the *Guardian, Daily Telegraph,* and *Independent*.

A native of Dublin, Ireland, **Catherine Yiğit** met her Turkish husband, Özcan, while studying economic geology at Colorado School of Mines in the United States. Her first experience of Turkey was the wild and wonderful eastern Black Sea region, from where her husband hails—a land of hazelnuts, lonely monasteries hidden in the steep mountains, and a warm and generous people. Living for three years in Çanakkale, in northwestern Turkey—just north of mythical Troy—she writes in snatches while her daughter, Ezgi Orla, sleeps.

Dutchwoman **Eveline Zoutendijk** left her country eighteen years ago to pursue a hotel management career abroad. After working in Manhattan and Paris, she fell in love with İstanbul, and despite the hopeless job market at the time, she decided to move to the city. She now owns and manages the Sarnıç Hotel in İstanbul's historic district of Sultanahmet. With the hotel in operation since 2002, Eveline has found setting up a business in Turkey a continuous challenge and welcome adventure. A Cordon Bleu–trained chef, she also gives Turkish cooking classes to tourists and residents. Between hectic workdays and the busy social life of a single woman, she struggles to find time for her hobbies of painting, writing, and traveling.

About the Editors

Anastasia M. Ashman is a career essayist specializing in personal tales of cultural adventure. *Tales from the Expat Harem* is her first anthology, adding a new facet to ten years of experience evaluating and editing creative material in New York and Los Angeles media and entertainment, working for literary agents and producers of film, television, and Broadway theater. She is also at work on *Berkeley to Byzantium: The Reorientation of a West Coast Adventuress*, a cultural memoir charting the peaks and valleys of her adventurous life spent in hybrid places of heightened texture and possibility, from the mean elevators and subways of Manhattan to the gilded palaces of Asia Minor and Southeast Asia, where she lived for five years. For *Cornucopia*, a glossy magazine for connoisseurs of Turkey worldwide, Anastasia has written about joining a Turkish family. She has encapsulated the vanishing cuisine of a Chinese–Malayan subculture, as well as covered Malaysia's architectural heritage movement for Asia's oldest newsweekly magazine, *Dow Jones' Far Eastern Economic Review*. For art and literary sections of newspapers like the *Asian Wall Street Journal* in Hong Kong and the *Village Voice* in New York City, she has reviewed historical nonfiction scribes, avant-garde multimedia poets, and multicultural travel commentators like Pico Iyer. Born and raised in the progressive California town of Berkeley, Anastasia studied classical clarinet and Kodokan judo for more than a decade each. She holds a degree in Classical Greek, Roman, and Near Eastern archaeology from Bryn Mawr College in Pennsylvania, and has been living in İstanbul with her husband, Burç Şahinoğlu, for three years.

Jennifer Eaton Gökmen is an American writer captivated by the people and customs of Turkey, her home for more than a decade. A proponent of the integrated, adventurous expatriate life, Jennifer began hers as an exchange student in England, later returning to the U.K. as a chef's assistant, working her way through the silver-service dining rooms of London's financial district before extensively backpacking Europe. In college, her love life and her wanderlust converged when a whirlwind romance with a young Turk resulted in a move to the Eastern Hemisphere. An active supporter of and participant in Turkish cultural activities, for the past six years she has served as International Coordinator for the Kadıköy Municipality Annual Folkdance Festival, showcasing two hundred ethnic dancers and musicians each summer. A native of Michigan, she holds a degree in creative writing and American and English literature from Western Michigan University. Her literary career began with the expatriate humor magazine *İstanbull...*, where she served as staff writer for two years. Her writing has appeared in the anthology *Strange Intimacies,* an exhibit at the 9th International İstanbul Biennial, and she has been a contribuor to the monthly city guide *Time Out İstanbul.* She is currently penning her myriad Turkish adventures in a comical transcontinental confessional, *Midwest Goes Middle East: Adventures of a Drama Queen Abroad.* Jennifer lives her idea of a charmed life with her husband, Bilgehan, in İstanbul. *Nazar değmesin ...*

Jennifer and Anastasia can be reached through their website, www.expatharem .com.

Photo by Zumrut Photography Studio

Praise for *Tales from the Expat Harem*

"Follow the journeys of 29 women as they discover Turkey and its people in this collection of stories designed to reveal a culture often veiled in mystery and mystique."
—National Geographic Traveler

"This compilation of real-life stories entertains and informs."
—International Herald Tribune

"In this collection of essays, 29 foreign women share their tales of conflict and discovery in Turkey. Spanning four decades and most of the country's regions, pieces take readers to weddings, workplaces, boisterous bazaars and deep into the feminine power bases of hamam bathhouses as expats redefine their identities in an unfamiliar cultural landscape." *—Globe and Mail*

"An excellent holiday read." *—Lonely Planet Turkey (10th Edition)*

"Beautifully written, thought-provoking and inspiring. Every essay is spot on, literary and insightful. Be ready to book a flight to Istanbul afterwards."
—Daily Telegraph (UK)

"Fascinating... A smart look at different levels of Turkish society through the perspectives of a variety of women." *—The Oregonian*

"Insights from women who learn to read the cultural fine print... Valuable today as an antidote to bigotry, it will serve as an even more valuable corrective to the blinkered historians of tomorrow." *—Cornucopia*

"A must read for anyone planning a visit." *—Curve*

"Comic, romantic, and thought-provoking." *—Cosmopolitan (Turkey)*

"Not only aesthetically pleasing but instructive. Written with a sharp eye for details, provides many ethnographic insights...A great read! Don't miss it."
—Journal of Middle East Women's Studies

"Rip-roarer of a guide to understanding Eastern and Western social values. [The editors are] Alexa de Tocquevilles." *—The Gulf Today (UAE)*

"Charming, warm-hearted and vivid...a definite must-read for everyone pondering the question of what it is we call 'home'." *—NRC Handelsblad (The Netherlands)*